# 101 CHANGEMAKERS

## Rebels and Radicals
## Who Changed US History

Edited by
• Michele Bollinger and Dao X. Tran •

Haymarket Books
Chicago, IL

*To Jacob, Quyen, and Sasha,*
*and the changemakers of today.*
*Occupy history!*

© 2012 Michele Bollinger and Dao X. Tran

Published in 2012 by
Haymarket Books
PO Box 180165
Chicago, IL 60618
www.haymarketbooks.org
773-583-7884

ISBN: 978-1-60846-156-1

Printed in Canada by union labor.

Library of Congress cataloging-in-publication data is available.

10 9 8 7 6 5 4 3 2

Trade distribution:
In the US, Consortium Book Sales and Distribution, www.cbsd.com
In Canada, Publishers Group Canada, www.pgcbooks.ca
In the UK, Turnaround Publisher Services, www.turnaround-uk.com
In Australia, Palgrave Macmillan, www.palgravemacmillan.com.au
All other countries, Publishers Group Worldwide, www.pgw.com

Cover and interior design by Ragina Johnson.

Published with the generous support of Lannan Foundation
and the Wallace Global Fund.

"To be hopeful in bad times is not just foolishly romantic. It is based on the fact that human history is a history not only of cruelty, but also of compassion, sacrifice, courage, kindness.

What we choose to emphasize in this complex history will determine our lives. If we see only the worst, it destroys our capacity to do something. If we remember those times and places—and there are so many—where people have behaved magnificently, this gives us the energy to act, and at least the possibility of sending this spinning top of a world in a different direction.

And if we do act, in however small a way, we don't have to wait for some grand utopian future. The future is an infinite succession of presents, and to live now as we think human beings should live, in defiance of all that is bad around us, is itself a marvelous victory. "

*—Howard Zinn*

# Contents

Preface v

Acknowledgments viii

Read This First ix

1. Crispus Attucks 1
2. Tom Paine 3
3. Tecumseh 5
4. Sarah and Angelina Grimké 7
5. David Walker 9
6. Nathaniel "Nat" Turner 11
7. John Brown 13
8. William Lloyd Garrison 15
9. Elizabeth Cady Stanton 17
10. Frederick Douglass 19
11. Lucy Stone 21
12. Harriet Tubman 23
13. Susan B. Anthony 25
14. Geronimo 27
15. Sitting Bull 29
16. Mark Twain 31
17. Mary "Mother" Jones 33
18. Queen Liliuokalani 35
19. Albert and Lucy Gonzalez Parsons 37
20. Mary Elizabeth Lease 39
21. Eugene Debs 41
22. Clarence Darrow 43
23. Jane Addams 45
24. Ida B. Wells 47
25. W. E. B. Du Bois 49
26. William "Big Bill" Haywood 51
27. Albert Einstein 53
28. Joe Hill 55
29. Frances Perkins 57
30. Helen Keller 59
31. Henry Wallace 61
32. A. Philip Randolph 63
33. Elizabeth Gurley Flynn 65
34. Paul Robeson 67
35. Langston Hughes 69
36. Ella Baker 71
37. Clifford Odets 73
38. Rachel Carson 75
39. Anita Andrade Castro 77
40. Richard Wright 79
41. Harry Hay Jr. 81
42. Bayard Rustin 83
43. Studs Terkel 85
44. Rosa Parks 87
45. Genora Dollinger 89
46. Carlos Bulosan 91
47. Grace Lee Boggs 93
48. Billie Holiday 95
49. Jacob Lawrence 97
50. Fannie Lou Hamer 99

51. Fred Korematsu 101

52. Betty Friedan 103

53. Del Martin and Phyllis Lyon 105

54. Philip and Daniel Berrigan 107

55. Howard Zinn 109

56. Mary and Carrie Dann 111

57. James Baldwin 113

58. Shirley Chisholm 115

59. Malcolm X 117

60. Elizabeth Martinez 119

61. Cesar Chavez 121

62. Noam Chomsky 123

63. Martin Luther King Jr. 125

64. Dolores Huerta 127

65. Harvey Milk 129

66. Lorraine Hansberry 131

67. Daniel Ellsberg 133

68. Richard and Mildred Loving 135

69. Audre Lorde 137

70. Ralph Nader 139

71. Gloria Steinem 141

72. Edward Said 143

73. Sylvia Mendez 145

74. Claudette Colvin 147

75. John Lewis 149

76. Bob Dylan 151

77. Jesse Jackson 153

78. Joan Baez 155

79. Stokely Carmichael 157

80. Muhammad Ali 159

81. Huey P. Newton 161

82. Billie Jean King 163

83. Angela Davis 165

84. Leonard Peltier 167

85. Alice Walker 169

86. Fred Fay 171

87. Wilma Pearl Mankiller 173

88. August Wilson 175

89. Barbara Young 177

90. Sylvia Rae Rivera 179

91. Mary Beth Tinker 181

92. Judy Bonds 183

93. Cleve Jones 185

94. Lam Duong 187

95. Fernando Suarez del Solar 189

96. Tony Kushner 191

97. Chuck D 193

98. Bhairavi Desai 195

99. Elvira Arellano 197

100. Laila Al-Arian 199

101. Constance McMillen 201

Glossary 203

About the Contributors 208

# Preface

Whenever struggles for social justice find their way into the classroom, both teaching and learning are transformed. The social upheavals of the 1960s left their imprint on the classroom, as students fought for everything from free speech rights to affirmative action. At the very least, the collective impact of these struggles was to transform the relationship between student and teacher in the years that followed.

Today, as more people mobilize against corporate control of our schools, the potential to reclaim our curriculum grows. As an institution, education has become increasingly scripted and "data-driven" rather than a way for children to explore and analyze their community and create ways to change it. In fact, such exploration is now openly discouraged. In April 2011, David Coleman, a primary author of the Common Core State Standards that have been adopted by forty-four states, argued against the usefulness of children's personal experiences and opinions. Coleman explained, "As you grow up in this world you realize people don't really give a **** about what you feel or think." More notorious has been the Republican Party of the state of Texas, which stated in its 2012 platform that "we oppose the teaching of Higher Order Thinking Skills (HOTS) (values clarification), critical thinking skills and similar programs . . . which focus on behavior modification and have the purpose of challenging the student's fixed beliefs and undermining parental authority." Increasingly, social justice educators and progressive parents have to carve out our own spaces to share empowering history and ideas with our children.

We created *101 Changemakers: Rebels and Radicals Who Changed US History* to aid this process. Thankfully, we are not the first to blaze this path. Radical historian Howard Zinn argued that history should be explored from the perspective of the mass of ordinary people who made it—and his book *A People's History of the United States* changed how millions of people understand US history. A genuine people's history would not be complete without a comprehensive and thoroughgoing analysis of the experience of oppressed people in the United States. Many pioneering scholars—John Hope Franklin, Elizabeth Martinez, and Ronald Takaki to name a few—have enriched our understanding of US history through their groundbreaking work. Like Zinn, we find an inextricable link between the history of the oppressed in US history and a genuine people's history.

In 2007, Rebecca Stefoff adapted Zinn's work for young readers in *A Young People's History of the United States*. In *Lies My Teacher Told Me*, James Loewen helped us identify which textbooks to leave behind and explained how the truth about history, though sometimes brutal, is always more thought-provoking than the stultifying patriotic myths. Bill Bigelow of *Rethinking Schools* has helped teachers create lessons with *A People's History for the Classroom*. And in 2009, William Holtzman, with Rethinking Schools and Teaching for Change, launched the Zinn Education Project, an invaluable online resource for teaching people's history.

These resources are great for high school students and for the youngest readers, stories of social justice and groundbreaking individuals such as Martin Luther King Jr., Cesar Chavez, and Rosa Parks have made their way into picture books. But we felt that a more comprehensive resource accessible to middle school students was needed. We have been inspired by middle school students who draw picket signs to protest budget cuts to their schools. Shouldn't they, too, be able to learn lessons from the rich history of social protest in this country?

The increasing corporate control of education has deeply affected social science curriculum. Students are taught that our "heroes" are the "great" presidents—even the likes of Andrew Jackson, who personally murdered countless Native Americans—or the "captains of industry," like the notoriously anti-Semitic Henry Ford. At the same time, thorough representations of the victims and survivors of Indian removal, the impact of the growth of industry on US workers, and the effects of environmental devastation are often absent.

Children do learn in school about a handful of advocates for social change. But their stories are often sanitized or oversimplified in a way that makes them seem much less threatening and definitely less interesting. For example, most students today often learn about Helen Keller as a courageous young woman who overcame her disabilities. But few know about her antiwar activism or her staunch advocacy for women's and workers' rights. Many students learn about Martin Luther King Jr. in a way that fails to include his views on the war in Vietnam or that outright misrepresents the relationship between his politics and those of Malcolm X. And of course, many more are taught little or nothing about Malcolm X, because radical figures are often completely sidelined from the curriculum.

We aimed to provide more for the young readers and activists of today. Through these brief, accessible, and dynamic profiles of various "changemakers" throughout US history, students can learn about the power that ordinary people have to change the world and the circumstances that give them opportunities to do so.

Since no single person changes the world alone, we tried to relate each person's story in the context that gave rise to it. Even though each changemaker inspired and led others to challenge society, they were each in turn influenced—and sometimes challenged—by people around them who were gravitating toward protest and who raised questions about how best to make social change.

Likewise, many of our changemakers are products of their times and have their own political flaws and human complexities. We aimed to depict them as completely as we could in five hundred words—while staying true to the essence of each changemaker's contribution. At the same time, we found ourselves challenged by how to represent mature and sensitive issues to young readers. We did tread somewhat lightly around particular issues of violence, repression, and sexuality, but only when we feared that those discussions would distract the reader from the overall lessons of the changemaker's life. We also adapted to current trends around explicit language, including not spelling out racial slurs, even when used in a quote with historic context. Discussing issues such as racism in the classroom can be fraught with pain for children whose lives are shaped by that oppression; we want this book to contribute to discussions that are constructive and empowering.

Selecting our changemakers was not easy. There are those champions whose legacies have fundamentally altered the course of our society—Frederick Douglass, Harriet Tubman, Muhammad Ali—whose stories we tried to tell in a more dynamic way. But there are also scores of influential and decisive people, sometimes controversial, often radical, who have been marginalized from the mainstream versions of US history. These are the lesser-known changemakers to whom we hope to introduce young readers in this book—from Crispus Attucks, Nat Turner, Carlos Bulosan, Ella Baker, and Del Martin and Phyllis Lyon on down to modern-day fighters like Fred Fay, Sylvia Rivera, Judy Bonds, and Elvira Arellano. We could easily have filled two volumes.

We also aspired to integrate the groundbreaking contributions of people of color, immigrants, women, and LGBT people, those whose roles have been ignored or underplayed in our children's schoolbooks because of ignorance and bigotry, as fully as possible. We recognize that there are many stories that have yet to be told and need to be told—and we look forward to the time when a genuinely liberated history can fully represent all our histories.

Finally, we believe that young people are routinely underestimated in our society. Far from being "apathetic" or obsessed with texting and playing video games, they are increasingly engaged in figuring out how to change the world around them. In the past few years, we have seen young people organizing for LGBT rights, for the DREAM Act, fighting for justice for Trayvon Martin, marching against sexism, and occupying Wall Street. We hope to inspire more young changemakers to shape their own history, and to fill future books with their stories. •

## Acknowledgments

A book is always a collective work, and *101 Changemakers* is no exception. We owe heartfelt thanks to the many who initiated it and nurtured it into being.

Thanks to Randall Wallace and the Wallace Global Fund for having the insight that this book was needed and investing the resources to complete it. Brenda Coughlin, your attentive and critical advice helped us get over some big bumps in the road.

The crew at Haymarket Books—Anthony Arnove, Rachel Cohen, Rory Fanning, Julie Fain, Eric Kerl, Sarah Macaraeg—you put the *rad* in *radical* and are the hardest-working bunch of book people ever. Ragina Johnson, your design work is brilliant. Sarah Grey (with whom Dao loves to be detailed, nuanced, and word-nerdy), our appreciation of your copyedit and sensitivity to the content cannot be expressed enough.

Badia AlBanna, Bill Bigelow, Akunnah Eneh, Rob Geremia, Jesse Hagopian, Brian Jones, Deborah Menkart, Tricia Obester, David Rapkin, and Marissa Torres all gave perceptive feedback and invaluable perspectives on elementary and middle school education. Nadya Ali, Pedro Lahoz Wolfe, and Daisy Maass shared the valued insights of the under-eighteen crowd for some key profiles.

Jason Farbman, Akiko Ichikawa, James Illingworth, Alex Tronolone, and Erik Wallenberg all pitched in with research and review. Michael Darrow, the Fred T. Korematsu Institute for Civil Rights and Education, Dr. Sherna Berger Gluck, Trish Irons, and Margaret Randall went the extra mile for us.

David Meketon (who introduced Dao to *A People's History of the United States*) and Debbie Wei, teachers and comrades, helped shape Dao's longtime commitment to radical social change and gave intuitive advice early on in the project. Peter Lamphere, your warm support of and patience with a certain grumpy editor and our offspring are hugely appreciated.

Ed and Susan Bollinger, Jane and Marvin, Jim and Marlene, Sasha and Jacob, and Michele's colleagues and students at Woodrow Wilson High School in Washington, DC, have been a source of support and inspiration to her. Dave Zirin: Michele thanks you for all that extra parenting but mostly for your love, humor, and great taste in television shows.

Finally, we thank all the contributors, for writing with flair the stories of these amazing changemakers—and of course the changemakers themselves, without whom this book could not exist. •

# Read This First

**For too many young people, history is just plain boring. History can seem like it is all about random dates and facts about powerful kings and important presidents making long-winded speeches. History can appear to be about events that happened so far in the past that they seem to have no connection to our world today.**

It doesn't have to be this way. History should be exciting. It should be thrilling. It tells us the greatest stories ever told, and those stories contain lessons from the past that can help us create a better future. But we can only do that if we know who *really* made our history—and what exactly they did.

In this book, you'll learn about rebels and radicals. You'll learn about people who defied ugly stereotypes and stood up against bigotry. You'll learn about musicians who spoke for millions through their music and athletes who changed the world on and off the field. You'll learn about young people—like Claudette Colvin, Mary Beth Tinker, and Constance McMillen—who didn't wait for someone else's permission to stand up for themselves and others.

Change is at the heart of history. But the world doesn't just change out of nowhere. Change happens when ordinary people decide—for all kinds of reasons—to take action. Sometimes they end up remaking the world. Often, this experience is not easy. People who challenge commonly held ideas and demand the right to take charge of their own lives face anger, hostility, and even violence. However, when people refuse to back down—because of their own courage and because they have the support of a broader movement of people—they can win amazing victories that change the course of history.

To help make this history real, we wanted to share the stories of 101 "changemakers." For us, changemakers include people who shaped struggles for social justice and inspired others to join in. The impact of these struggles on our society goes far beyond the people and places involved in them, touching all our lives. Because so much of the history of the United States has been shaped by racism, sexism, and other kinds of discrimination, this book spends a lot of time looking at the diverse experiences of people who resisted those forces.

Some of these people unexpectedly found themselves in the middle of a specific conflict that required them to take action. But many of them devoted their entire lives to the goal of completely transforming society. Some of them you have probably heard of—but there are lots of people in this book who will be new to you. They are the unsung heroines and heroes of US history.

When you read this book, we hope you will be challenged to rethink what you know about history—and what you know about the United States. You may or may not agree with all of the beliefs and actions of the 101 people profiled here, but we can promise you this: you won't be bored. We hope that you will take these stories as a starting point for thinking about your own ideas and how you, too, can be a changemaker. This is *your* book. This is *your* history. •

# Crispus Attucks
## (ca. 1723–1770)

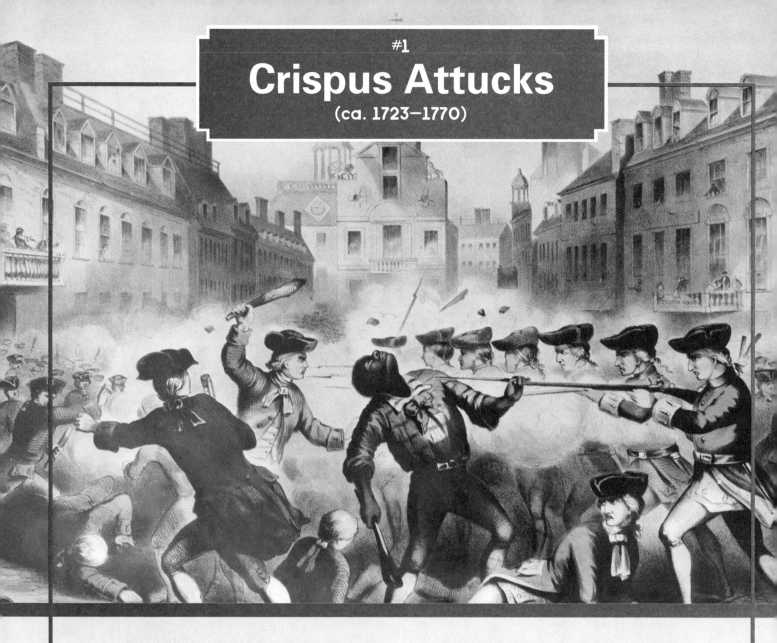

**Did you know that the first person to die for the cause of the American Revolution was a black man? His name was Crispus Attucks.**

We know very little about him for sure, but historians believe he was born around 1723 in Framingham, Massachusetts. His mother was a Natick Indian and his father was an enslaved African.

Crispus was born into slavery, but he longed to be free. He worked trading cattle for his master, William Brown. Eventually he escaped and got a job on a whaling ship. His master put out a notice and a reward for his capture. Crispus was never caught. He worked on ships for the next twenty years. It was hard and dangerous work, but at least he was free.

In 1770 Crispus happened to be in Boston when he heard about a confrontation brewing with some British soldiers. The people of Boston were becoming more and more frustrated with England's King George for imposing unfair taxes and sending soldiers to police the streets. Sailors like Crispus were also angry because the soldiers were taking part-time work that locals used to do.

All this came to a head when a British soldier pushed a young boy down in the street. An angry crowd began to gather and more soldiers arrived as well. The town's bells rang in alert and Crispus pushed to the front of the crowd. He led them, armed with clubs and snowballs, toward the Old State House.

No one is sure exactly what happened next, but at some point the British troops opened fire on the crowd. Crispus was hit two times in the chest and was the first to die. Four others were also killed in what came to be known as the Boston Massacre.

John Adams, who later became president of the United States, defended the British soldiers in court. He criticized the mob's actions and Crispus in particular, "whose very looks was enough to terrify any person." Later, Adams changed his mind. He recognized Crispus as a hero who stood up for freedom and exposed the brutality of British rule. "On that night," wrote Adams, "the foundation of American independence was laid."

Ironically, the revolution that Crispus died for did not bring freedom for those born into slavery like himself. Inspired by the slogan "Liberty or Death," thousands of African Americans fought in the war and signed petitions asking for their freedom. But in the end, slavery continued in America for almost a century after independence.

After the war, Crispus was largely forgotten until many decades later. He became a symbol for abolitionism, the movement to end slavery. In 1858 the abolitionists declared the first "Crispus Attucks Day" and in 1888 a Crispus Attucks memorial was put up on the Boston Common. Martin Luther King Jr. remembered Crispus as well. He noted that although Crispus "shed blood" to free this country from British rule, Crispus's "great-great-grandson" would face racism.

**—Leela Yellesetty**

## Timeline:

| | |
|---|---|
| 1723(?) | Born in Framingham, MA |
| 1750 | Sept 30, escapes slavery to work on a whaling ship |
| 1770 | March 5, shot by the British in the Boston Massacre |
| 1858 | March 5, first Crispus Attucks Day celebrated in Boston |
| 1888 | Crispus Attucks memorial put up on Boston Common |

## More you can do:

- **Read these books:** *Crispus Attucks, Patriot* by James Neyland; *America's Black Founders: Revolutionary Heroes and Early Leaders* by Nancy Sanders; and *Revolutionary Citizens: African Americans, 1776–1804* by Daniel Littlefield
- **Design a poster to promote learning more about Crispus Attucks**

## What do you think?

- If you were an African American during the Revolutionary War, would you have supported it? Why or why not?
- Why do you think slavery continued after the revolution?
- Why do you think Crispus became an important figure for the abolitionist and civil rights movements?

# Tom Paine
## (1737–1809)

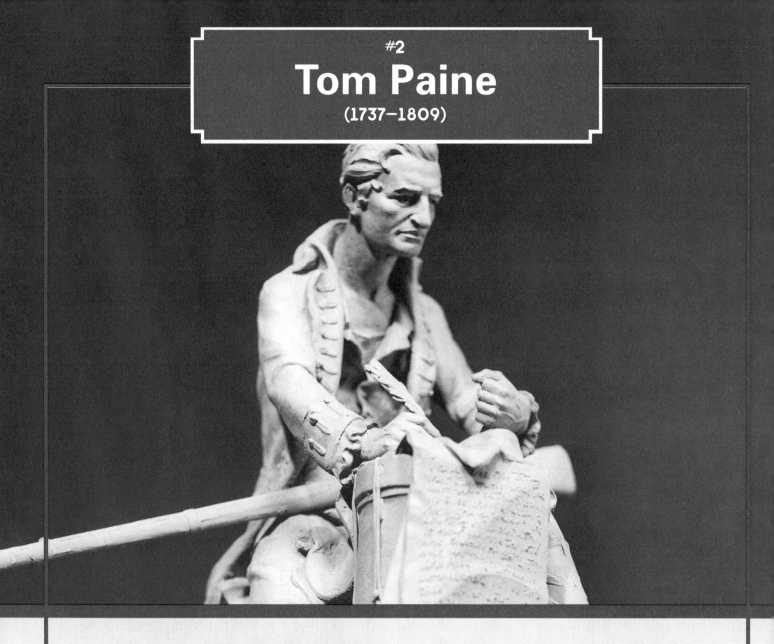

**In January 1775, Tom Paine was just another poor Englishman sailing to the North American colonies in hopes of a better future.**

One year later this English nobody became a hero by writing *Common Sense*, a short book that helped start a war for independence against the country he had just left.

Most famous writers in those days came from rich families, but Tom had to leave school at age thirteen to get a job. For twenty years he worked in England as a dressmaker and a tax collector, sometimes facing real poverty.

When Tom arrived in Philadelphia, colonists were angry about English taxes but still loyal to King George III. In *Common Sense*, Tom wrote that the problem was not the laws of the English king but that England had a king at all: "For as in absolute governments the King is law, so in free countries the law ought to be King; and there ought to be no other."

*Common Sense* urged colonial settlers to create a republic, a government based on elected representatives of the people: "The sun never shined on a cause of greater worth." Written in a plain style for workers and farmers, *Common Sense* sold one hundred fifty thousand copies. Few other books have ever been bought by such a big portion of the American people. On July 4, 1776—six months after Tom wrote *Common Sense*—the colonists declared independence from England. Of

> "These are the times that try men's souls: The summer soldier and the sunshine patriot will, in this crisis, shrink from the service of his country; but he that stands it now, deserves the love and thanks of man and woman."
>
> —*Tom Paine,* Common Sense

course, England did not agree. The War for Independence lasted seven years and at first the small and poor Continental Army was in deep trouble.

Tom wrote a series of articles called "The American Crisis" to keep Americans from giving up by reminding them what they were fighting for. "Tyranny, like hell, is not easily conquered," he wrote, "yet the harder the conflict, the more glorious the triumph. . . . Heaven knows how to set a proper price upon its goods; and it would be strange . . . if FREEDOM should not be highly rated." General George Washington found these words so inspiring he had them read to his soldiers the night before the important battle of Trenton.

After the war ended, many of the new nation's leaders were slave owners like Washington and wealthy lawyers like John Adams who did not want to see any more radical changes.

Tom was different. He saw the American Revolution as part of a worldwide movement for fairness. He wrote against slavery and poverty. When France revolted against its king, Tom moved to France and was elected to the new government even though he only spoke English. Later, when his allies lost power, he was thrown in jail and almost executed.

In 1791 Tom wrote *The Rights of Man* to support the French Revolution. Two years later he wrote *The Age of Reason* to argue that society should be based on science rather than religion. Like *Common Sense*, these books were widely read by working people in France, England, and the United States.

These books, however, also made Tom many enemies who thought his ideas were dangerous to governments and religions. When he died in 1809 outside New York City, few people came to the funeral of one of the great leaders of the American Revolution.
—**Danny Katch**

## Timeline:

| 1737 | Born in Thetford, England |
|---|---|
| 1775 | Arrives in Philadelphia |
| 1776 | Writes *Common Sense*, which helps convince American colonists to fight for independence from Great Britain |
| 1776–83 | Writes "The American Crisis" articles to inspire American troops during the Revolutionary War |
| 1791–92 | Writes *The Rights of Man* in support of the French Revolution |
| 1792 | Moves to France and is elected to the revolutionary National Convention |
| 1793 | Arrested and jailed when his allies in the French Revolution are thrown out of power, and is angry that President Washington doesn't do more to win his freedom |
| 1793–94 | Writes *The Age of Reason* in support of science and reason over organized religion |
| 1794 | Released from prison |
| 1802 | Returns to United States |
| 1809 | Dies in New Rochelle, New York |

## More you can do:

- Think about what Tom said about "summer soldiers" and "sunshine patriots." What do you think he meant? Can you think of who might be considered such today? What about their opposite, "winter soldiers"?
- Read some of Tom's *Collected Writings* and write an essay about something you feel passionate about and want to convince others to change

## What do you think?

- How do you think Tom's childhood in England influenced his ideas as an adult in America?
- Why do you think *Common Sense* was so popular?
- What would Tom Paine think about conditions in the United States today?

# Tecumseh
## (1768–1813)

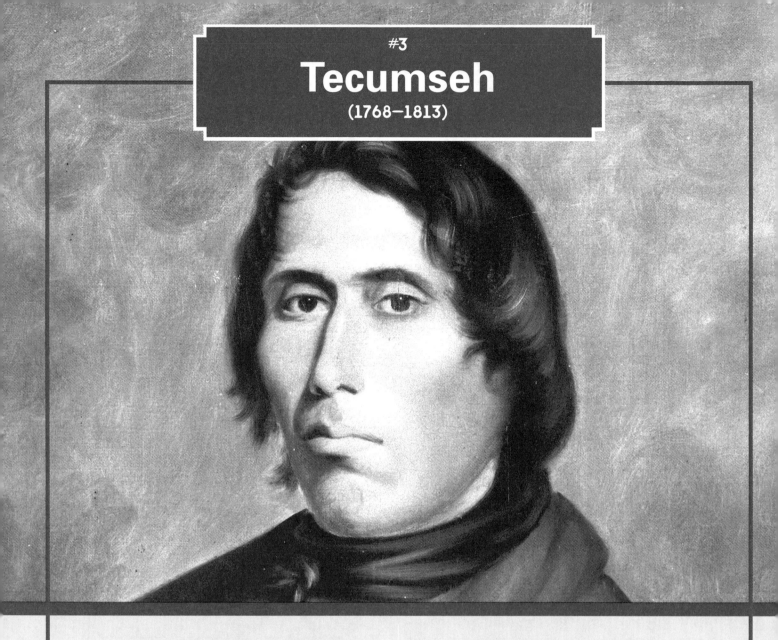

**Tecumseh was a leader of the Shawnee Nation. From 1805 to 1813 he helped to unify different tribes against US settlement.**

Tecumseh grew up watching his people forced from their homes by the fur trade. British and French armies fought for control to make more money from fur. Other tribes fought, too. Settlers like Daniel Boone led invasions that pushed the Shawnee even further west. Disease, sometimes caused on purpose by whites, killed many. Alcohol, also brought by whites, caused abuse and made Shawnee society weaker.

In 1805, Tecumseh's brother, Tenskwatawa, led a religious movement that began to unite different tribes. Called "the Prophet" by his followers, he wanted a return to traditional ways rather than farming.

By 1810 Indian leaders had signed a treaty giving away millions of acres of land. Many local chiefs were corrupt. Tecumseh tried to negotiate with the white governor William Henry Harrison. He sat with the governor on a bench and kept pushing him over. When Harrison said there was no room, Tecumseh laughed and said that was what whites were doing to the Indians.

But it was clear that Harrison would not give the land back. Instead, Tecumseh relied on uniting various Native nations together. Tecumseh was known as a great speaker. He

> **"** No tribe has the right to sell, even to each other, much less to strangers. . . . Sell a country! Why not sell the air, the great sea, as well as the earth? Did not the Great Spirit make them all for the use of his children? **"**
>
> —*Tecumseh, address to General William Henry Harrison, 1810*

said that the tribes must eat out of a "bowl with one spoon." This meant that no tribe by itself had the right to give away land that belonged to everyone. Tecumseh traveled to various Native nations across the Midwest and South.

He formed the largest confederation of nations ever. He went south where the Cherokee Nation was, in what is now Georgia. He said to the Osage: "Brothers, we must be united; we must smoke the same pipe; we must fight each other's battles." He went east to New York to speak to the Iroquois. He traveled as far north as Wisconsin to speak to the Sioux.

Native Americans from many nations had great respect for Tecumseh. Many joined him. This was even more amazing since most spoke different languages.

While Tecumseh was away, Harrison attacked the Shawnee. He defeated Tecumseh's brother and burned their supplies. But Tecumseh continued to build his alliance. Tecumseh also used the British Empire against the white settlers in the War of 1812. He led a large Native army against the whites. He hoped to win independence. When the whites tried to invade Canada, Tecumseh's army helped to stop them. He helped to capture Fort Detroit.

However, the British did not need to win more victories. Even though Tecumseh wanted to capture land from the white settlers, the British retreated. In 1813, Tecumseh was killed trying to slow the US Army's attack.

Tecumseh is known for leading and uniting many Native nations. He thought everyone should be equal within a nation. He also thought that no group should sell land that belonged to all. His war for independence set a great example for Native resistance for the future.

**—Peter Lamphere**

## Timeline:

| | |
|---|---|
| 1763 | Pontiac leads a confederation of tribes against the British, inspiring Tecumseh's later actions |
| 1768 | Born |
| 1774–82 | Five invasions of settlers push the Shawnee back to the area near Detroit |
| 1780s | Leads his own band of warriors |
| 1794 | Defeated at the battle of Fallen Timbers |
| 1805 | Tecumseh's brother has a vision, renames himself the Prophet, and begins a religious movement |
| 1810 | The treaty of Ft. Wayne gives up 2.1 million acres of land to the Americans |
| 1811 | Travels to various Native nations to build his alliance |
| 1811 | November, Governor Harrison attacks the Prophet at the Battle of Tippecanoe |
| 1812 | Helps to capture Ft. Detroit with the British |
| 1813 | British supply lines are cut and they begin a retreat from Detroit |
| 1813 | October, is killed covering British retreat at the Battle of the Thames |

## More you can do:

- **Watch the PBS documentary *American Experience: We Shall Remain:* "Tecumseh's Vision"**
- **Visit the Tippecanoe Battlefield Museum in Indiana**

## What do you think?

- **What were the economic and political changes that created Tecumseh's rebellion?**
- **Why was Tecumseh able to unite so many people, even though they spoke different languages?**
- **Why did Tecumseh fight on the side of the British in the War of 1812? Do you agree with his decision?**

# Sarah and Angelina Grimké

## (1792–1873; 1805–1879)

**The Grimké sisters were rebels with a cause. They were born into a wealthy family in Charleston, South Carolina, an important and powerful city in the slave-holding South before the Civil War.**

The sisters had everything two girls could want. They had slaves to wait on them, a rich father to buy them things, and invitations to all the best parties. But these perks were based on the labor of enslaved people, who were forced to raise cotton and perform the work that made the Grimké family and others like them rich. While this terrible fact was clear, most chose not to see the brutal treatment of those enslaved.

But Sarah and Angelina were different. At age five, Sarah saw an enslaved person being whipped. She was so upset she tried to get on the next ship headed to a place without slavery.

From early on, Sarah's smarts were obvious to those around her. But while their brothers studied and planned for college, Sarah and Angelina were told to stay home and learn "womanly" skills like cooking and sewing.

At twelve, Sarah began to teach Bible lessons to the young enslaved people in her home, even though her parents forbade it. Ignoring her parents (and breaking the law), Sarah taught her "personal" slave, a young woman, to read. Upon finding out, her furious father threatened to whip the young woman,

> "As a Southerner I feel that it is my duty to stand up here tonight and bear testimony against slavery. I have seen it — I have seen it. I know it has horrors that can never be described. I was brought up under its wing: I witnessed for many years its demoralizing influences, and its destructiveness to human happiness."
>
> —From Angelina Grimké's speech at Pennsylvania Hall

so Sarah stopped. But she didn't give up on learning or challenging the wrongs around her. When her brother Thomas returned from university, she insisted that he teach her everything he knew.

In 1835, William Lloyd Garrison wrote an article in the *Liberator* about the violence of pro-slavery forces in Britain. Angelina wrote him a personal letter praising his efforts. Garrison was so impressed that he published the letter without telling her. It quickly made Angelina and her sister stars in the national antislavery movement. As Southerners from a slave-holding family, they were an important voice for the movement. But they also drew attacks from many who thought their message was too radical.

Both Sarah and Angelina spoke out against slavery at public events. In 1837, over twenty-three weeks, they spoke in sixty-seven cities. They stood up for the enslaved, but also to those who attacked their rights as women to speak in public. Sarah wrote in *Letters on the Equality of the Sexes*, "All I ask our brethren is, that they will take their feet from off our necks, and permit us to stand upright on that ground which God designed us to occupy."

On May 17, 1838, Angelina Grimké gave a speech at Philadelphia's Pennsylvania Hall. As she spoke a pro-slavery mob formed outside and began to smash windows. Later that night, the hall was burned down.

In 1863, the sisters wrote "An Appeal to the Women of the Republic," rallying women to support the North in the Civil War to end slavery. After the war, the two opened a school teaching both girls and boys, and they continued to speak out for the rights of black people. In 1870, the two, by then quite elderly, risked arrest by voting in an election.

Both Sarah and Angelina continued to fight for equality until they passed away. Sarah died on December 23, 1873, and Angelina died on October 26, 1879.
—**Mike Stark**

## Timeline:

**1819** Sarah goes to Philadelphia; meets Israel Morris, who introduces her to Quaker faith

**1835** Angelina's letter published in the *Liberator*

**1836** Angelina writes *An Appeal to the Christian Women of the South* to encourage Southern women to join the movement against slavery; Sarah writes the "Epistle to the Clergy of the Southern States"

**1837** Angelina invited to speak before the Massachusetts State Legislature; testifies in February the following year, becoming the first woman in the United States to speak before an elected body

**1837** Angelina writes "Letters to Catherine Beecher" and Sarah writes "Letters on the Equality of the Sexes," defending their right to speak

**1848** Angelina speaks at Pennsylvania Hall hours before it is burned down by a pro-slavery mob

**1861** The Civil War begins

**1863** Angelina and Sarah write "An Appeal to the Women of the Republic," calling on women to support the North in the war; this same year, Abraham Lincoln issues the Emancipation Proclamation, ending slavery in the South

**1870** Angelina and Sarah, along with forty-two others, break the law and cast votes in a local election

**1873** Sarah Grimké dies

**1879** Angelina Grimké dies

## More you can do:

- **Find and read aloud part of Angelina's speech at Pennsylvania Hall: www.pbs.org/wgbh/aia/part4/4h2939t.html**

## What do you think?

- **Why do you think people objected when Sarah and Angelina began to speak out publicly against slavery?**
- **Do you think their Southern upbringing helped them in their fight against slavery?**
- **What do you think the Grimké sisters would be doing today if they were alive?**

WALKER'S

## APPEAL,

IN FOUR ARTICLES,

TOGETHER WITH

## A PREAMBLE,

TO THE

### COLORED CITIZENS OF THE WORLD,

BUT IN PARTICULAR, AND VERY EXPRESSLY TO THOSE OF THE

## UNITED STATES OF AMERICA.

*Written in Boston, in the State of Massachusetts, Sept. 28, 1829.*

SECOND EDITION, WITH CORRECTIONS, &c.

BY DAVID WALKER.

1830.

**Slavery in the United States was a barbaric practice. Slave traders brought millions of people from Africa and shipped them across the Atlantic Ocean chained together like cattle.**

Many died during the voyage. Those who survived lived a life of hard labor without any political freedoms or human rights. Slavery made some in this country very rich.

But there were also heroes who rejected racism and the injustice of slavery. David Walker was one of them. As a black man who was born free, he grew up with a staunch hatred for the slave system. He left the South and moved to Boston, claiming, "I cannot remain where I must hear slaves' chains continually and where I must encounter the insults of their hypocritical enslavers." David demanded swift and radical action to end slavery.

In 1829, David wrote and published a pamphlet titled *David Walker's Appeal to the Colored Citizens of the World*. What was so shocking about *Walker's Appeal*? David wrote that America was not living up to its ideals of freedom and democracy. He targeted leaders like Thomas Jefferson, who wrote the Declaration of Independence but also owned slaves and defended racism. The *Appeal* destroyed many common racist ideas that served to justify slavery. It also emphasized the achievements of people of African descent and encouraged black pride. Unlike anything that had come before it, the *Appeal* urged enslaved and free black people to unite and rebel against their masters and oppressors. David also felt that the United States belonged more to blacks than to whites because "we have enriched it with our blood and tears."

David took risky and covert steps to spread his ideas. Above all else, he wanted his *Appeal* to reach the enslaved men and women of the South. At his secondhand clothing shop, David sewed copies of the pamphlet into the clothing of sailors and naval officers who took them to Southern ports. There, they distributed the *Appeal* through black churches and other networks.

*Walker's Appeal* struck fear into Southern slave society. Alarmed slave owners threatened David with death and even put a $10,000 bounty on his head. Southern leaders outlawed antislavery writings and banned blacks from learning to read. They had reason to be scared: slave rebellions were growing.

*Walker's Appeal* was an inspiring call to enslaved people to fight for freedom. David's pamphlet played a key role in founding the national abolitionist movement. In the early 1830s, small antislavery groups came together to form one united movement. The *Appeal* shaped the ideas of the movement's first leaders.

Unfortunately, David himself did not live to see the movement grow. He died only a year after the *Appeal* was published, probably from tuberculosis. However, his brave and firm call for racial justice helped create a movement that culminated in the Civil War and the abolition of slavery.

—Zach Zill

## Timeline:

| | |
|---|---|
| 1797 | Born to an enslaved father and a free mother in Wilmington, North Carolina |
| 1810s | Moves to Charleston, South Carolina, a haven for free blacks, and affiliates himself with the African Methodist Episcopal Church |
| early 1820s | Moves to Boston, owns and operates a used clothing store |
| 1826 | Marries Eliza Butler and helps found the Massachusetts General Colored Association; Thomas Jefferson, defender of slavery, dies |
| 1827 | A group of African Americans in New York City creates one of the first abolitionist publications, *Freedom's Journal*; David is an early supporter and writer |
| 1829 | *Walker's Appeal* first published |
| 1830 | Dies; pamphlet in wide circulation among blacks in the United States |

## More you can do:

- Find and read *Walker's Appeal* and describe some of the arguments David made against slavery
- Watch the PBS series *Slavery and the Making of America*

## What do you think?

- Why did David condemn Thomas Jefferson? Do you think this was an effective tactic?
- David sewed his pamphlet into sailors' garments at his shop. What else would having his own shop allow him to do?
- During David's time, some abolitionists thought the country should free and deport all blacks in the United States back to Africa or the Caribbean. Why did David oppose this?

# Nathaniel "Nat" Turner
## (1800–1831)

**Few enslaved leaders have become as legendary as Nat Turner. In 1831, Nat led an armed slave revolt in the small farm community of Southampton, Virginia.**

"Turner's Rebellion" shocked the young American nation and warned of the coming civil war.

As was the custom at his birth in 1800, Nat was given the same last name as his "owner," Benjamin Turner. Nat's father escaped from slavery when Nat was just a boy. Nat's mother and grandmother raised him. His paternal grandmother's people were the Coromantee of Ghana. They were known as a defiant people who resisted enslavement. Nat lived up to this reputation.

Young Nat learned to read and write from the Turners. This was unusual for many enslaved people at the time. He used his education and deep religious beliefs to develop himself as a leader. He spent much of his time preaching to other enslaved people, who nicknamed him "the Prophet."

In the 1820s, Nat started hearing voices and seeing visions of black and white angels clashing in the sky. He believed God was sending him messages to "slay [his] enemies with their own weapons." After seeing a solar eclipse, Nat thought the time had come to rise up against the injustice of slavery. On August 21, 1831, he and several trusted fellow enslaved Africans began the deadly rebellion. They traveled from house to house, killing slave owners and their families with knives and axes. Freeing enslaved people they met, Nat and his band seized weapons, horses, and money. Nat led more than seventy rebels in this "explosion [of] black rage."

The rebels focused their rage on slave-owning households. They spared one home where a poor white family lived, and the home of Nat's childhood friend. White authorities wasted no time in responding. Militias were assembled and quickly surrounded Nat and the rebels. Within two days, several battles weakened and finally defeated the rebellion. However, it took twice as many white soldiers to defeat the small but defiant group of black rebels. Many rebels were captured and executed.

Nat himself escaped capture for two months. He hid in a small hole that he dug in a field. On October 30, a dog discovered his hiding spot and Nat was caught. He was quickly tried, convicted, and sentenced to death by hanging. The state of Virginia executed as many as fifty-one enslaved people for the rebellion, even though many were not involved.

The rebellion terrified white slaveowners in Virginia and beyond. Most thought that those they enslaved were less than human and were happy to be slaves. White people were shocked at how quickly the rebellion spread. After the uprising, harsh slave laws were enacted from Southampton County to Georgia, the Carolinas, and Alabama. After Nat's execution, the white population of Southampton went on a rampage. Mob violence killed close to two hundred black people in Virginia and North Carolina.

Nat and the rebellion he led inspired those opposed to slavery. Long after the end of slavery, black leaders took inspiration from the strength and bravery Nat and his fellow rebels showed. Despite its bloody and failed ending, people would never forget Turner's Rebellion.

—Zach Zill

## Timeline:

| | |
|---|---|
| 1800 | Born in Southampton County, Virginia, on October 8 |
| 1802–10 | Father escapes from slavery |
| 1821 | Runs away but returns to the Turner farm after hearing a voice, marries enslaved girl Cherry |
| 1822 | Sold to Thomas Moore, who drives him hard as a field hand |
| 1825 | Begins conducting his own praise meetings |
| 1827 | Ministers to and baptizes a white man |
| 1830 | Moves to the home of Joseph Travis, husband to Thomas Moore's widow |
| 1831 | August 21, begins rebellion with other enslaved Africans after seeing solar eclipse |
| | August 22, the group turns toward the county seat, Jerusalem, is confronted by militia, and scatters |
| | August 23, several rebels are captured; the remainder meet in a fight with state and federal troops in which three die |
| | October 30, discovered and captured |
| | November 5, tried, convicted, and sentenced to death in Southampton County |
| | November 11, executed |
| 1832 | Virginia, Alabama, and other Southern states enact laws forbidding the education of enslaved people |

## More you can do:

- **Read *The Confessions of Nat Turner* and Stephen Oates's *The Fires of Jubilee: Nat Turner's Fierce Rebellion***

## What do you think?

- **At the time of Turner's Rebellion, enslaved and free blacks outnumbered whites in Southampton County. Did this contribute to the rebellion's failure? How?**
- **Why would the Virginia authorities execute enslaved people who were not part of the uprising? Can you think of any current-day examples of anything similar?**

# John Brown

### (1800–1859)

**John Brown was the most radical white activist for the abolition of slavery before the US Civil War. John was born in Connecticut and raised in Ohio.**

He grew up in a very religious home. His father Owen called slavery "a great sin." John was a failed businessman and had twenty children by two wives. Three of his grown sons later died fighting by his side against slavery.

John became interested in the abolitionist movement in his thirties when he first read newspapers like William Lloyd Garrison's *Liberator*. More liberal abolitionists called for returning blacks to Africa and paying the slaveholders for loss of "property." But John believed slavery should be immediately ended without paying slaveholders. He did not rule out using violence if needed.

In a period of intense racism when many blacks were enslaved, John Brown was considered crazy for his antiracism. Even other abolitionists had a hard time with his ideas and actions. He would only go to a church if it allowed blacks and whites to sit together. He invited blacks to his home. He called them "Mr." and "Mrs.," titles of respect. Most of all, his personal sacrifice and dedication to the cause of ending slavery made him stand out. Like many of the people in this book, his "insanity" had to do with his vision of social change.

> **" I, John Brown, am now quite certain that the crimes of this guilty land will never be purged away but with Blood. I had (as I now think) vainly flattered myself that without very much bloodshed, it might be done. "**
>
> *—John Brown, from a note he wrote just before his execution*

When abolitionist Elijah Lovejoy was lynched in 1837, John pledged his life to ending slavery. As the United States expanded into the West, numerous attempted compromises on the issue of slavery failed. During those years, John moved around and developed his ideas during this time. He settled his family on a farm in North Elba, New York.

In 1854, the Kansas-Nebraska Act opened up settlement of Kansas. The question of whether slavery would be allowed was to be decided by a vote of the settlers. Supporters of both sides poured into the state, including John and three of his sons. A pro-slavery mob attacked the antislavery town of Lawrence. John led a raid that killed five pro-slavery activists. This act gave the abolitionists confidence and turned the tide against slavery in Kansas.

John spent the next three years traveling to Canada and New England to rally his supporters and raise funds. He also took the fight directly into the slave South. This began with a raid on Harpers Ferry, Virginia, on October 16, 1859. John led nineteen men in an attempt to capture the federal arsenal there. He planned to set up armed encampments and set up a section of the Underground Railroad to help enslaved people in the area escape. The raid was defeated. John was arrested by Colonel Robert E. Lee, the future leader of the Confederate Army.

John was executed by the State of Virginia just six weeks later. But his trial and writings from prison made slavery the key issue of the 1860 election. John himself noted, "Had I interceded . . . on behalf of the rich, powerful, and intelligent . . . it would have been right. Every man in the court would have deemed it an act worthy of reward rather than punishment." The Civil War began sixteen months after his death.
—**Brian Chidester**

## Timeline:

| | |
|---|---|
| 1800 | Born in Torrington, Connecticut |
| 1820 | Marries Dianthe Lusk |
| 1826 | Moves to Pennsylvania, opens a tannery, farms, becomes first postmaster of the village of New Richmond, opens a school, and helps found a church |
| 1834 | Dianthe dies in childbirth |
| 1837 | Pledges to fight for abolition of slavery after the lynching of abolitionist Elijah Lovejoy; remarries to Mary Day |
| 1847 | Meets abolitionist Frederick Douglass |
| 1854 | Kansas-Nebraska Act starts race to settle Kansas |
| 1855 | Arrives in Kansas; defends town of Lawrence against pro-slavery mob |
| 1856 | Leads a raid that kills five pro-slavery settlers near Pottawatomie Creek in May |
| 1857–58 | Tours New England and Canada, raising funds and gathering recruits |
| 1859 | October 16, leads the raid on Harpers Ferry. October 25–November 2, put on trial. December 2, executed |
| 1861 | April 12, Civil War starts |

## More you can do:

- **Read Henry David Thoreau's "A Plea for Captain John Brown" and consider what you would write in John's defense**
- **Visit the John Brown Museum State Historic Site in Osawatomie, Kansas**

## What do you think?

- **Was John Brown justified in using violence in his attempt to end slavery?**
- **In your opinion, why did John think that his attempt to free the enslaved would not require too much bloodshed? Why did he change his mind later?**
- **What impact did John's actions have on the start of the Civil War?**
- **Do you think it was significant that John, a white man, fought to liberate enslaved people?**

# William Lloyd Garrison

## (1805–1879)

William Lloyd Garrison was one of the most famous whites to try to end slavery. He was a journalist and a public speaker. He also tried to gain full equality for black people and for women.

William was born in 1805 in Newburyport, Massachusetts. His father was a sailor who lost his job when William was young. The family became very poor and his father left them. From a young age, William wanted to help end slavery. He became an abolitionist.

William worked as a reporter for several abolitionist newspapers. Then, in 1831, he started his own newspaper called the *Liberator*. In 1833, William cofounded the American Anti-Slavery Society. He stood for an immediate end to slavery. He wanted total equality for black people—and for women. He was also against working with any of the major political parties. He thought that while some politicians might say they opposed slavery, they did little to end it. These were not popular positions, even in the North. While making a speech in Boston in 1835, a mob tried to attack him and lynch him. He narrowly escaped with his life.

Not all abolitionists agreed with him either. One of William's best friends in the abolitionist movement was Frederick Douglass. Frederick had been enslaved, and he agreed with William on many things. But Frederick thought abolitionists should use the Constitution to condemn slavery. He thought the

> On this subject [slavery], I do not wish to think, or to speak, or write, with moderation. No! No! Tell a man whose house is on fire to give a moderate alarm . . . but urge me not to use moderation in a cause like the present. I will not retreat a single inch —AND I WILL BE HEARD.
>
> —*William Lloyd Garrison, "To the Public,"* Liberator, *January 1, 1831*

Constitution was supposed to be about freedom, so slavery was really unconstitutional and anti-American. William disagreed. He pointed out that the Constitution at the time actually backed the return of enslaved people who had escaped. The original Constitution also considered those enslaved to be only three-fifths of a person. To William, the Constitution was a pro-slavery document and should be abolished. Once he even burned the Constitution in public.

William used angry words, but he always said slavery should be abolished peacefully. He just wanted to convince slave owners and the government to stop it. This attitude began to change when the North and the South got closer to war. In 1859, a white abolitionist named John Brown attacked an army base to get guns to give to enslaved people. He was put on trial and hanged. William responded: "As a peace man—an 'ultra' peace man—I am prepared to say, 'Success to every slave insurrection at the South, and in every slave country.'" When the Civil War broke out in 1861, it was clear to William that the North was going to abolish slavery and the South was fighting to preserve it. He was convinced that violence was now necessary and supported the Northern side.

William risked his life many times in order to end slavery. After the Civil War, he continued to speak out for justice for everyone. Slavery was over, but blacks were now trying to get equal rights in the United States. William wrote and gave speeches seeking equal rights for all black people. He also spoke more often about women's equality and getting women the vote. William showed everyone what a difference dedicated journalists can make to history.

—Jon Van Camp

## Timeline:

- **1805** Born in Newburyport, Massachusetts
- **1831** Founds the abolitionist newspaper, the *Liberator*
- **1833** Cofounds the American Anti-Slavery Society
- **1844** Publicly burns a copy of the Constitution
- **1859** John Brown raids an armory in Harpers Ferry, Virginia, in order to start a slave uprising; William supports the effort
- **1861** The Civil War begins; William declares it a war against slavery and supports the North
- **1870s** Becomes active in the suffrage movement, which promoted voting rights for women

## More you can do:

- William Lloyd Garrison was known for inspiring people to act through his newspaper. Write a newspaper editorial that tries to get people to act on a modern issue
- Visit the *Liberator* photo gallery at www.theliberatorfiles.com to see and read about William and his fellow abolitionists

## What do you think?

- Why was William was attacked for being an abolitionist? Is there any issue you would speak out about, even if it meant you might be physically harmed?
- Whose side would you take in the debate between William and Frederick? Why?
- William eventually realized that nonviolence would not end slavery. Do you think he was right in this conclusion?
- William went from opposing slavery to defending women's rights. Do you think there is a connection between the two issues?

# Elizabeth Cady Stanton

## (1815–1902)

**The struggle for women's rights began more than one hundred years ago. One of the most influential leaders of that movement was Elizabeth Cady Stanton.**

Elizabeth's father was a lawyer who taught her about law. Elizabeth was a strong believer in individual rights. She thought every woman should have the right to vote or to have any job for which she is qualified. She wanted to be a lawyer but was not allowed to enter law school because she was a woman. Throughout her life, Elizabeth spoke publicly, wrote, and was an active promoter of women's rights.

In 1840, Elizabeth went to the World's Anti-Slavery Convention with her husband to support the abolitionist movement. However,

when she arrived, she was denied entry because she was a woman. Women were asked to sit in a separate area and were not allowed to speak or to vote. In London, Elizabeth met fellow activist Lucretia Mott. Based on their experiences at the Anti-Slavery Convention, they decided to do something drastic to bring women together to fight for their rights. Elizabeth said, "We resolved to hold a convention as soon as we returned home, and form a society to advocate the rights of women." In 1848, the Women's Rights Convention was held in Seneca Falls, New York.

The Seneca Falls Convention was a meeting for women and men to discuss the role of women in society. Elizabeth presented a three-hundred-person audience with the

> **"**The best protection any woman can have, one that will serve her at all times and in all places, is courage, and this she must get by experience, and experience comes by exposure.**"**
>
> *—Elizabeth Cady Stanton, in a letter to the Akron Women's Convention, May 16, 1851 (in* Women's Letters, *ed. Stephen Adler)*

"Declaration of Rights and Sentiments." She modeled this document after the Declaration of Independence. Elizabeth argued that women deserved social, economic, and political equality. She listed the complaints that women had as well demands women wanted. Elizabeth's list of demands included the right to vote, which was unheard of at the time. This shocked even many of the women's rights activists at the convention. By the end of the two-day conference, one hundred people had signed the declaration.

The conference was national news; many people thought that it was ridiculous for women to demand rights. The abolitionist Frederick Douglass, who attended the conference, described their reaction afterward in his newspaper: "A discussion of the rights of animals would be regarded with far more complacency by many of what are called the wise and the good of our land, than would be a discussion of the rights of woman."

Elizabeth made other important contributions to the women's rights movement. In 1868, she worked with Susan B. Anthony to publish a weekly political newspaper called the *Revolution*. She was the president of the National American Woman Suffrage Association for twenty years.

She said: "The strongest reason why we ask for woman a voice in the government under which she lives; in the religion she is asked to believe; equality in social life, where she is the chief factor; a place in the trades and professions, where she may earn her bread, is because her birthright to self-sovereignty; because, as an individual, she must rely on herself." Elizabeth died in 1902.

In 1920, the US government passed the Nineteenth Amendment, granting women the right to vote. Although Elizabeth did not live to see this event, she is remembered as a leader in the struggle for women's rights.

—Rose Golder-Novick

## Timeline:

**1815**  November 12, born in Johnstown, New York

**1840**  Marries Henry Brewster Stanton; attend World's Anti-Slavery Convention in London

**1848**  Organizes the Women's Rights Convention at Seneca Falls with Lucretia Mott

**1852**  Founds the Women's State Temperance Society to fight to ban alcohol, which she sees as the main cause of domestic violence; argues that women should have the right to divorce their husbands if they abuse alcohol

**1868**  Establishes the political weekly *Revolution* with Susan B. Anthony

**1890**  Elected president of the National American Woman Suffrage Association

**1902**  October 26, dies in New York City

## More you can do:

- Read the "Declaration of Rights and Sentiments" from the Seneca Falls Conference, 1848
- One way that Elizabeth worked to change things was by asking people to sign petitions saying that they supported a change. Think of an issue you want to change and create a petition for people to sign
- Watch the PBS documentary *Not for Ourselves Alone: The Story of Elizabeth Cady Stanton and Susan B. Anthony*

## What do you think?

- What gains have women made toward equality in the twenty-first century? In what ways are women still unequal?
- What do you think is the connection between the abolition of slavery and women's suffrage?
- Why did Elizabeth and Frederick Douglass disagree about whether to demand voting rights for both women and African Americans? What would you have done?

# Frederick Douglass
## (1818–1895)

Frederick Douglass tugged nervously at the sailor's uniform he wore. As the train raced north, away from his home in Baltimore, he could hardly contain himself.

He felt desperately afraid he would be caught. Frederick was wearing another man's clothes and carrying identification that belonged to a free black sailor named Stanley. The young man's heart was filled with hope and excitement. It was September 3, 1838. Frederick was twenty years old and still officially a slave. And he was stealing his way to freedom.

This launched the career of one of the greatest freedom fighters in US history. It was Frederick's third time trying to escape. The first two had ended in bitter punishment. But the third, planned with the help of a free black woman named Anna Murray, ended differently. Within twenty-four hours, Frederick had made it to freedom in New York City.

He was born Frederick Augustus Washington Bailey near the Chesapeake Bay. He never knew his white father and he hardly knew his mother. He spent much of his young life working for his "master," Hugh Auld, in Baltimore.

Auld tried to prevent Frederick from learning to read, but he could not be stopped. Frederick picked up reading in bits and pieces—from white children and from letters and newspapers. Eventually, he learned

> **If there is no struggle, there is no progress. Those who profess to favor freedom and deprecate agitation are men who want crops without plowing up the ground, they want rain without thunder and lightning.**
>
> —*Frederick Douglass, in a speech given in Rochester, New York, 1857*

enough to teach other slaves. But slave owners found out about the lessons and violently broke them up. Frederick was sent to live with a poor white farmer named Edward Covey. Covey was cruel and beat Frederick brutally and often. Though his spirit was nearly broken, at age sixteen, Frederick fought back against Covey and won. Covey never beat him again.

Frederick's courage only grew once he escaped. As a free man, Frederick committed himself to resisting not just individual slave owners but the whole slave system. In doing so, he came to oppose all injustice and inequality. He fought for the rights of the poor, women, immigrants, and Native Americans.

Frederick toured the nation speaking against slavery. He was a brilliant speaker. His speeches drew large, supportive crowds. But several times, he barely escaped from angry pro-slavery mobs that tried to kill him. His ideas were dangerous to a country still built on slavery. He exposed the hypocrisy of slavery in his speech "What to the Slave Is the Fourth of July?" He also spoke out against the racism that made poor whites see slaves as their enemies. In Frederick's words, the rich slave owners "divided both to conquer each."

When the war came in 1861, Frederick understood that it would become a war to end slavery. He was an avid supporter of the Union side. He met with and advised President Lincoln. He also helped recruit black soldiers to fight.

Frederick wanted freedom for enslaved people. But he wanted equality for all, no matter a person's gender or skin color. So he fought for integration of schools and for the right to vote. After the war, he held a number of political offices. He never stopped speaking out against racism, sexism, and injustice.
—Zach Zill

## Timeline:

| 1818 | Born in February |
|------|------------------|
| 1826 | Sent to work for the Aulds in Baltimore, Maryland |
| 1830(?) | Begins to learn to read |
| 1836 | First two escape attempts |
| 1838 | Successfully escapes Covey; marries Anna Murray; takes the name Frederick Douglass |
| 1841 | Began speaking at abolitionist meetings |
| 1845 | Publishes his first autobiography; travels to Ireland, England, and Scotland, where he is treated "not as a color, but as a man" |
| 1847 | Publishes the *North Star* |
| 1848 | Is the only African American to attend the first women's rights convention at Seneca Falls, New York |
| 1855 | Publishes *My Bondage and My Freedom* |
| 1859 | Flees US briefly because of association with John Brown |
| 1861 | Civil War begins |
| 1863–65 | Advises Lincoln; recruits for one of the first black units in the war, including his two sons |
| 1865 | War ends; Lincoln is assassinated |
| 1868 | Black men win the right to vote |
| 1882 | Anna dies |
| 1884 | Marries white feminist Helen Pitts |
| 1895 | Dies of heart attack |

## More you can do:

- **Read Frederick's autobiographies, *My Bondage and My Freedom* and *Narrative of the Life of Frederick Douglass, an American Slave*, and Jon Sterngass's *Frederick Douglass***

## What do you think?

- **What made Frederick's third escape attempt successful where prior ones had failed?**
- **Why did Frederick commit himself to resisting not just individual slave owners but the whole slave system?**
- **Explain why Frederick asked "What to a slave is the Fourth of July?"**

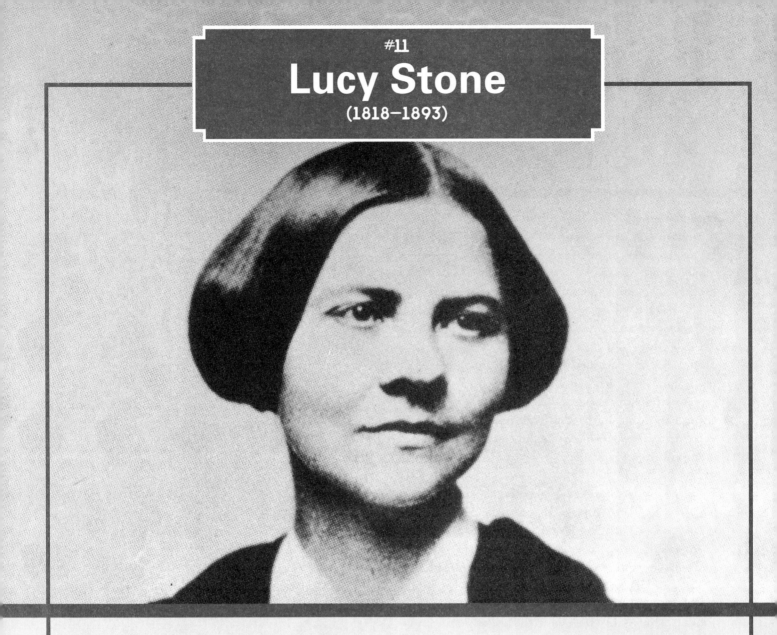

# Lucy Stone
## (1818–1893)

**Lucy Stone was a writer, editor, and activist for women's rights and against slavery. She was born in West Brookfield, Massachusetts.**

Sadly, her father used to spend the family's money on alcohol. When she saw her mother suffer she began to question why men were in charge. At sixteen, she began teaching school. She demanded a raise when she found out she was making less money than one of the male teachers.

After nine years Lucy had saved enough to go to Oberlin College—the only college in the country that would admit women. Women weren't allowed to be in the school's debating society, so she started a women's debating society that met secretly in the woods at night. In 1847 she became the first woman from Massachusetts to graduate from college.

Lucy thought that slavery was wrong. After college she began working as an organizer for William Lloyd Garrison's Anti-Slavery Society. Garrison published an antislavery newspaper called the *Liberator*. She traveled around giving speeches, even though many people were upset that a woman was speaking at all—especially on such a controversial topic. People threw rotten eggs and other things at her, but Lucy refused to be silenced. Lucy thought that women and slaves had a lot in common. Both were forced to work for others instead of living up to their potential. Both were told they were stupid and

> " Now all we need is to continue to speak the truth fearlessly, and we shall add to our number those who will turn the scale to the side of equal and full justice in all things. "
>
> —Lucy Stone, "The Progress of Fifty Years," speech at World's Fair Chicago, May 15, 1893

beaten when they disobeyed. Neither could vote or own property. Many people in the antislavery movement, including Garrison, thought that she talked too much about women's rights during her speeches against slavery. She left the group so that she would be free to fight for women's rights.

Throughout her life, Lucy stood up against what society thought women should do. She even wore "bloomers," or loose pants under a knee-length skirt. People were so shocked by this that they would yell and point her out wherever she went. She finally stopped wearing them after a few years because they distracted people from what she was saying.

Lucy organized the first National Women's Rights Conference in Worcester, Massachusetts, in 1850. She became well known as a feminist. When she married Henry Blackwell, she was the first American woman in recorded history to keep her maiden name. When their daughter was born, they gave her both last names: Alice Stone Blackwell.

During the Civil War, Lucy continued working to end slavery. She helped to found the Women's National Loyal League in 1863, which lobbied President Lincoln and the Union states to pass the Thirteenth Amendment to end slavery.

After slavery was ended, Lucy worked for women's rights for the rest of her life. She fought for women's right to vote—a right that was not won until after her death. She founded the *Woman's Journal*, in which she wrote about how women could take action to win their rights. She died in 1893. But her daughter Alice helped win the right to vote in 1920. Lucy's last words were, "Make the world better."

—Sarah Grey

## Timeline:

| | |
|---|---|
| 1818 | Born in West Brookfield, Massachusetts |
| 1837 | Demands equal pay at her teaching job |
| 1843 | Begins attending Oberlin College; organizes women's debating society |
| 1847 | Becomes first Massachusetts woman to graduate from college |
| 1848 | Begins working as an organizer for the Anti-Slavery Society |
| 1850 | Organizes first National Women's Rights Conference |
| 1852 | Begins wearing bloomers in public |
| 1855 | Marries Henry Blackwell but keeps her name |
| 1856 | A former slave, Margaret Garner, is accused of killing her baby rather than allowing it to be sold into slavery; Lucy is accused of sneaking a knife into Margaret's jail cell so that she could kill herself rather than be forced back into slavery |
| 1857 | Birth of daughter Alice Stone Blackwell |
| 1859 | Birth of premature son, who died shortly after birth |
| 1863 | Founds Women's National Loyal League to lobby for Thirteenth Amendment to end slavery |
| 1869 | Organizes the American Woman Suffrage Association to lobby for the right to vote |
| 1872 | Founds, with Henry, the feminist *Woman's Journal* |
| 1893 | Dies of stomach cancer and is the first person in Massachusetts to be cremated |

## More you can do:

- **Read Kathy Wilmore's play *Lucy Stone, Crusader for Freedom***

## What do you think?

- **Why was it so shocking for a woman to speak in public? What other "radical" things did Lucy do?**
- **Why did Lucy think that women's rights and the rights of enslaved Africans were connected? Do you agree?**
- **Why was it important to Lucy to keep her name when she got married?**

# Harriet Tubman

## (ca. 1820–1913)

Harriet Tubman was one of the greatest "conductors" on what was called the Underground Railroad. The Underground Railroad was not underground and it was not a railroad.

It was a secret way of helping enslaved persons to freedom. Some called Harriet "Moses." John Brown called her "General Tubman" and said that she was "one of the bravest persons on this continent." The great abolitionist Frederick Douglass sang her praises.

Harriet came into this world as an enslaved person sometime between 1820 and 1822 in Maryland. Her birth name was Araminta Moss. She later took the name Tubman from her first husband and changed her first name to Harriet.

She was not a large woman, standing little more than five feet tall. Throughout her life, she suffered from seizures and sleeping fits from a blow to her head as a teenager. She never learned to read and had no formal education. But Harriet was one of the most intelligent people who ever lived in the United States.

When she escaped from slavery in 1849, her husband and two brothers were too afraid to go with her. So she went alone. She then risked travel back to the South thirteen times to free her entire family. She also helped dozens of other enslaved people escape. When the US government started tracking down escapees in the Northern states, she led the freedom seekers even further north—into Canada.

> **"** I was conductor of the Underground Railroad for eight years, and I can say what most conductors can't say—I never ran my train off the track and I never lost a passenger. **"**

*—Harriet Tubman, from* Harriet Tubman: Imagining a Life *by Beverly Lowry*

Harriet was deeply religious and her faith helped give her courage. She always traveled at night, often in the dead of winter. She would steal away on a Saturday evening—because she knew the newspapers would not print "runaway" notices until Monday morning.

Harriet carried a gun, which she was always prepared to use. She kept a special potion to keep babies quiet, in case they had to hide from a slave catcher. She often disguised herself. She even pretended to read a newspaper once to avoid being seen by a former master.

When the Civil War started, Harriet joined the Union cause. After working as a nurse, cook, and laundress, she became a spy. The Union Army used her knowledge to gather intelligence and launch raids. In fact, Harriet became the first woman in US military history ever to lead an armed expedition. In the Combahee River Raid, Harriet led a group of mostly black soldiers in a daring attack that liberated more than 750 enslaved persons.

After the war, Harriet continued working to help newly freed people. Despite her widespread fame, she still faced racism and poverty. She never received pay from the government for her service during the war. She mostly had to rely on money collected by her supporters. But her fighting spirit remained, even as she grew old. With slavery abolished, Harriet took up the cause of women's rights. She worked with women like Susan B. Anthony to fight for women's right to vote.

In 1913, at more than ninety years old, she fell ill with pneumonia and died. Though small physically, Harriet Tubman made an enormous impact on the country and our history.

**—Zach Zill**

## Timeline:

| | |
|---|---|
| 1820–22 | Born in Dorchester County, Maryland, to enslaved parents |
| 1840 | Father granted freedom |
| 1844 | Marries John Tubman |
| 1849 | Escapes from slavery |
| 1849–60 | Makes thirteen return trips to free other slaves |
| 1858 | Purchases a house in Auburn, New York; meets John Brown and shares with him her practical knowledge about the Virginia countryside |
| 1859 | Raid on Harpers Ferry fails; Brown is executed |
| 1861 | Civil War starts, works as nurse |
| 1863 | January, Emancipation Proclamation goes into effect; Southern blacks are freed from slavery |
| 1863 | June, leads Combahee River Raid |
| 1869 | Marries soldier Nelson Davis, who was also formerly enslaved |
| 1890s | Undergoes brain surgery in Boston |
| 1913 | Dies on March 10 |

## More you can do:

- **Read Ann Petry's *Harriet Tubman: Conductor on the Underground Railroad***
- **Research the narratives of "passengers" on the Underground Railroad and draw a map of a possible route to freedom**

## What do you think?

- **Would you have risked your life to escape enslavement or be a "conductor" on the Underground Railroad? Why or why not?**
- **Harriet once said, "I freed thousands of slaves. I could have freed thousands more, if they had known they were slaves." Explain what she might have meant.**

# Susan B. Anthony

## (1820–1906)

**Susan B. Anthony was a feminist activist who fought for women in the United States to have the right to vote.**

She was also an abolitionist for more than a decade before the Civil War did away with slavery. Susan was often fearless, refusing to back down from what she believed even in the face of resistance or ridicule.

Susan helped to form a weekly journal on women's rights called the *Revolution* in 1868. The journal's motto was "The true republic— men, their rights and nothing more; women, their rights and nothing less." The *Revolution* supported suffrage, or the right to vote, for both women and African Americans, and many other rights for women, such as equal pay.

A year later, she helped found the National Woman Suffrage Association (NWSA). Suffrage was the main cause to which Susan would devote her life. But she also believed oppressed people should fight together for their liberation. In the late 1850s she attempted to merge the civil rights struggles of women and blacks by joining the Anti-Slavery Society. From the beginning of the NWSA, Susan worked to unite women fighting for equality at work with those fighting for the right to vote.

Susan's life was not without controversy or missteps. She worked hard to bring women workers into the struggle for suffrage. But when Susan encouraged women to gain independence by working in print shops where

"Where, under our Declaration of Independence, does the Saxon man get his power to deprive all women and Negroes of their inalienable rights?"

—Susan B. Anthony, speech at Ninth National Women's Rights Convention, 1859

men were striking, she was expelled from the National Labor Union. She also left the Anti-Slavery Society when it supported the Fifteenth Amendment, which granted blacks but not women the right to vote. This ended her long friendship with abolitionist Frederick Douglass.

Susan's early life helped shape her outlook and politics. She was born into a Quaker family. Many Quakers, including her brother, were against slavery long before the Civil War. When she was sixteen, Susan collected enough anti-slavery petitions to fill several boxes. Her mother and her sister were also involved in the struggle for women's rights. So when men were paid four times more than women at her first job as a teacher, she began to fight for equal pay.

Despite her eagerness to defeat injustice, Susan was at first far from confident. She was nervous about how she looked and whether she was a good enough public speaker. She eventually got over these fears to become a respected orator and a leader in the fight for women's rights.

Susan won a much bigger following when, in 1872, she was arrested for the crime of voting in the presidential election. She was convicted and fined $100. She publicly announced, "I shall never pay a dollar of your unjust penalty"—and never did. Nearly forty years later, in 1920, women finally won the right to vote with the passage of the Nineteenth Amendment to the US Constitution. It was called the Susan B. Anthony Amendment.

—Jason Farbman

## Timeline:

| 1820 | February 15, born in Adams, Massachusetts |
| 1854 | Begins circulating petitions for married women's property rights and women's suffrage |
| 1854 | Begins organizing conventions on women's rights throughout New York State |
| 1861 | Travels across upstate New York on an antislavery campaign with the slogan "No Union with Slaveholders, No Compromise" |
| 1868 | January 8, begins publishing the *Revolution*, a journal of women's rights |
| 1869 | Founds the NWSA, with Elizabeth Cady Stanton |
| 1872 | November 18, arrested for voting |
| 1873 | A judge orders the jury to find Susan guilty of voting and imposes a $100 fine; Susan never pays |
| 1884–87 | Susan and three coauthors publish the four-volume *History of Woman Suffrage* |
| 1906 | March 13, dies of heart disease and pneumonia |
| 1920 | August 26, women win the right to vote, as granted in the Nineteenth Amendment to the US Constitution |

## More you can do:

- Read *The History of Woman Suffrage* and the lecture Susan delivered after her arrest and trial for voting: "Is it a Crime for a Citizen of the United States to Vote?"

## What do you think?

- Why was Susan expelled from the National Labor Union? Was it wrong to encourage women to take the jobs of striking men?
- The Fourteenth Amendment to the Constitution says in part, "All persons born or naturalized in the United States . . . are citizens of the United States" and are entitled to certain rights—including voting. But women weren't allowed to vote until the Nineteenth Amendment was passed in 1920. Why did it take so long for women to gain this right?

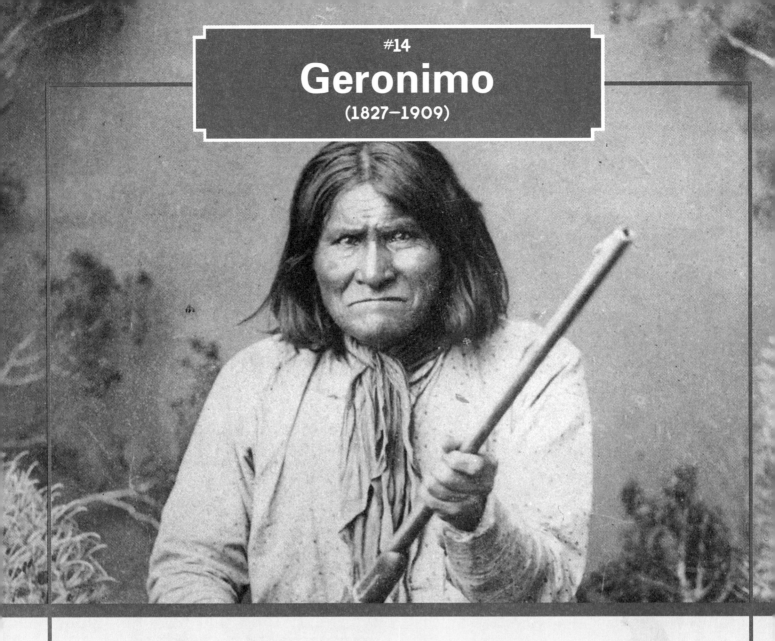

# Geronimo
## (1827–1909)

**Geronimo was a Chiricahua Apache. He led a struggle against Mexico and the United States to defend the Apaches' land and way of life after 1850.**

The Apache lived in what is today the southwestern United States. Geronimo's people grew corn, hunted wild game, and gathered wild fruits and nuts. For generations, the Spanish captured and sold Apache people into slavery. They offered gold to anyone who killed an Apache. These attacks drove the Apaches into the mountains. When they were short of supplies they raided Spanish settlements.

Once, when Geronimo and other members of his tribe were trading in a Mexican town,

soldiers attacked the Apache camp near the town and killed Geronimo's wife and three small children. Geronimo appealed to other Native nations to help him to seek justice. He led his fellow warriors on an attack that wiped out a large group of Mexican soldiers.

After a war with Mexico that ended in 1848, the United States claimed the Southwest. Relations with the new white intruders were friendly at first, but turned sour. Eager for land and gold, the government in Washington sent soldiers to force the Apache bands to give up their lands.

In 1860, the great Chiricahua Apache chief Mangas Coloradas went to a gold mining camp to talk peace. The miners tied him to a tree and lashed him with bullwhips. Mangas began leading attacks on white settlements.

In the following year, the Chiricahua Apache chief Cochise, along with his wife, young son, brother, and two nephews, came to parley with American troops. The commanding officer accused Cochise of kidnapping a white boy. Cochise had not taken the boy, but the whites did not believe him. He escaped from the soldiers by cutting a hole through a tent. Then the soldiers hung his brother and his two nephews. "After this trouble," Geronimo recalled, "all of the Indians agreed not to be friendly with the white men any more."

A few years later, General Joseph R. West's volunteer forces lured Mangas into their camp under a flag of truce and then shot him. At the same time, soldiers attacked and destroyed Mangas's camps. Geronimo called this "the greatest wrong ever done to the Indians." In retaliation, the Chiricahua Apaches killed many white settlers and then retreated into the mountains.

Constantly on the run, the Apaches couldn't survive. Thousands were forced onto the San Carlos reservation in Arizona in 1876. Geronimo fled San Carlos, escaping into Mexico and eluding troops for many years. Scouts discovered his refuge and he agreed to go back to the reservation in 1884. He escaped again for one last time the next year.

General Miles promised that Geronimo and his people could live at the San Carlos reservation. Instead, he and hundreds of other Chiricahua Apaches were imprisoned in Florida. Geronimo was held prisoner for twenty-three years until his death in 1909. He told General Miles, the day he gave himself up, "Once I moved about like the wind."

**—Paul D'Amato**

## Timeline:

| | |
|---|---|
| ca. 1827–29 | Geronimo (whose original name was Goyahkla, meaning "one who yawns") is born in what is today southwestern Arizona |
| 1837 | Mexican State of Chihuahua offers $100 for an Apache warrior's scalp, $50 for a woman's, and $25 for a child's |
| 1850 | Slaughter of Geronimo's family, along with many others, by Mexican soldiers |
| 1850 | Leads an attack on Mexican soldiers; gets name "Geronimo" |
| 1863 | January 18, Mangas Coloradas is captured and killed by US soldiers |
| 1871 | Congress votes to give $70,000 for "collecting the Apaches of Arizona and New Mexico upon reservations"; Apaches who refuse to move are to be considered "hostile" |
| 1876 | Thousands of Chiricahua Apaches move to San Carlos; Geronimo settles on reservation but escapes to freedom several times |
| 1886 | Surrenders to General Miles |
| 1909 | Dies and is buried in the Apache cemetery in Fort Sill, Oklahoma |

## More you can do:

- **Read** *Geronimo: My Life*, edited by S. M. Barrett
- **Watch** the documentary *We Shall Remain*, episode 4: "Geronimo"

## What do you think?

- **Who do you think started the war between the Indians and the white settlers?**
- **Why were the settlers and the US government so determined to force the Apache people onto reservations?**
- **Why did Geronimo and his band try to elude capture for so long?**

28

# Sitting Bull

## (ca. 1831–1890)

**Sitting Bull was a great leader of the Lakota Nation. He remains an important symbol for Native American resistance to the US conquest of the North American continent.**

In the area that is now South Dakota, Sitting Bull was born into a leading Hunkpapa Lakota family. As a very young man, his father gave him the name Tatanka-Iyotanka (Sitting Bull), which reflected his bravery and reliability.

Between 1850 and 1890, US society experienced enormous growth. New businesses took over land in the West in order to build railroads and mine for gold and other minerals. White settlers moved west with them—into the lands of the Lakota, Cheyenne, and Arapaho peoples. The US Army used brutal force against the Native Americans to push them out of the way. This led to war.

Native leaders like Sitting Bull courageously defended their people. In 1866, the Oglala Lakota chief Red Cloud led Native American warriors in an attack on US Army forts and settlers on the lands around the upper Missouri River. Another Lakota leader, Crazy Horse, won an important victory at the Battle of One Hundred Slain. This war ended when the US government signed the Fort Laramie Treaty of 1868, which granted a 25-million-acre territory to the Sioux Indians and set aside millions more acres as hunting grounds.

The most important part of the treaty was

a promise that the Black Hills, an area that is holy to the Lakota people, was to be theirs forever. The Lakota wished to live peacefully on the same lands where their people had been for generations. But the United States did not want to honor the treaty. Mining companies believed there was gold in the Black Hills and they wanted it. They tried to convince the Lakota to sell their land.

The Lakota did not want to sell their land. In fact, the idea of selling the land was alien to them. Sitting Bull spoke about the difference in values between Native tribes and American society, saying that "the love of possessions is a disease with them. These people have made many rules that the rich may break, but the poor may not. . . . They claim this mother of ours, the Earth, for their own use, and fence their neighbors away from her, and deface her with their buildings and their refuse."

Time and time again, Sitting Bull refused to agree to the sale of Lakota land. When US officials could not convince the Lakota to sell, war broke out again. Sitting Bull and Crazy Horse led Lakota, Cheyenne, and Arapaho warriors in a strong victory over the 7th Calvary of the US Army in the Battle of Little Big Horn on June 25, 1876. The US Army was shocked that they lost and sought harsher revenge. US officials captured Native American leaders and arrested them. Sitting Bull was able to escape.

A few years later, he returned to defend his people once again. In 1890, the US Army was worried that Sitting Bull might help lead a new war against white settlers in order to protect the Lakota way of life. Instead of recognizing the rights of the Lakota, the US government resorted to violence once again. On December 15, 1890, Sitting Bull was killed by one of the dozens of Indian Affairs policemen sent by the US government to arrest him.

—**Michele Bollinger**

## Timeline:

| | |
|---|---|
| 1831(?) | Born in what is now South Dakota |
| 1845 | Granted name "Sitting Bull" by his father |
| 1866 | Red Cloud's War begins |
| 1868 | Fort Laramie Treaty is signed; Black Hills granted to the Lakota "exclusively" and "in perpetuity"; Great Sioux Reservation is established |
| 1874 | General George Armstrong Custer leads campaign for gold into the Black Hills in violation of the Fort Laramie Treaty |
| 1876 | June 25, the Lakota, Cheyenne, and Arapaho defeat the United States at the Battle of Little Big Horn |
| 1877 | May 5, Crazy Horse meets with US officials |
| 1877 | September 5, Crazy Horse is killed in US custody |
| 1881 | July 19, returns to US from Canada; detained by US officials |
| 1883 | May, returns to Standing Rock |
| 1884 | Participates in Buffalo Bill Cody's Wild West show; returns to Standing Rock |
| 1890 | Lends support to Ghost Dance movement |
| | December 15, taken prisoner and killed |
| | December 26, 7th Calvary of the US Army kills three hundred unarmed Lakota at the Wounded Knee Massacre |

## More you can do:

- **Find and read a copy of the order to arrest Sitting Bull**
- **Explore resources on the Black Hills and the Lakota people, such as www.dlncoalition.org**
- **View the PBS documentary** *We Shall Remain*

## What do you think?

- **In what ways did white society and Native Americans view land differently?**
- **Why did the United States use force and set its military against Native Americans?**
- **Why were Indian tribes victorious at Little Big Horn?**
- **What were the outcomes of the Fort Laramie Treaty? Did the United States honor this treaty?**

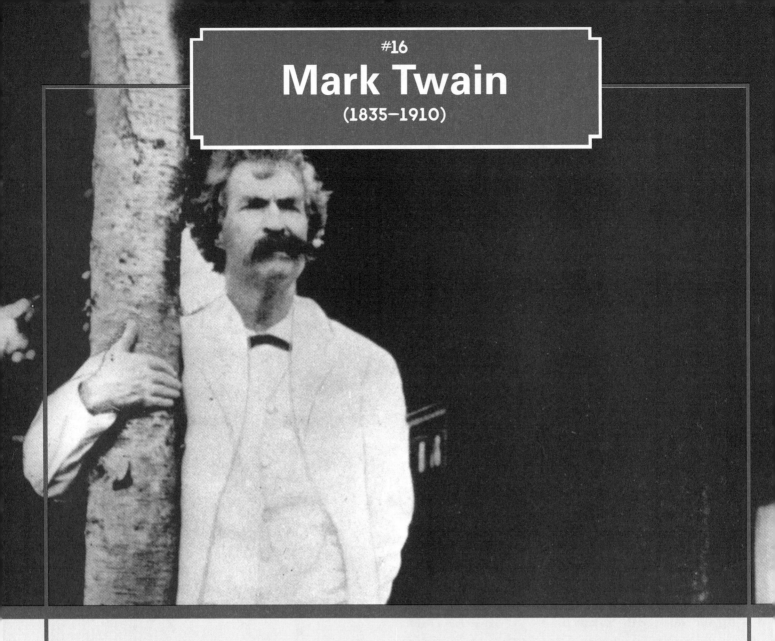

# #16
# Mark Twain
## (1835–1910)

Mark Twain was born Samuel Langhorne Clemens in Missouri. He had a humble childhood in a frontier town near the Mississippi River.

He drew on this experience for his best-known books, *The Adventures of Tom Sawyer* and *The Adventures of Huckleberry Finn*.

When his father died, twelve-year-old Samuel left school to earn money. He first worked as a printer's apprentice in East Coast cities, in horrible conditions and without pay. He returned to the Midwest in the 1850s, where he had another miserable apprenticeship on the riverboats. He was a trade union activist in both jobs.

By his mid-twenties, he had become a successful steamboat pilot. But the Civil War halted that career. Samuel briefly joined a group of soldiers fighting for the South. But within weeks he left and joined his brother Orion, who supported the North, in Nevada.

Next came his "wild years out West" as a failed silver and gold prospector. He mixed with a group of artists and writers called the Bohemians. He became a journalist in San Francisco, publishing articles protesting unfair treatment of Chinese immigrants, police brutality, and a legal system that favored the rich over the poor. He started a lifelong career as a popular, entertaining public speaker, using the name "Mark Twain." On the steamboats this was a measure of depth—two fathoms. But in bars it meant "write down two drinks for me."

He met the Langdons, a wealthy coal family from upstate New York who were committed abolitionists. He got to know socialists and activists against racism and for labor and women's rights, including Helen Keller and Frederick Douglass. A whole new world was opened to him. He fell in love with Olivia Langdon and they were married in 1870.

Mark found fame and fortune through writing and public speaking. His work—especially his humor and wit—was loved by ordinary people, but not by the literary elite. For example, the Library Committee of Concord, Massachusetts, called *Huckleberry Finn* "rough, course, inelegant . . . trash, suited for the slums." The book has sparked disagreements in recent decades. It uses the racist language and stereotypes of its time, which are now rightly considered hateful and wrong. But the novel is against racism. In an era when African Americans were losing the rights they won when slavery ended, racists hated the story because it sympathizes with the runaway slave Jim. The book was published in installments in *Century* magazine, alongside an essay calling for equality for former slaves. In the same year, Mark argued that African Americans should be compensated for the crime of enslavement.

Mark was also an inventive but unsuccessful businessman. He faced bankruptcy several times, especially during the financial crises of the 1880s. He spent many years traveling the world, digging himself out of debt through tiring but wildly popular speaking tours. Toward the end of his life, his wife and two of his three daughters died, causing him much grief. He became ever more critical of US social and economic inequalities at home and wars abroad.
—Helen Scott

## Timeline:

| | |
|---|---|
| 1835 | November 30, born Samuel Langhorne Clemens in Florida, Missouri |
| 1853 | Moves to East Coast to work in print industry |
| 1858 | Starts work as a pilot on Mississippi River |
| 1863–34 | Adopts the name "Mark Twain" and moves to San Francisco to work as a journalist |
| 1867 | First public lecture in New York City; publishes *Celebrated Jumping Frog of Calaveras County and Other Sketches*. Begins a lifelong career of traveling, public speaking, and writing |
| 1870 | Marries Olivia Langdon in Buffalo, New York |
| 1876 | Publishes *The Adventures of Tom Sawyer* |
| 1910 | Dies April 21; buried in Elmira, New York |
| 2010 | Volume one of the *Autobiography of Mark Twain* published, a hundred years after his death, as he wished |

## More you can do:

- Read the first few chapters of *Tom Sawyer* and pick out which details you think Mark might have drawn from his boyhood experiences
- Visit the Mark Twain Boyhood Home & Museum in Hannibal, Missouri

## What do you think?

- To what extent are Mark Twain's life and works at odds with the image of him as a national hero and "father of American literature"?
- Do you think that the language of Huckleberry Finn should be read and discussed by students? What are some ways you can think of to talk about the book's language in the classroom?
- The Civil War destroyed slavery and brought with it the promise of greater democracy and freedom. But by the late 1870s, Reconstruction was abandoned and corporations grew powerful. Racist segregation and a growing divide between rich and poor created new tensions in society. How did Mark's work reflect the contradictions of the Gilded Age?

# Mary "Mother" Jones

## (1837–1930)

**Mother Jones was a legendary union organizer. She was born Mary Harris in 1837 in Ireland.**

Mary moved to Canada as a teenager and then to the United States when she was twenty years old. Mary worked as a seamstress for wealthy families in Chicago. She was shocked by the suffering of the poor and how little the rich seemed to care. In 1860, Mary moved to Memphis, Tennessee, where she met George E. Jones, who was a union activist. They got married in 1861 and had four children together.

Then tragedy struck this happy family. In 1867, a yellow fever epidemic swept through Tennessee. Mary's husband and all her small children caught the disease and died within a week. After losing her family, Mary moved back to Chicago and opened a dress shop. But tragedy struck again just four years later. The Great Chicago Fire of 1871 destroyed Mary's home, her shop, and all her belongings.

Despite her own suffering, Mary decided to dedicate her life to helping poor and working people. Many workers were trying to form unions, but their employers did their best to prevent this. Most workers had to go on strike to try and win union recognition.

Mary became a union organizer. Soon she began traveling around the country, visiting workers who were on strike. She joined their picket lines and used humor and storytelling

> **In Georgia where children work day and night in the cotton mills they have just passed a bill to protect songbirds. What about the little children from whom all song is gone?**
>
> —Mother Jones, speaking at a demonstration in New York City, 1903

when she spoke to large crowds of strikers to keep their spirits up.

By 1897, when she was sixty years old, Mary began calling herself Mother Jones. From then on she was a legend. Her white hair and old-fashioned clothes made her seem like a grandmother. Many workers called her "the miners' angel." It is believed that the folk song "She'll Be Coming 'Round the Mountain" is about her.

Mother Jones traveled wherever she was needed. As she said, "My address is like my shoes. It travels with me. I abide where there is a fight against wrong."

Mother Jones saw young children working long hours in textile mills and mines. In 1903, she organized a "Children's Crusade," a march of two hundred child strikers and their supporters from Pennsylvania to New York. The children held signs with slogans such as "We want time to play!" and "We want to go to school!"

Mother Jones was sent to prison many times, but she never gave up her fight for justice. She joined both the Socialist Party and the Industrial Workers of the World, two of the most important radical movements of the time.

In 1913, she told striking miners in Colorado, "Rise up and strike. . . . We are going to stand together and never surrender. Boys, always remember you ain't got a damn thing if you ain't got a union!"

Mother Jones continued organizing as long as her health would permit. She finally died on November 30, 1930, at the age of ninety-three. Up to fifteen thousand people attended her funeral, tearfully mourning the loss of "the miners' angel."
—Sharon Smith

## Timeline:

- **1837** Born Mary Harris in 1837 in Ireland
- **1861** Marries George E. Jones
- **1867** Loses her husband and four small children to yellow fever
- **1871** Loses her home and all her belongings in the Great Chicago Fire
- **1897** Begins calling herself Mother Jones and becomes a legend among workers
- **1903** Organizes the "Children's Crusade"
- **1930** Dies at the age of ninety-three, after more than forty years of union organizing

## More you can do:

- **Read The Autobiography of Mother Jones, by Mary Harris Jones, or listen to the audio recording at librivox.org**
- **Learn more about child workers today and make strike signs that they might carry**
- **Listen to the song "Workin' in the Coal Mine" by Allen Toussaint, sung by Lee Dorsey**

## What do you think?

- **What made Mary decide to dedicate her life to helping poor and working people?**
- **How did Mary become the legend known as "Mother Jones"?**
- **How did Mother Jones help children who were working long hours in textile mills and mines?**

Liliuokalani was the ruler of Hawaii until the islands were seized by the United States in 1898. She was the last monarch of the island nation.

Liliuokalani was born on Oahu to a royal family. As a child, she attended school and traveled. Liliuokalani had a gift for music. She wrote many songs, including "Aloha Oe" (Farewell to Thee).

Hawaii changed a great deal during Liliuokalani's life. Between the 1770s and 1840s, Europeans and whites from the United States began settling in Hawaii. At first, the white settlers were mostly missionaries who converted some native Hawaiians to Christianity.

Then, white settlers from the United States purchased Hawaiian land and began to grow sugar on plantations for export. White sugar growers brought in Chinese and Japanese workers who labored in horrible conditions for very low pay. Sugar production was a profitable business and Hawaii's white plantation owners became powerful businessmen.

At the same time, the original inhabitants of Hawaii had their own government, culture, and society. Hawaii was a kingdom ruled by an elected monarch. In 1874, King Kalakaua—Liliuokalani's brother—began his reign. Kalakaua negotiated with the sugar growers to keep the peace and to enrich Hawaii. But the sugar growers wanted more control over Hawaii in order to make better deals with US businesses. In 1887, white leaders forced the king to sign a new constitution that weakened the monarch and restricted voting rights for some Hawaiians.

In 1891, King Kalakaua died and Liliuokalani became queen. Hawaiians wanted her to fight to maintain native control over the government. She wrote, "To have ignored or disregarded so general a request I must have been deaf to the voice of the people, which tradition tells us is the voice of God." Liliuokalani planned a new constitution to restore the rights of Hawaiians and weaken the power of white residents.

White leaders opposed Liliuokalani's plans. On January 16, 1893, armed US troops backed the white leaders against the queen and overthrew her rule. They created a new government with Sanford Dole, who wanted the United States to annex Hawaii.

Hawaiians protested against the overthrow. In early 1895, allies of the queen led a three-day rebellion against the government but were defeated. Fearing Liliuokalani's leadership, white officials imprisoned her in the Iolani Palace. She gave up her throne in exchange for the release of her allies.

President Grover Cleveland opposed annexation. But most politicians, as well as many Americans, believed in "manifest destiny." This belief held that the United States was superior to other nations and should conquer other lands—including Hawaii. US newspapers that supported the overthrow printed racist and sexist images of the queen.

In 1898, the new president, William McKinley, annexed Hawaii against the wishes of the Hawaiians. The brutal plantation economy continued to grow in Hawaii. Liliuokalani died in 1917. In 1993, the US government formally apologized for the events of 1893.

**—Michele Bollinger**

## Timeline:

| | |
|---|---|
| 1778 | Captain James Cook arrives in Hawaii |
| 1838 | Born on the island of Oahu |
| 1881 | King David Kalakaua's reign begins |
| 1887 | The Bayonet Constitution is created |
| 1891 | Liliuokalani becomes queen |
| 1893 | Liliuokalani is overthrown |
| 1895 | Liliuokalani is imprisoned |
| 1897 | Liliuokalani travels to the US to speak out against annexation |
| 1898 | The United States annexes Hawaii; the Spanish-American War begins |
| | The American Anti-Imperialist League is founded |
| 1901 | James Dole, Sanford's cousin, establishes the Hawaiian Pineapple Company |
| 1917 | Queen Liliuokalani dies |
| 1959 | Hawaii becomes the fiftieth state of the United States |

## More you can do:

- Find the 1897 anti-annexation petitions signed by Hawaiians and presented to the United States
- Compare the experience of Hawaiians to American Indians during the same time period

## What do you think?

- Why did Liliuokalani pursue changes to the Constitution? Why did she not try to please the sugar growers?
- In what ways were Hawaiian society and culture damaged by the growth of the white settlers?
- In the late 1800s, how did the United States view nations that it sought to conquer? Why were these beliefs widespread?
- As the leader of her nation, how did Liliuokalani defy expectations for women held by many Americans at the time?

# Albert and Lucy Gonzalez Parsons

## (1848–1887; ca. 1853–1942)

**Albert and Lucy Gonzalez Parsons were firebrand organizers of workers in the United States in the late 1800s and early 1900s.**

Albert was the child of English immigrants. Lucy was of mixed Mexican, Native American, and African American descent. The couple met and married in Texas, but life there was difficult for an interracial couple. Albert couldn't find work, and he was shot in the leg by the Ku Klux Klan for trying to help African Americans vote. Lucy and Albert moved to Chicago and quickly became leaders of the labor movement there.

Lucy and Albert were both strongly affected by the Great Railroad Strike of 1877. Strikers were protesting low pay and unsafe working conditions. The strike lasted forty-five days and spread to four states. It included many clashes between strikers and security guards, with deaths on both sides. After the strike ended, unions began organizing many more workers than they had before.

The unions' next step was the fight for the eight-hour workday. Before 1886, women, men, and children often worked more than fifty hours a week (on Saturdays, too). The slogan of the eight-hour-day movement was "eight hours for work, eight hours for sleep, eight hours for what we will." In Chicago, Lucy, Albert, and their two children helped lead a march of eighty thousand people for the eight-hour day on May 1, 1886. Later

> Will you deny that your jails are filled with the children of the poor, not the children of the rich? Will you deny that men steal because their bellies are empty?

—*Lucy Parsons, 1890*

that same week, there was a small labor rally in Chicago's Haymarket Square against police killings of strikers. Someone threw a bomb into police lines that resulted in the deaths and injuries of many protesters and police. Albert was no longer even at the rally but, along with his codefendants, was tried and convicted of "conspiracy to murder."

Lucy threw herself into a defense campaign for the Haymarket martyrs, as they came to be known. Largely as a result of her tireless organizing, the Haymarket Affair gained national and international attention. Lucy explained to crowds that the accused men were innocent, and that it was really their political ideas that were on trial. Lucy said it was an attempt to stop the success of the eight-hour-day and labor movements. It was during this time that she was described by the Chicago police as being "more dangerous than a thousand rioters." Despite the public outcry, Albert was executed.

Lucy kept on being a spirited fighter for workers' and women's rights. She became a regular presence in the streets of Chicago. She sold revolutionary pamphlets, books, and newspapers while avoiding the police. She often spoke at trade union meetings and walked picket lines with striking workers. She helped organize the unemployed and poor to demand relief and better services.

Lucy last spoke publicly at age eighty-two in 1941, in frigid weather, on a picket line of striking workers at a machine shop in Chicago. After their victory she rode in a place of honor on their May Day parade float.
—**Alex Tronolone**

## Timeline:

| | |
|---|---|
| 1848 | Albert born in Montgomery, Alabama |
| ca. 1853 | Lucy born in Texas |
| 1870–73 | Albert and Lucy marry in Texas and move to Chicago |
| 1881 | Albert is a major figure in the Chicago Social Revolutionary Congress |
| 1884 | Albert becomes editor of the *Alarm* newspaper |
| 1886 | May 4, Haymarket Affair: Unidentified bomber kills eight and wounds many police |
| 1886–87 | Lucy goes on a speaking tour in seventeen states, speaking to about 200,000 people to defend the radicals accused of murder in the Haymarket Affair |
| 1887 | November 11, Albert is hanged |
| 1894 | Lucy helps organize Jacob Coxey's "Army of the Unemployed" |
| 1905 | June 27, Lucy is a founding member of the Industrial Workers of the World; is one of two women at the conference and the only one to speak |
| 1905 | Lucy begins editing the *Liberator* |
| 1917 | Lucy organizes "Hunger Demonstrations" in Chicago |
| 1927 | Lucy is elected to the executive committee of International Labor Defense |
| 1942 | March 7, Lucy dies in a house fire; Chicago police raid her apartment and take books and papers the fire did not destroy |

## More you can do:

- Learn more about Lucy at www.lucyparsonsproject.org
- Read primary source materials at the Haymarket Affair Digital Collection: www.chicagohistory.org/hadc

## What do you think?

- Is the eight-hour-day struggle still relevant today? Why or why not?
- Why do you think Albert and his codefendants were executed?
- What made Lucy "more dangerous than a thousand rioters"?

# Mary Elizabeth Lease

## (ca. 1850–1933)

Mary Elizabeth Lease was born in Pennsylvania around 1850. Her parents had fled Ireland because her father faced hanging as a rebel against English rule.

When Mary was a child, her father and two brothers were killed fighting against the South during the Civil War. Mary became a teacher. She moved to Kansas and married Charles Lease.

Mary and Charles started a small farm. This was a difficult time to be a farmer. Farmers borrowed money from banks to buy seed and equipment, hoping to pay it back when they sold their crops. If their crops failed or prices fell, they had trouble paying the high inter-est charged by banks. They also had to transport crops by rail, and the railroads charged farmers higher rates than they charged large corporations. Like many, Mary and Charles lost their farm because they couldn't pay their debts. They tried farming in Texas, but failed again. Mary and Charles moved back to Kansas with their four children.

Mary studied law and became one of the first women lawyers in Kansas. She also became active in politics. She fought for the right of women to vote, for the right of working people to join unions, and for Ireland to be free from English rule. Mary became a very good public speaker and spoke all over Kansas. She was quoted as saying that farmers should "raise less corn and more hell." She

> ❝ It is no longer a government of the people, by the people, and for the people, but a government of Wall Street, by Wall Street, and for Wall Street. The great common people of this country are slaves, and monopoly is the master. ❞
>
> —*Mary Elizabeth Lease, in a speech given in 1890*

later claimed that quote was made up by reporters, but it didn't bother her because she thought it was "a right good bit of advice."

Mary thought the Republican and Democratic Parties didn't care about farmers and workers. She helped start the Union Labor Party and ran for local public office. She came close to winning, which was remarkable when women weren't even allowed to vote. Mary then helped start a new party, the People's Party of America, which was known as the Populist Party.

Farmers and workers alone had no power to stand up to banks, railroads, and factory owners. Millions joined or supported the Populist Party hoping that they could make radical change to give control of the economy to working people. Mary became one of the most famous Populists and gave speeches across the country. She pointed out how politicians from the major parties were more interested in the profits of the industrialists than in the lives of working people. "The politicians said we suffered from overproduction. Overproduction, when 10,000 little children . . . starve to death every year in the United States." Opponents attacked her by calling her "unwomanly," but Mary's speeches brought many new members into the party.

The Populists won control of the state government in Kansas. The new Populist governor appointed Mary to office. But eventually, the Populists merged with the Democrats. Even though she didn't trust the Democrats, Mary campaigned for the Democratic-Populist candidate for president in the 1896 election. When the Democrats lost, the Populist movement collapsed.

Mary moved to New York to begin a new career as a journalist. She continued to work for some causes, including women's suffrage, Prohibition (making it illegal to make or sell alcoholic beverages), and making birth control legal.

—**Don Lash**

## Timeline:

| | |
|---|---|
| 1850 or 1853 | Born in Pennsylvania |
| ca. 1870 | Moves to Kansas to teach school |
| 1873 | Marries Charles Lease and begins farming |
| 1883 | After second farm fails, begins studying law |
| 1885 | Admitted to Kansas bar as a lawyer; gives first public speech |
| 1887 | Becomes lecturer for Farmer's Alliance |
| 1888 | Helps found Union Labor Party; runs for county office |
| 1890 | Helps found People's Party of America (Populist Party) |
| 1892 | Campaigns all over the West and South in presidential election; Populists get more than one million votes and win four states |
| 1893 | Populists win control of legislature and governor's office in Kansas; Mary appointed president of state board of charities |
| 1896 | Populists merge with Democrats to support William Jennings Bryan for president; Mary opposes merger but campaigns for Bryan |
| 1897 | Moves to New York with her children; becomes writer for *New York World* newspaper |
| 1902 | Divorces Charles Lease |
| 1933 | Dies in New York |

## More you can do:

- **Read Richard Stiller's *Mary Elizabeth Lease: Queen of Populists***
- **Find and read press accounts of Mary's speeches**

## What do you think?

- **What do you think Mary's opponents meant when they called her "unwomanly"?**
- **Why did Mary think that merging with the Democratic Party was a mistake for the Populists?**
- **Mary campaigned for women's suffrage, Prohibition, and birth control. Why did she think all three issues were important for American women? Do you agree or disagree? Why?**

# 21

# Eugene Debs
## (1855–1926)

It was the summer of 1894. The US Army had just opened fire into a crowd of five thousand railroad workers in Chicago. Dozens fell to the ground, injured or killed.

These men, along with two hundred thousand others in twenty-seven states, had walked off their jobs to protest low wages and the lack of dignity on the job. The event was known as the Pullman Strike. It pitted thousands of railroad workers against the federal government and some of the richest men in America.

One man helping to lead the strike was Eugene "Gene" Victor Debs. When the strike was declared illegal, Gene was arrested and sent to prison. In prison, he studied politics and became a socialist. In doing so, Gene joined the long line of American rebels who refused to accept the inequality and injustices of capitalism. He began to call for a society based on equality, cooperation, and workers' power. Gene's experience in the labor movement convinced him that capitalism was rigged in favor of the rich and against working people. So he dedicated himself to the socialist cause, helping to found the Socialist Party in 1901.

The early twentieth century was a time of great social change. This was the era in which the United States became a world power, a leader in industry and in military might. John D. Rockefeller, Jay Gould, Andrew Carnegie, J. P. Morgan, and other company owners made great fortunes.

> "I am not a labor leader; I do not want you to follow me or anyone else. . . . I would not lead you into the Promised Land if I could, because if I led you in, someone else would lead you out. You must use your heads as well as your hands, and get yourself out of your present condition."
>
> *—Eugene Debs, in a speech given in 1910*

But those who worked on the shop floor were left behind. These were the millions of workers who labored on the railroads and in the coal mines, steel mills, automobile plants, and textile factories. They included women, African Americans, and immigrants from all over the world.

These were the people who joined the Socialist Party, which soon had more than a hundred thousand members nationwide. They joined because they wanted to improve their own lives and fight for a better world. And they joined because they loved Gene Debs.

The United States has never had a socialist leader quite as popular as Gene. He ran for president five times on the Socialist ticket. He crisscrossed the country on his "Red Special" train, speaking in front of large, enthusiastic crowds.

Gene was also hated by many defenders of capitalism. The *New York Times* called him "a lawbreaker at large, an enemy of the human race." President Woodrow Wilson called him a "traitor to his country." But Gene's real legacy is very different. He helped lead a movement of working people who struggled to share in America's vast wealth. And though Gene didn't believe that socialism had anything special to offer blacks except as workers, he rejected racism and refused to speak to segregated crowds.

The second time Gene went to jail was for speaking out against World War I, which was considered a crime under the Espionage Act. Many others spoke out against this war, too. They felt that it was being fought for the benefit of the rich to increase the power of the elites. Even in prison, Gene managed to win almost one million votes for president.

—Zach Zill

## Timeline:

1855  November 5, born in Terre Haute, Indiana

1871  Leaves railroad yard work to work as a locomotive fireman

1875  Joins the Brotherhood of Locomotive Firemen

1884  Elected to the Indiana General Assembly; serves one term

1893  American Railway Union founded with Eugene as its leader

1894  Leads Pullman Strike; imprisoned in Woodstock, Illinois

1900  Runs for president for the first time

1901  Helps found the Socialist Party of America

1905  Aids in the founding of the International Workers of the World union

1918  Imprisoned again in Atlanta, Georgia, for opposing WWI

1920  Wins one million votes for president while in prison

1926  October 20, dies a few years after being released from prison, in Elmhurst, Illinois

## More you can do:

- Read *The Bending Cross: A Biography of Eugene Victor Debs* by Ray Ginger

## What do you think?

- Why do you think Gene saw World War I as a rich people's war?
- Six days after the Pullman Strike was broken, President Grover Cleveland, who declared the strike illegal, signed a bill to declare Labor Day a national holiday. He was not reelected president that year. Why do you think this might be?
- Look at the quotation above from Gene's speech in Utah in 1910. Why might someone like Gene want to discourage people from following him?

# 22

# Clarence Darrow

## (1857–1938)

**Clarence Darrow was a brilliant and controversial defense lawyer. He is best known for opposing the death penalty and defending academic freedom, especially the right to teach evolution.**

He worked for "the downtrodden," civil rights, and the right to strike. Clarence sometimes represented people who had committed horrible crimes, but he fought to get them a fair trial. He also used every trial as an opportunity to challenge and change public opinion.

As a young lawyer, Clarence made many powerful and influential friends, like the Illinois governor John Altgeld. He began his career as a lawyer for rich corporations and he was smart and well connected. He probably could have become rich and powerful himself. In his family, though, justice was more important than wealth and power. His father had opposed slavery and his mother fought for women's right to vote.

Clarence began to defend union leaders and working-class people who spoke out against corporate greed and poverty. He convinced Governor Altgeld to posthumously (after death) pardon August Spies and Albert Parsons, two radicals who were framed for bombing and killing policemen and hanged in 1887. He also defended strike leader Eugene Debs in 1894 and the coal miners who went on strike in Pennsylvania in 1902. Since strikes were mostly illegal before the 1930s,

" As long as the world shall last, there will be wrongs,
and if no man objected and no man rebelled,
those wrongs would last forever. "

—*Clarence Darrow*, Argument of Clarence Darrow in the Case of
the Communist Labor Party of Chicago in Criminal Court, *1920*

workers and strike leaders often faced prison time.

In 1925 Clarence defended Ossian Sweet and several others from Detroit. That year white mobs in that city were attacking black people. Sweet, a black doctor, had bought a house in a white neighborhood. One night, under the pressure of threats, nine of Sweet's friends came to defend the house from a white mob. When the mob attacked, a white person was killed. Eleven of the men defending the house were tried for murder. Clarence said, "I insist that there is nothing but prejudice in this case; that if it was reversed and eleven white men had shot and killed a black while protecting their home and their lives against a mob of blacks, nobody would dream of having them indicted. They would be given medals instead." The jury acquitted Sweet.

Around the same time, he lost another important case. According to Tennessee law, teaching that humans were the product of evolution was illegal. John T. Scopes was accused of teaching the theory of evolution in biology class. Clarence used the case to put the law, the theory of divine creation, and strict interpretation of the Bible on trial. Scopes was found guilty. It was still illegal to teach evolution in Tennessee. But as in so many of Clarence's other cases, he was able to do something just as important as win in court. He helped change public opinion about the issue.

Clarence was famous for making long arguments. In these statements, he tried to appeal to people's intelligence. He asked jurors to examine their opinions about corporate greed, mental illness, the social roots of crime, science and religion, racism, and justice. He believed that people could be rational and fair if they were given all the facts.

—Sarah Knopp

## Timeline:

| | |
|---|---|
| 1857 | Born in Ohio to a farming family |
| 1880s | Works as lawyer for Chicago & Northwestern Railroad Company |
| 1894 | Represents Eugene V. Debs, who led the Pullman Strike of 1894 |
| 1896 | Runs (unsuccessfully) for Congress as a Democrat; active in the Populist Party |
| 1902 | Represents striking coal miners in Pennsylvania |
| 1911 | Defends the McNamara Brothers after they bomb the Los Angeles Times building; is accused of bribing jurors; ends his career as labor lawyer |
| 1924 | Defends Leopold and Loeb, two wealthy teenagers accused of killing a fourteen-year-old |
| 1925 | Loses Scopes "Monkey Trial" |
| 1925 | Wins Ossian Sweet case in Detroit |
| 1932 | Loses Massie trial, a racially charged case in which he defended white residents of Hawaii accused of killing a native Hawaiian who they said raped a white woman |
| 1938 | Dies in Chicago |

## More you can do:

- **Watch the film** *Inherit the Wind*
- **Find and read transcripts from the trials of Bill Haywood and John Scopes, and a primary source account of how Ossian Sweet defended his home**

## What do you think?

- **Why did Clarence say that if eleven white men had killed a black man, they "would have been given medals instead"? Do you think that courts are "colorblind"?**
- **Pick two cases that Clarence took and give your opinion about why he chose them.**
- **Clarence thought that influencing public opinion was just as important as winning trials. Why? Do you agree with him?**

# 23

# Jane Addams

## (1860–1935)

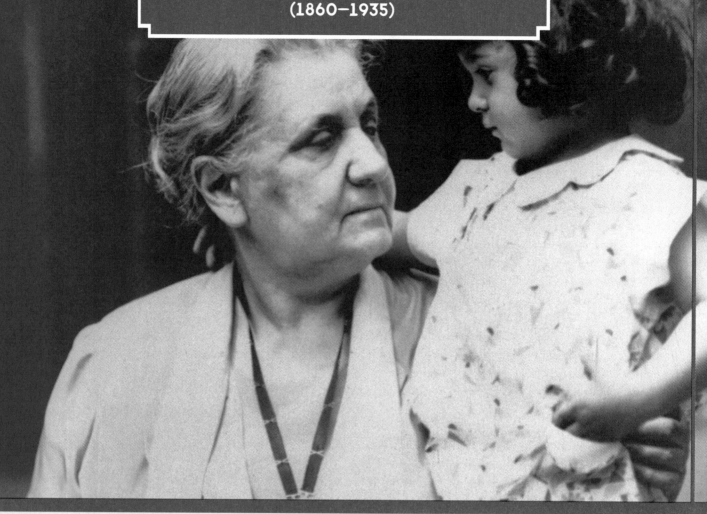

In 1919, the FBI labeled Jane Addams "the most dangerous woman in America." They wanted to smear Jane because she was a pacifist.

She gave speeches and organized meetings against World War I. This angered the US government, which was trying to rally patriotic support for the war.

Prior to the start of the war, Jane was best known as the founder of Hull-House in Chicago. Jane came from a wealthy family and wanted to do her part to help poor people. Hull-House was located in a poor neighborhood with many immigrants on Chicago's West Side. Jane and other

volunteers opened the house to the public in 1890.

Almost immediately, neighbors started to come to the house to take classes in cooking or sewing. They came to attend lectures, to see the artwork in the house, or just to spend time with their neighbors. Eventually, Jane and the settlement workers opened a kindergarten and a nursery, where working women could leave their children daily. They started boys' clubs and girls' clubs to give older children something to do during the day. Hull-House was a resource for the whole community.

Jane hosted meetings at the house with leaders

of the labor movement, immigrant activists, and suffragists. She also became involved with all these movements herself. When forty thousand textile workers went on strike in 1910, Jane raised money to help them. She was a friend of labor, but refused to join picket lines because she thought that they were too confrontational. Jane helped organize campaigns to keep immigrants from being deported. She also put together resources to help immigrant families in her community, and wrote about the burdens that immigrant women face. In 1912, at the height of her popularity and influence, Jane became a leader in the fight for women's suffrage. She insisted that the right to vote must be extended to all women, including immigrants and the poor. She also advocated for women's right to an education and a job outside of the home.

When World War I started in 1914, Jane started to focus her energy on the antiwar movement. She became a leader of the Women's Peace Party and helped organize conferences of peace activists. She also set up meetings with political leaders to try to convince them to end the war. Her pacifist position was controversial because it challenged President Woodrow Wilson's foreign policy. As a result, the government and the media slandered Jane's reputation. She was labeled a socialist and an anarchist. In reality, she was neither of these things.

It wasn't until a decade after the war that Jane gained popular recognition for the work she had done. By the early 1930s, at the start of the Great Depression, Jane started receiving awards and was included on lists of great American heroes. In 1931, she received her proudest honor. For her work at Hull-House, and for being a leader in the peace movement, she became the first American woman to win the Nobel Peace Prize.

—Caitlin Sheehan

## Timeline:

| | |
|---|---|
| 1860 | Born Laura Jane Addams to a wealthy mill owner and state senator in the farming village of Cedarville, Illinois |
| 1877–81 | Attends college at Rockford Female Seminary and becomes one of the first graduates of the school |
| 1890 | Opens the Hull-House settlement on the West Side of Chicago |
| 1905 | Helps found the American Sociological Society |
| 1909 | Publishes *The Spirit of Youth and the City Streets* |
| 1910 | Receives honorary degree from Yale University; publishes *Twenty Years at Hull-House* |
| 1912 | *American Magazine* dubs Jane the "Foremost Woman in America" |
| 1915 | Appointed chair of the Women's Peace Party |
| 1931 | Becomes the first American woman to win the Nobel Peace Prize |
| 1935 | Thousands of supporters and admirers turn out to her funeral at Hull-House |

## More you can do:

- **See photographs of Hull-House at the University of Illinois at Chicago's online archive: www.uic.edu/jaddams/hull/**
- **Read Hilda Satt Polacheck's *I Came a Stranger: The Story of a Hull-House Girl***

## What do you think?

- **Do poor neighborhoods today still need the sorts of services that Hull-House provided?**
- **Women now have the right to vote. Does that mean that women have equal rights to men?**
- **Can you think of other times in history when the government has used patriotism to drum up support for war? Or to stop people from speaking against war?**

# 24

# Ida B. Wells

## (1862–1931)

**Ida B. Wells was an African American activist and journalist who fought fearlessly against lynching and for women's rights.**

She was born into slavery in Holly Springs, Mississippi on July 16, 1862, the oldest of eight children. Six months later, President Abraham Lincoln signed the Emancipation Proclamation, which officially declared all enslaved people free. Ida's parents worked hard to help newly freed black people win their rights and get an education, and encouraged Ida to study hard. But when Ida was sixteen, while she was away visiting family, a disease called yellow fever swept the South and killed both her parents and her youngest brother.

Ida lied about her age so that she could get a job teaching to support her brothers and sisters. She was frustrated because white teachers got $80 a month and she was only paid $30. In 1883, she and three of her siblings moved to Memphis to live with her aunt.

When Ida was young, many African Americans used their freedom to go to school, start businesses, and even run for office. White people in the South were furious that the people who used to be enslaved were now their competition. They reacted with violence. All over the country, white mobs accused African Americans of crimes and murdered them in public. They called this "lynching." Some white people treated lynchings like parties. White children would

> ## "Somebody must show that the Afro-American race is more sinned against than sinning, and it seems to have fallen upon me to do so."
>
> —*Ida B. Wells*, Southern Horrors: Lynch Law in All Its Phases, *1892*

even have picnics and pose for pictures with the bodies of the victims.

Lynching was a way to keep African Americans "in line" by making them afraid. Whites used this fear to start a system of segregation, which became known as Jim Crow. Under Jim Crow, whites and blacks had to do everything separately. African Americans had to sit in the back of the bus, drink from separate water fountains, and eat in different restaurants. In 1884 Ida refused to move to the back of a train. The conductor picked her up and threw her out. She sued the railroad and won, but the Tennessee Supreme Court overturned her victory.

Ida was horrified at the racism that was growing around her. In 1887 she became a journalist and wrote angry editorials that showed the horrors of lynching and racism. She was fired from her teaching job for writing about racism in the schools, but she never stopped writing. In 1892 three African American men, Ida's friends, were lynched. Ida published a furious editorial. While she was out of town a white mob destroyed her newspaper office. She never came back to Memphis.

From her base in Chicago she toured the country speaking against lynching. She showed people graphic pictures to shock them into taking action.

In 1895 Ida married Frederick Barnett and kept her own name. They had four children together. Ida struggled to keep up with her work while also raising children. She started several groups to fight for women's and African Americans' rights, including the important National Association for the Advancement of Colored People (NAACP). Ida also began to write an autobiography but died of kidney failure before she finished. Her book ends in the middle of a word.

—Sarah Grey

## Timeline:

| | |
|---|---|
| 1862 | Born enslaved on July 16 in Holly Springs, Mississippi |
| 1863 | January 1, Emancipation Proclamation |
| 1878 | Parents and several siblings die of yellow fever while Ida is away; lies about her age to get a teaching job |
| 1883 | Moves to Memphis; gets a teaching job |
| 1884 | Buys first-class train ticket and refuses to sit in Jim Crow car; is bodily removed by conductor; sues the railroad and wins |
| 1887 | Becomes part owner of and reporter for *Memphis Free Speech and Headlight* |
| 1891 | Fired from her teaching position because of her fiery editorials about the schools |
| 1892 | Three friends lynched by a white mob; after Ida responds in an editorial, the paper's office is destroyed by a mob and Ida flees town |
| 1893 | Organizes boycott of the World's Columbian Exposition in Chicago because of its treatment of African Americans |
| 1894 | Tours Britain; has public debates about racism |
| 1895 | Marries Frederick Barnett and keeps her own last name |
| 1896 | Helps found National Association of Colored Women, National Afro-American Council, and Women's Era Club |
| 1931 | Dies of kidney failure, her autobiography only half finished |

## More you can do:

- Read Ida's writings in the book *Southern Horrors and Other Writings: The Anti-Lynching Campaign of Ida B. Wells, 1892–1900*, edited by Jacqueline Jones Royster

## What do you think?

- Why did Ida's editorials make people so angry? Why did she keep writing even when it put her in danger?
- Why wasn't Ida allowed to stay in her seat on the train? What would you have done if you were in her position?

# 25

# W. E. B. Du Bois
## (1868–1963)

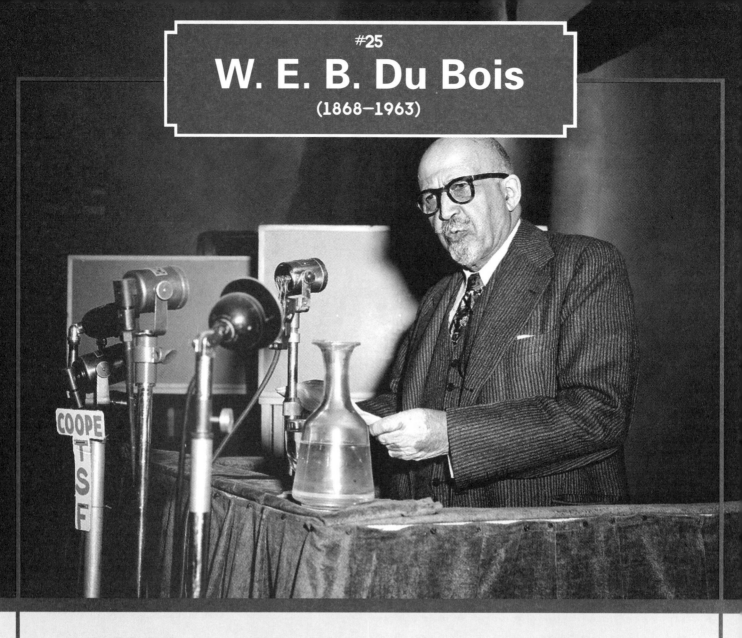

**W. E. B. Du Bois was an African American scholar and journalist. He was one of the most famous civil rights leaders of the twentieth century.**

William Edward Burghardt Du Bois was born in Massachusetts in 1868. His father left home when he was only two, and his mother had a stroke, so young William had to work in order to support the family.

William worked hard at his studies, too. He got a scholarship to Fisk University and later Harvard University. In 1896, he became the first African American ever to earn a PhD from Harvard. He became one of the most famous, well-respected, and controversial professors in the country.

In 1903 William published *The Souls of Black Folk*. In it, he criticized the ideas of Booker T. Washington, who believed that blacks should just obey the laws, get an education, and stay out of politics. This was the only way, he thought, they would get the respect of white people. William thought getting respect was not the point and urged blacks to pressure the government to end discrimination and pass laws against lynching.

In 1910 William helped to found the National Association for the Advancement of Colored People (NAACP). It became the largest civil rights organization in the country. William edited the NAACP's paper, *Crisis*. He reported on lynching in the South and the attacks on black people in the years after World War I.

> ## "The problem of the twentieth century is the problem of the color line."
>
> —*W. E. B. DuBois*, The Souls of Black Folk, *1903*

In the 1930s, William wrote several books about African Americans and their history. At the time, most historians argued that it was wrong to give blacks rights after the Civil War because they abused these rights. William argued in *Black Reconstruction in America* that this was not true. Blacks had won many rights after the Civil War, but whites violently took those rights away from them.

William was not only famous in the United States but all over the world, especially in Africa. He believed that all Africans around the world should come together. He helped organize five Pan-African Congresses from 1919 to 1945.

William always considered himself a socialist. He sympathized with the poor and favored workers' rights. Although he praised the Russian Revolution, he often criticized the Soviet Union and the US Communist Party. However, he also condemned the US government and capitalism, and many of his friends were members of the Communist Party.

After World War II ended in 1945, the Cold War began. William advocated peace with the Soviet Union and an end to nuclear weapons. The US government accused William of being an agent for the Soviet government and put him on trial in 1951. Even though the judge threw out the charges, this made William even angrier with the government.

After being accused of being a communist for so long, in 1961, William finally joined the Communist Party. That same year, he and his wife moved to Ghana in West Africa to work on the *Encyclopedia Africana*. He died there in 1963.

**—Jon Van Camp**

## Timeline:

| | |
|---|---|
| 1868 | Born in Great Barrington, Massachusetts |
| 1884 | Enters Fisk University in Nashville, Tennessee |
| 1896 | Becomes the first African American to get a PhD from Harvard |
| 1899 | Publishes *The Philadelphia Negro* |
| 1903 | Publishes *The Souls of Black Folk* |
| 1910 | Cofounds the NAACP; is named the editor of the *Crisis* |
| 1934 | Resigns from the NAACP because of disagreements with the leadership |
| 1935 | Publishes *Black Reconstruction in America* |
| 1940 | Becomes chairman of the Peace Information Center (PIC) |
| 1943 | Rejoins the NAACP |
| 1948 | Leaves the NAACP for the second time because of his friendship with Communists |
| 1951 | Goes on trial for not registering the PIC as an "agent of a foreign state"; case is thrown out |
| 1961 | Joins the Communist Party |
| 1961 | Moves to Ghana with his wife to work on the *Encyclopedia Africana* |
| 1963 | Dies in Ghana at the age of 95 |

## More you can do:

- In *Black Reconstruction in America*, William told the history of the period after the Civil War from the viewpoint of black people. Pick another historical event and write about it from the viewpoint of a group that has not been able to write its own history

## What do you think?

- What do you think William meant by the "color line" being the most important divide? Is it still true today?
- Is it more important for oppressed people to try to better themselves or to fight for their rights?
- How do you think most African Americans felt about William moving to Ghana?

# #26
# William "Big Bill" Haywood
## (1869–1928)

**"Big Bill" Haywood was a working-class hero of his time. He was born in 1869 in Salt Lake City, Utah.**

His family was very poor, and his father died when he was just three years old. When Bill was only nine, he lost an eye in an accident and began to work as a miner. Miners suffered from very harsh working conditions, long hours, and low pay. Mining was extremely dangerous, and many miners died at work.

In 1896, Bill joined a new union, the Western Federation of Miners, and soon became a leader. People called him "Big Bill" Haywood because he stood more than six feet tall, weighed more than two hundred pounds,

and was known for his fearless dedication to the fight for workers' rights.

Although he had very little formal education, Bill was able to explain complicated ideas in plain language. As he once said, "For every dollar the boss has and didn't work for, one of us worked for a dollar and didn't get it."

By 1900, Bill became convinced that socialism could better the lives of working people. He helped to form the Socialist Party of America in 1901. Bill also believed in the need for "one big union" of workers. In 1905, he helped to found the Industrial Workers of the World (IWW). As he explained, "The aims and objects of this organization should be to put the working class in possession of the economic power . . . without regard to capitalist masters."

The IWW wanted all workers to become members. At the time, this was a revolutionary idea because most unions excluded unskilled workers. Most unions also refused to allow women, African Americans, and immigrants to join. Some of the IWW's most important struggles involved female, African American, and immigrant workers—including children.

One of the union's most famous victories took place in Lawrence, Massachusetts, in 1912. The Lawrence textile workers went on strike when the bosses decided to lower their pay in January. Their families were already going hungry, so they decided to shut down their machines in protest. They marched from one building to the next, calling other workers out on strike.

When Big Bill arrived in Lawrence, fifteen thousand strikers enthusiastically greeted him, along with three marching bands. After two long winter months on strike, the bosses finally agreed to the strikers' demands. The workers celebrated their victory by singing the workers' solidarity song, the "Internationale," in fourteen different languages.

Like most radicals, Bill opposed the United States entering World War I in 1917. But Congress passed espionage and sedition laws, making it illegal to protest against the war. In 1918, Bill was sentenced to twenty years in prison. In 1921, he escaped to Russia instead of going to prison.

He was welcomed into Russia, where workers had recently formed a socialist government. Bill lived there until his death in 1928. An urn with his ashes was sent to Chicago and is buried near the Haymarket Martyrs' Monument.

—Sharon Smith

## Timeline:

| | |
|---|---|
| 1869 | Born in Salt Lake City, Utah |
| 1878 | Goes to work in a mine at age nine |
| 1886 | Joins the Knights of Labor after the Haymarket Affair |
| 1896 | Elected secretary of Western Federation of Miners |
| 1901 | Joins the Socialist Party of America |
| 1902 | Second Cripple Creek miners' strike |
| 1905 | Launches the IWW with other union leaders |
| 1906 | Charged with conspiracy to murder the governor of Idaho |
| 1907 | Acquitted; embarked on lecture tour |
| 1908 | First visit to New York City; greeted by thousands at Grand Central Station |
| 1911 | Gives a fiery speech at Cooper Union in New York City |
| 1912 | Helps to win the Lawrence textile strike; expelled from Socialist Party |
| 1918 | Is sentenced to twenty years in prison for opposing World War I |
| 1921 | Flees to Russia |
| 1928 | Dies |

## More you can do:

- Find and read Big Bill Haywood's speech, "The General Strike," given in New York City on March 16, 1911

## What do you think?

- Why did Bill think it was necessary to build "one big union"?
- Why did the state governments in Colorado and Idaho side with the mine owners in their disputes with the miners?
- Why did the federal government find it necessary to make criticism of World War I a crime? Did that violate the First Amendment to the US Constitution? Why or why not?
- Do workers have a right to the wealth created by their labor? Why or why not?

# 27

# Albert Einstein
## (1879–1955)

**Albert Einstein was the most famous scientist of the twentieth century. He transformed our understanding of the physical world with his theories of special and general relativity and made many other outstanding contributions to science.**

Albert was born in Germany in 1879. As a boy he excelled at math, but he hated the rigid rules and rote learning of his high school and dropped out when he was fifteen. He finished school in Switzerland and got a diploma in math and physics but was unable to find a teaching position.

Albert took a job at a patent office while working on an advanced degree in physics at Zurich University. In 1905, while still at the patent office, Albert published four ground-breaking articles dealing with several issues in physics. One of them contained the famous equation $e = mc^2$, which shows the equivalence of energy and mass. It was another three years before Albert was offered an academic position, but within a very short time his theories of relativity had transformed physics.

Albert argued that nothing could move faster than the speed of light and that measurements of space, time, and mass depend on the relative motion of the measurer (this is called relativity theory). His general theory of relativity predicted that the force of gravity would bend light. Observations of light from distant stars during a total eclipse of the sun

> ## "Imagination is more important than knowledge."
> —*Albert Einstein, interview in the* Saturday Evening Post, *1929*

in 1919 seemed to support this prediction and Albert became an international celebrity. In 1921, he was awarded the Nobel Prize for Physics.

Albert remained active in scientific research for the rest of his life, but he also used his fame to speak out on social and political issues. He was a democratic socialist who called capitalism the "predatory phase of human development." He also rejected the top-down government of the Soviet Union. Because of his politics, Albert was watched by the FBI for decades.

From the early 1920s Albert was an outspoken Jewish opponent of the Nazi Party. When Hitler came to power in 1933, he fled Germany and settled in the United States for the rest of his life. Shortly before the start of World War II, Albert wrote a letter to President Roosevelt urging him to develop a nuclear weapon before the Nazis did. Later, he regretted sending the letter. He became a leading opponent of nuclear weapons.

For more than twenty years, Albert was also a vocal opponent of racism and segregation in the United States. He joined the National Association for the Advancement of Colored People and was a personal friend of leading African American activists like W. E. B. Dubois and Paul Robeson.

A few years after the founding of Israel in 1948, Albert was asked to become its president, but he declined. While he favored a Jewish homeland, he disliked the idea of a Jewish-only state. He supported a state in Palestine in which Jews and Arabs could maintain their own cultural identities and live together with equal rights.
—**Phil Gasper**

## Timeline:

| | |
|---|---|
| 1879 | Born in Ulm in southern Germany |
| 1903 | Marries Mileva Marić |
| 1905 | Publishes four historic scientific articles, including one on the special theory of relativity |
| 1915 | Publishes his general theory of relativity |
| 1919 | Divorces Mileva and marries Elsa Löwenthal |
| 1921 | Awarded Nobel Prize for Physics |
| 1933 | Emigrates to the United States |
| 1952 | Declines the presidency of Israel |
| 1955 | Dies in Princeton, New Jersey |

## More you can do:

- Read Albert's article "Why Socialism?" from the May 1949 issue of *Monthly Review* www.monthlyreview.org/2009/05/01/why-socialism
- Albert's first wife, Milvea Marić, was also a scientist. Research what it was like to be a woman scientist in Albert's time. How did Milvea contribute to Albert's groundbreaking research in 1905?

## What do you think?

- After World War II, Albert said that urging President Roosevelt to build an atomic bomb was the worst decision he ever made. Why do you think he later changed his mind?
- Why did Albert turn down the offer to become president of Israel in 1952? Do you think he made the right decision?
- In 2000, *Time* magazine named Albert "Person of the Century," but in its description of his life, the magazine never mentioned that he was a socialist. Why was this?
- What did Albert mean when he called capitalism the "predatory phase of human development"? Do you agree with him?

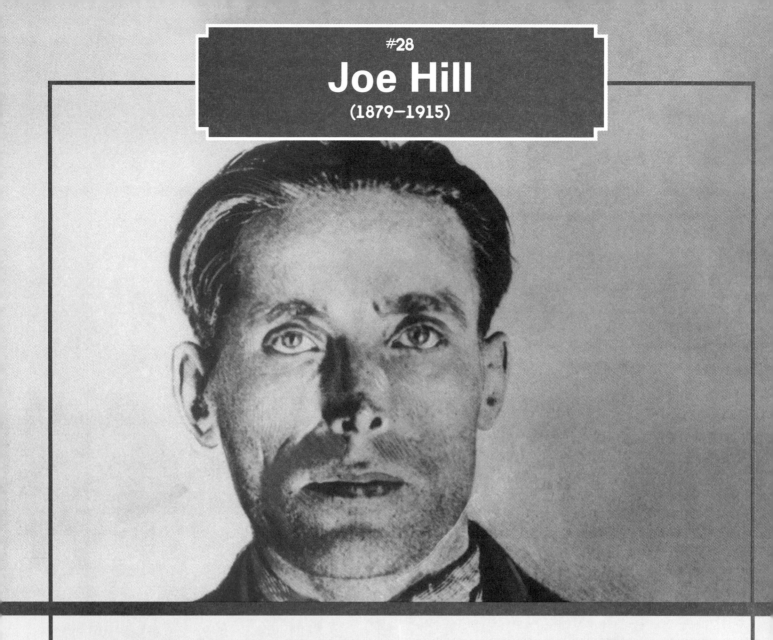

# 28

# Joe Hill
## (1879–1915)

**Joe Hill was a labor organizer and legendary songwriter. His music has inspired famous musicians such as Woody Guthrie and Bob Dylan. Joe was born Joel Hägglund in Gävle, Sweden.**

At an early age, he sang songs with his family and taught himself to play the organ and violin. He wrote songs poking fun at his family and mashing up news stories. By the time Joe was twenty-one, both his parents had died. The family sold their house and Joe and his brother left Sweden for America.

In 1902 Joe arrived in New York and traveled westward. He moved to Portland, Oregon, where 2500 sawmill workers were out on strike for a shorter workday and higher pay.

The strike was organized by the Industrial Workers of the World (IWW). Joe became one of their many new recruits.

Over the next several years, Joe participated in three major IWW free speech fights on the West Coast. Members of the IWW often gave speeches on busy streets. The employers they were organizing against used their political influence to pass laws banning street speaking. In response, the IWW sent hundreds of members from across the country. One by one, IWW members would mount a soapbox and begin speaking. The police would then yank them off the box and take them to jail. This filled the jails with more prisoners than they could hold. The IWW also demanded individual trials for each person arrested, creating a logjam in the courts.

> ## "Don't waste any time in mourning—organize."
> —Joe Hill, on the eve of his execution in 1915, to Big Bill Haywood

Joe went north and ended up in British Columbia, Canada, where IWW organizers were leading a strike of railroad construction workers. He wrote songs about the struggle for the striking workers to sing. Joe had already published several songs in the IWW's *Little Red Songbook*. But after helping to lead a failed strike in San Pedro, California, he took a year to focus on writing music. In the 1913 edition of the songbook, Joe had composed ten out of the twelve songs included.

Joe followed his friend to Utah in search of a job. There, Joe was arrested and convicted of murdering a local grocer. Joe did suffer a gunshot wound on the same night that the grocer was killed. But he maintained that he was shot in a dispute over a woman. The IWW led such an effective publicity campaign that it gained the support of the king of Sweden and the president of the United States. In several cities, tens of thousands marched and boycotted to demand Joe's freedom. Thousands of letters poured into the Utah governor's office.

Despite the heroic efforts to save Joe's life and a case based on weak evidence, Utah's political elite was determined to kill him. Joe was executed at the age of thirty-six.

At Joe's funeral in Chicago, as many as thirty thousand people marched in a mile-long procession singing his songs. A year later, 150 IWW delegates took packets of Joe's ashes home with them and scattered them over five continents and forty-seven of the lower forty-eight states—all except Utah.
—Adam Sanchez

## Timeline:

| | |
|---|---|
| 1879 | Born on October 7 in Sweden |
| 1902 | Emigrates to America with his brother |
| 1906 | Travels to the West Coast and witnesses the great 1906 San Francisco earthquake |
| 1907 | Joins the IWW in Portland, Oregon |
| 1908–1910 | Travels West Coast participating in free speech fights |
| 1911 | Participates in armed rebellion in Baja California to overthrow the Mexican dictatorship of Porfirio Díaz |
| 1911 | First song, "The Preacher and the Slave," is printed in the fourth edition of the *Little Red Songbook* |
| 1912 | March, participates in the San Diego Free Speech Fight and then travels north as a speaker and representative for the newly formed California Free Speech League |
| | April, travels to British Columbia; writes songs for striking railroad construction workers |
| 1914 | January 14, arrested for the murder of John G. Morrison in Utah |
| 1915 | November 19, executed by Utah firing squad |

## More you can do:

- **Check out the Joe Hill Project website at www.joehill.org**
- **Read *The Man Who Never Died: The Life, Times and Legacy of Joe Hill, American Labor Icon* by William M. Adler**

## What do you think?

- **What is the role of music in social movements?**
- **Can you think of other political movements in which music and song have played a crucial role?**
- **Are people still jailed and executed because of their political views?**

# #29
# Frances Perkins
## (1880–1965)

**Frances Perkins was a reformer who became the first woman Cabinet member. She was appointed secretary of labor by President Franklin D. Roosevelt (FDR) in 1933.**

As a young woman, Frances participated in the women's suffrage movement. She worked as a professor and in politics, although she could not vote herself, and became head of the New York Consumers League in 1910. Throughout her career, Frances broke new ground for women. After getting married, she kept her birth name, which was highly unusual at the time.

Frances observed the poverty and horrible living conditions in America's cities. In New York City in 1911, she personally witnessed the Triangle Shirtwaist Factory fire. The factory owner had locked the doors so the workers could not take breaks. When a fire broke out, they could not escape. Tragically, 146 garment workers, mostly teenage girls, were killed.

After the fire, Frances heard a speech by socialist organizer Ruth Schneiderman. Ruth argued for unions, explaining, "This is not the first time girls have been burned alive in this city. . . . The life of men and women is so cheap and property is so sacred!" This experience was a turning point for Frances. She helped pressure the state government for new labor laws that improved working conditions.

In 1929 the United States entered the Great

Depression, a period of unheard-of hardship for Americans. Millions of people were thrown into desperate poverty. That year, FDR, who was the governor of New York, appointed Frances as the state's first commisioner of labor. Frances fought for a minimum wage and shorter hours for women workers, and investigated how factories treated their workers.

In 1932 FDR was elected president. Frances had become an advocate for a minimum wage, an eight-hour workday, an old-age pension, a ban on child labor, and rights for immigrants. Although FDR did not agree with all her views, he appointed Frances secretary of labor. Frances worked on New Deal legislation such as the Social Security Act, which provided financial assistance to the elderly, widows, and their children.

The Great Depression brought serious conflicts between owners and workers to the forefront of society in a way that went beyond Frances' ability as a government official to address. Workers occupied plants and organized strikes. They demanded jobs, fair wages, and the right to organize into unions. When they won these victories, Frances helped write the new laws that improved working conditions and the standard of living for millions of ordinary Americans.

While Frances defended many workers' rights, she sometimes used her power to pressure unions to stop striking and negotiate with company owners. She did this even though many owners did not plan to follow the new laws that granted workers the right to unionize. However, she also prevented others in FDR's administration from taking more harsh action against striking workers. She stood up to criticism from Republicans, businessmen, and some male trade union leaders.
—Michele Bollinger

## Timeline:

| | |
|---|---|
| 1880 | Born in Boston |
| 1902 | Graduates from Mt. Holyoke College |
| 1911 | Witnesses the Triangle Factory fire in New York City |
| 1913 | Marries economist Paul Wilson |
| 1916 | Daughter Susanna is born |
| 1929 | The stock market crashes on October 29; the Great Depression begins |
| 1933 | Accepts FDR's offer to become secretary of labor |
| 1934 | General strikes occur in San Francisco, Toledo, and Minneapolis |
| 1935 | Social Security Act passes |
| 1937 | Autoworkers carry out "sit-down" strikes in Flint, Michigan, and organize the United Auto Workers |
| 1938 | Fair Labor Standards Act passed |
| 1945 | FDR dies; Harry Truman becomes president; Frances leaves office |
| 1952 | Serves on US Civil Service Commission |
| 1957 | Begins teaching at Cornell University |
| 1965 | Dies at age 85 |

## More you can do:

- View the PBS documentary *Triangle Fire*
- Explore resources at www.francesperkinscenter.org

## What do you think?

- In what ways was Frances influenced by the Progressive reform movement (1890s–1910s) and the growing labor movement (1900s–1930s)?
- In what ways was Frances a groundbreaking figure for women? What challenges did she face?
- Describe the events surrounding the Triangle Shirtwaist Factory fire in New York. Why did this leave such an impression on Frances?

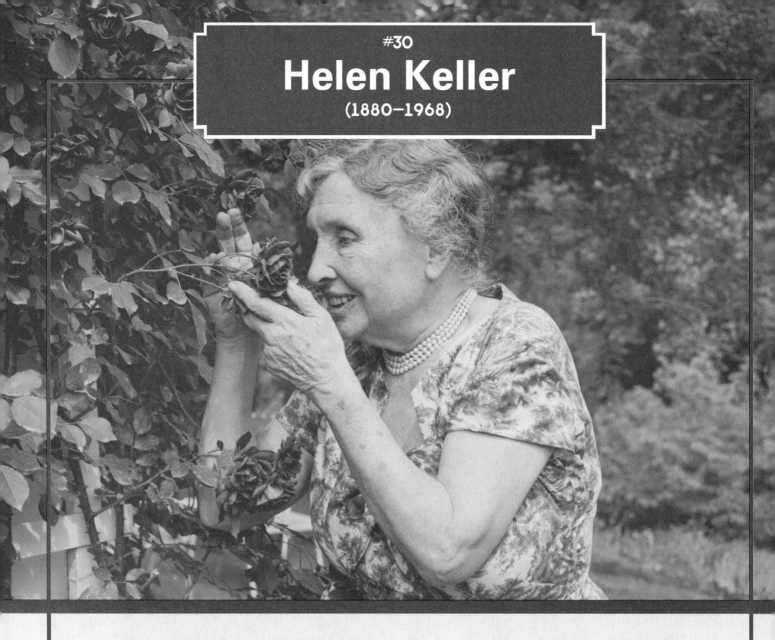

# 30

# Helen Keller
## (1880–1968)

**Helen Keller is famous for her work as a disability rights activist. She wasn't born disabled, but became deaf and blind after she got very sick as a toddler.**

Fortunately for Helen, her parents consulted many doctors and teachers, and she eventually learned to communicate. But she didn't do it alone. She might not have done it at all if she hadn't met Anne Sullivan. Helen's parents hired Anne as her teacher. Anne eventually broke through Helen's shell by spelling words with her finger on Helen's hand. One famous moment occurred when she made the connection between the letters (w-a-t-e-r) Anne was signing on her hands and the water falling on her other hand. Helen began to learn words and sentences. Then she

began to communicate by signing the manual alphabet.

Helen attended Radcliffe College in Cambridge, Massachusetts. She was becoming well known, meeting people like Mark Twain. She became the first deaf and blind person to earn a Bachelor of Arts degree.

As a disability rights activist, Helen was invited to speak across the United States and all over the world. But Helen's views were not limited to rights for those living with disabilities. She lived in a time of war and change, and she supported the labor movement and became a socialist.

Not everyone approved of this, however. For

> "I must face unflinchingly a world of facts—a world of misery and degradation, of blindness, crookedness, and sin. . . . How to reconcile this world of fact with the bright world of my imagining? My darkness had been filled with the light of intelligence, and, behold, the outer day-lit world was stumbling and groping in social blindness."
>
> —*Helen Keller*, Out of the Dark

example, the editor of the Brooklyn Eagle disagreed with Helen's political opinions. He quickly reminded his readers that Helen was disabled. In his view, her politics were mistakes that "spring out of the manifest limitations of her development."

In her essay "How I Became a Socialist," Helen wrote: "Now that I have come out for socialism he reminds me and the public that I am blind and deaf and especially liable to error. I must have shrunk in intelligence during the years since I met him. . . . Oh, ridiculous *Brooklyn Eagle*! Socially blind and deaf, it defends an intolerable system, a system that is the cause of much of the physical blindness and deafness which we are trying to prevent."

Helen supported women's right to vote and opposed World War I. She supported Eugene Debs, who was imprisoned for his opposition to the war. In a letter to Debs in 1919, Helen said, "I write because I want you to know that I should be proud if the Supreme Court convicted me of abhorring war, and doing all in my power to oppose it. When I think of the millions who have suffered in all the wicked wars of the past, I am shaken with the anguish of a great impatience. I want to fling myself against all brute powers that destroy life and break the spirit of man."

Helen spoke out for social justice. She joined the Industrial Workers of the World and helped found the ACLU. Her legacy as a disability rights activist continues, but her life as a radical is an important part of her story that should not be forgotten.
— Jessie Muldoon

## Timeline:

| | |
|---|---|
| 1880 | Born in Tuscumbia, Alabama on June 27 |
| 1887 | Anne Sullivan becomes Helen's teacher |
| 1903 | Publishes her autobiography *The Story of My Life* |
| 1904 | Graduates from Radcliffe College, becoming the first deaf and blind person to earn a college diploma |
| 1912 | Publishes *How I Became a Socialist* |
| 1916–18 | Is an active writer for the Industrial Workers of the World |
| 1919 | Writes letter defending Eugene Debs and opposing his imprisonment |
| 1920 | Helps to found the American Civil Liberties Union |
| 1936 | Anne Sullivan dies |
| 1961 | Suffers a number of strokes |
| 1964 | Awarded the Presidential Medal of Freedom by Lyndon B. Johnson |
| 1968 | Dies in Connecticut |

## More you can do:

- Read Helen's books *The Story of My Life* and *How I Became a Socialist*
- Find and read the *Brooklyn Eagle* editor's piece and write a response in defense of Helen

## What do you think?

- When Helen was a child, there were very few programs for people with disabilities. Today we have special education and the Americans with Disabilities Act, but there is still a struggle for disability rights in this country. What are some areas where people with disabilities are still fighting for justice?
- Helen Keller was concerned with social justice issues such as war, imperialism, and poverty. What do you think you she would say about the world today?

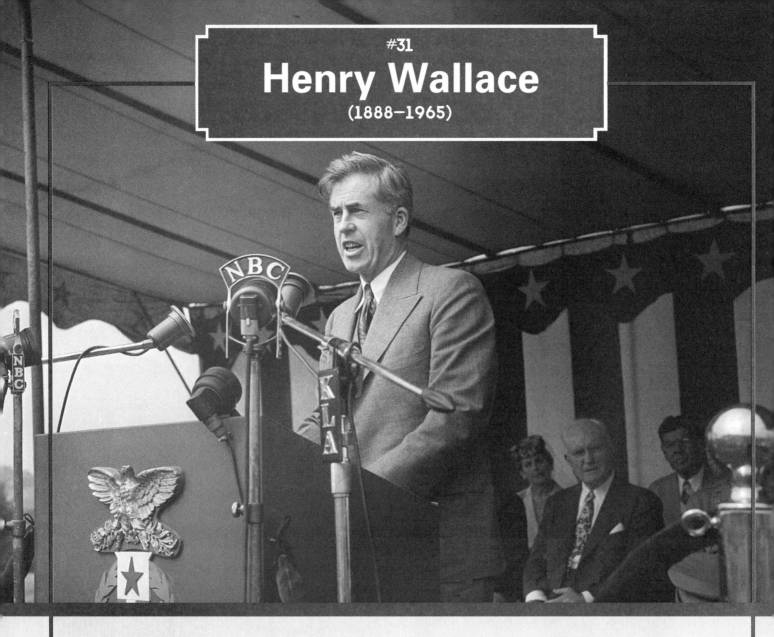

# 31

# Henry Wallace
## (1888–1965)

**Henry Wallace was a farmer, human rights advocate, and visionary.**

Henry grew up on a family farm in Iowa. He learned about agriculture with the African American botanist George Washington Carver. Later he went to Iowa State College. He developed a kind of hybrid corn that produced very high-yield crops. Based on this, he started the successful company Pioneer Hi-Bred. His father was secretary of agriculture from 1921 to 1924. Henry held that same office from 1933 to 1940.

He also served as secretary of commerce under President Truman and as vice president of the United States under President Franklin Delano Roosevelt. Many people thought Henry would follow Roosevelt as president of the United States. But conservative forces in the Democratic Party worked against his nomination.

In 1942, Henry gave his best-known speech, in which he spoke of the "march of freedom for the common man." Henry went beyond attacking the enemies of the United States in the Second World War (Germany, Italy, and Japan). He didn't agree that the United States should build an empire around the world. He said: "We cannot perpetuate economic warfare without planting the seeds of military warfare."

Powerful forces in the United States wanted to roll back the reforms known as the "New Deal"— programs like Social Security, unemployment

> ❝ The cause of liberty and the cause of true science must always be one and the same. For science cannot flourish except in an atmosphere of freedom, and freedom cannot survive unless there is an honest facing of facts. ❞
>
> —*Henry Wallace*, Democracy Reborn

insurance, and the minimum wage that made people's lives better. Henry did not agree. He said: "We cannot fight to crush Nazi brutality abroad and condone race riots at home. . . . We cannot plead for equality of opportunity for peoples everywhere and overlook the denial of the right to vote for millions of our own people."

Henry's progressive views and defense of the New Deal made him many enemies, including some in the Democratic Party. In 1944, just before he could be nominated for vice president (which many understood would mean he could very likely become president if President Roosevelt, who was then in poor health, passed away or resigned the presidency), party operatives closed the convention for the night so they would have more time to lobby against him. The plot worked and Harry Truman became the party's nominee and, soon after, when President Roosevelt died on April 12, 1945, the next president.

Truman's election was a turning point in our nation's history. Truman made relations between the United States and the Soviet Union worse and made the decision to drop atomic bombs on Japan. To offer an alternative, Henry ran for president on the Progressive Party ticket in 1948. Many activists supported his campaign. Henry called for an end to segregation and lynching of African Americans. And he supported a system of health insurance for all. The legendary activist folksingers Paul Robeson and Pete Seeger sang at numerous campaign stops for Henry, and Woody Guthrie wrote songs for his campaign. Well before the civil rights movement of the 1950s, Henry's party ran African American candidates. Henry refused to speak to any audience that was segregated or to stay at any segregated hotels. Henry was far ahead of his time, though, and only earned 3 percent of the popular vote.

Henry died in 1965, leaving behind a remarkable legacy of a politician who was willing to work toward peace and justice.
—**Anthony Arnove**

## Timeline:

| | |
|---|---|
| 1888 | Born in Iowa |
| 1910 | Graduates from Iowa State University |
| 1921 | Becomes editor of *Wallace's Farmer* |
| 1926 | Founds Hi-Bred Corn (later renamed Pioneer Hi-Bred) |
| 1933 | Appointed secretary of agriculture |
| 1940 | Resigns as secretary of agriculture to join Roosevelt's presidential campaign |
| 1941 | Becomes vice president |
| 1942 | Gives his "Century of the Common Man" speech |
| 1944 | Pushed aside by Democratic Party insiders, who nominate Harry Truman for vice president |
| 1945 | Becomes secretary of commerce |
| 1946 | Resigns as secretary of commerce |
| 1946 | Becomes editor of the *New Republic* |
| 1947–48 | Runs for president on the Progressive Party ticket |
| 1965 | November 18, dies in Danbury, Connecticut |

## More you can do:

- **See the New Deal Network's collection of Henry's writings at http://newdeal.feri.org/wallace**

## What do you think?

- **How did Wallace's experience as a farmer impact his political platform?**
- **What contradictions between American foreign and domestic policy did Wallace point out?**
- **Why did some people in the Democratic Party not want Wallace as their presidential candidate?**

# 32

# A. Philip Randolph
## (1889–1979)

**Asa Philip Randolph was one of the most important African American leaders of the labor movement.**

He founded the first labor union for black workers, the Brotherhood of Sleeping Car Porters. He was also a fighter for civil rights and against racism.

Philip was the son of a minister in Florida. He moved to New York in 1911. He attended City College and became a socialist. Socialism to him meant economic equality for everyone. In the *Messenger* magazine, he wrote that capitalism was at the root of segregation: "Prejudice is the chief weapon in the South which enables capitalists to exploit both races." He felt that blacks and whites were divided in or-

der to prevent them from organizing. This meant that they worked for lower wages while businesses got richer.

Philip opposed World War I. He ran for office on the Socialist Party ticket. But later in the 1920s, he believed that business interests did not have to oppose black or labor rights. He also attacked other socialists who organized in the Communist Party.

Sleeping car porters were black men who worked on overnight trains for the Pullman Company. They acted as servants to the mostly white passengers. They worked long hours for little pay, earning mostly tips. They also faced racism on the job. The porters wanted a union to push for better pay and

**66** Treason of the slave to his master is a virtue.
Loyalty of a slave to his master is a vice. **99**

—*A. Philip Randolph, in the* Messenger, *1919*

respect on the job. Because of his belief in civil rights for workers, Philip was asked to become its president.

The American Federation of Labor (AFL) was the main organization of unions in the country. But it did not admit black members. Philip was a major critic of this segregation. By 1929, he helped win entry for African Americans into the AFL.

Philip worked hard to build community support for the idea of a union. Many blacks treated unions with suspicion because of the unions' previous racism. Philip got the support of churches and community groups. After a twelve-year struggle, the brotherhood finally won its first contract with the Pullman Company. It was the first black union to win a contract.

This did not end Philip's fight for civil rights. When the United States fought in World War II, many blacks got jobs in industry. But they were still segregated, with blacks working the hardest or lowest-paying jobs. Also, blacks and whites could not serve in the same units in the war. In 1941, he organized a movement to march on Washington against segregation. This movement was one of the first national civil rights struggles. President Franklin Roosevelt eventually agreed to end segregation in the war industries, and the march was called off. By 1948, the military was formally integrated.

In 1963, civil rights leaders again took up the idea for a march on Washington. At this march, which Philip also helped organize, Martin Luther King Jr. gave his "I Have a Dream" speech. Philip was a strong leader fighting for civil rights for black workers. He was involved in almost every major battle against racism in his lifetime.

**—Peter Lamphere**

## Timeline:

| | |
|---|---|
| 1889 | Born in Crescent City, Florida |
| 1911 | Moves to New York hoping to become an actor |
| 1913 | Marries Lucille Campbell Green; helps found the Harlem Shakespearean Society |
| 1914 | Becomes a member of the Socialist Party |
| 1917 | Starts the *Messenger* with Clifford Owen |
| 1922 | Runs for New York State comptroller on the Socialist Party ticket, unsuccessfully |
| 1925 | Becomes leader of the Brotherhood of Sleeping Car Porters; runs for New York secretary of state on the Socialist Party ticket, unsuccessfully |
| 1929 | Brotherhood affiliates with the American Federation of Labor |
| 1937 | Brotherhood wins a contract with the Pullman Company |
| 1941 | Organizes the March on Washington Committee to fight for desegregation of war industries |
| 1950 | Helps found the Leadership Conference on Civil Rights |
| 1963 | Organizes the March on Washington for Civil Rights along with Martin Luther King Jr. |
| 1979 | Dies in New York City |

## More you can do:

- **Read the *Messenger*, available in many academic libraries around the country**
- **Watch the 1996 documentary *A. Philip Randolph: For Jobs and Freedom***

## What do you think?

- **In what ways was Philip a pioneer?**
- **Why do you think the passengers treated porters in racist ways?**
- **Why do you think Philip changed his mind about whether business interests would oppose black rights? What do you think?**
- **How did Philip's activism help inspire and shape the later civil rights movement of the 1950s and 1960s?**

# 33

# Elizabeth Gurley Flynn
## (1890–1964)

When she was sixteen years old, Elizabeth Gurley Flynn gave her first speech, on "What Would Socialism Do for Women?," to the Harlem Socialist Club.

She became a tireless fighter in defense of working people, women, and the right to free speech.

In 1907 Elizabeth joined the Industrial Workers of the World (IWW). The IWW believed in bringing together workers of every job, every ethnic and racial group, male and female, into "one big union" to gain better pay and working conditions. Elizabeth was well known for her fiery talks against poverty and unfairness. She met with miners in Montana and silk weavers in New Jersey.

She inspired thousands to take action. IWW songwriter Joe Hill penned "Rebel Girl" in her honor.

Elizabeth helped lead the famous Lawrence Textile Strike of 1912, also known as the Bread and Roses strike. Workers walked off the job to protest the poverty wages and brutal working conditions. Most of the workers were women and nearly half were teenagers. Despite speaking more than twenty-five different languages, the workers stayed united and won their demands for bread and roses, too. That is, they wanted fair pay *and* dignity.

IWW members used public speaking to help energize workers. City officials passed laws against public speech to try to keep the movements from becoming popular. Elizabeth and others organized free speech campaigns to protest those laws. Hundreds would get arrested speaking on street corners. They would then clog up the jails. Elizabeth was arrested at least ten times doing this.

When the United States entered World War I, thousands of activists were arrested, including Elizabeth. The government accused her of spying, but there was no proof. She claimed that she was in jail because of her political beliefs, which is against the Constitution. She became a founding member of the American Civil Liberties Union (ACLU).

In 1919, inspired by the 1917 revolution in Russia, millions of workers went on strike across the United States. The government cracked down again. Many left-wing activists were arrested or forced to leave the country in what were known as the Palmer Raids.

Elizabeth was also an outspoken organizer for the rights of political prisoners. Most famously, she worked in defense of Sacco and Vanzetti, anarchists who were framed for murder and executed in 1927.

Elizabeth joined the Communist Party (CP) in 1937 and served as one of its top leaders for the rest of her life. During World War II she pushed for the creation of day care centers to support women who wanted to work outside the home. In 1942 she ran for Congress in New York and got fifty thousand votes.

During the anticommunist panic of the 1940s and 1950s known as McCarthyism, Elizabeth was once again targeted for her political views. She was kicked out of the ACLU. In 1951, she was arrested and spent two years in prison. A rebel girl until the end, Elizabeth struggled for more than half a century for a better world. She was never afraid to speak out for what she believed in, no matter the personal cost.

—Leela Yellesetty

## Timeline:

| | |
|---|---|
| 1890 | Born in Concord, New Hampshire |
| 1907 | Joins the Industrial Workers of the World |
| 1909 | First free speech battle in Spokane, Washington |
| 1912 | Helps lead the Lawrence Textile Strike |
| 1915 | Joe Hill writes the song "Rebel Girl" in Elizabeth's honor |
| 1920 | Helps found the American Civil Liberties Union |
| 1937 | Joins the Communist Party |
| 1942 | Runs for Congress and wins fifty thousand votes |
| 1951 | Arrested for being a Communist |
| 1964 | Dies on a trip to the Soviet Union; receives a state funeral attended by twenty-five thousand people |

## More you can do:

- Listen to the song "Rebel Girl" by Joe Hill and identify the traits that led him to write that song in Elizabeth's honor
- Read Elizabeth's speech at her trial

## What do you think?

- What do you think about the IWW's idea of "one big union"? Why do you think so many workers went on strike back then?
- Were you surprised to learn that the government arrested so many people for their political beliefs? Why did this happen?
- Can you think of a time when you wanted to speak out but were afraid of the consequences? What did you do?
- How do you think the struggles Elizabeth was a part of impacted her life?

# 34

# Paul Robeson
## (1898–1976)

**Paul Robeson was an African American actor and singer. He became famous in the 1930s and '40s. At this time, it was very rare for a black performer to be so successful.**

Many African Americans and workers around the world loved him for supporting their rights. Many others hated him because he was accused of being a Communist and "un-American."

Paul was born in Princeton, New Jersey, in 1898. His father was a minister, but he was fired for preaching about the mistreatment of blacks. Then, when Paul was only six, his mother died in a house fire. After that, Paul's life was difficult. He had to work many hard jobs as a teenager to help the family.

In 1915, Paul won a four-year scholarship to Rutgers University. He excelled at singing, acting, public speaking, and even sports. He also got excellent grades and finished at the top of his class.

Paul went to law school. He quit his first job when one of the secretaries refused to work with him because he was black. Paul soon began acting in plays in New York. After a few years, he moved to Britain where it was easier for blacks to get acting jobs. He lived there from 1928 to 1939. He acted in several leading roles, most famously as Shakespeare's Othello. He also starred in some films and became very famous.

> ❝ I will function as an artist, but no longer stand . . . up there, doing just acting and concerting. I am going to sing, yes, as an artist. . . . But I give my talents to the people. . . . I come from the people, and from the side of the people. ❞
>
> —*Paul Robeson, speech at the Council on African Affairs, April 1947*

At this time Paul began to support causes that he cared about. He sang for miners in Wales who were on strike for better pay and working conditions. He also supported the democratic government of Spain, which was under attack by fascists in Spain.

After Paul returned to the United States, he became even more famous. On the radio and in films, he sang and spoke in support of US troops during World War II. During the Cold War that began soon after, the Communist government of the Soviet Union was the enemy of the United States. Paul supported many of the same causes as the Communists, like fighting racism and workers' rights. Paul even visited the Soviet Union several times.

So in 1956, Paul was called before Congress and accused of being a member of the Communist Party. This was very dangerous because many people lost their jobs or even went to prison for being suspected of being a Communist. Paul was one of the few people called before Congress who was not afraid. When a Congressman asked why Paul did not just go and live in the Soviet Union, he responded: "Because my father was a slave, and my people died to build this country, and I am going to stay here, and have a part of it just like you. And no fascist-minded people will drive me from it. Is that clear?"

Many African Americans and activists respected his defiance, but the US government did not. They took away Paul's passport and would not allow him to travel, which made it hard for him to work. He gave many concerts at the Canadian border during these years, but it was very tough on him. Paul could finally travel in 1961, but fell ill on a trip to Moscow. By 1963, he had retired and lived a quiet life until his death in 1976.

—Jon Van Camp

## Timeline:

| | |
|---|---|
| 1898 | Born in Princeton, New Jersey |
| 1904 | His mother dies when he is only six years old |
| 1919 | Graduates at the top of his class at Rutgers University |
| 1923 | Graduates from law school |
| 1924 | Gets his first major lead in Eugene O'Neill's play *All God's Chillun Got Wings*; racists threaten to riot |
| 1928 | Stars in the London production of *Show Boat* and sings the song he makes famous, "Ol' Man River" |
| 1930s | Stars in several films including *Show Boat*, *The Emperor Jones*, and *King Solomon's Mines* |
| 1940s | Stars for many years as the lead in Shakespeare's *Othello*, in both London and New York, as one of the first black men to play the role in a major production |
| 1950s | Holds several yearly concerts at the Canadian border |
| 1956 | Testifies before the House Un-American Activities Committee; refuses to apologize for any of his political activities and accuses the committee of racism |
| 1976 | Dies at the age of seventy-eight |

## More you can do:

- Paul Robeson made "Ol' Man River" into a protest song by changing the lyrics. Take a popular song that you know and change the lyrics or the style to make a protest song about an issue today

## What do you think?

- Why was Paul so loved? Why was he so hated?
- How do you think Paul's hard life when he was a child affected him?
- Do you agree with Paul that "an artist must take sides"? Why or why not?
- Why do you think Paul spoke up in Congress when most other people did not? Was he right to speak to them so harshly?

# 35

# Langston Hughes
## (1902–1967)

**Langston Hughes was an African American poet, author, and playwright. He wrote poems, plays, and books about racism and how black people fought against it.**

James Mercer Langston Hughes was born in Joplin, Missouri, in 1902. From an early age, he wanted to be a writer. Langston went to college, but had a hard time getting work.

In the early 1920s, he was working as a busboy at a hotel in Washington, DC. A frequent visitor to the hotel was the famous poet Vachel Lindsay. One day, while clearing tables, Langston wrote one of his poems on a napkin and gave it to Lindsay. Lindsay was very impressed and told all his friends (especially

book publishers) about Langston. In a few years, Langston Hughes was one of the most famous poets in the country.

This was at the beginning of the Harlem Renaissance, a time when blacks in the United States created a lot of outstanding literature, art, and music. Langston would become a major part of this renaissance.

Many poets and authors at the time wrote about other rich, educated people that they knew. Langston wrote about poor people, blacks, and immigrants. His poetry also describes his pride at being African American. This was fairly unusual in his day.

Langston also warned that blacks and others

> Hold fast to dreams
> For if dreams die
> Life is a broken-winged bird
> That cannot fly.
>
> —*Langston Hughes, "Dreams"*

would rebel if they continued to suffer. In one of his most famous poems, "Harlem," he asks:

> What happens to a dream deferred?
>
> Does it dry up
> like a raisin in the sun?
> Or fester like a sore
> And then run?
> Does it stink like rotten meat?
> Or crust and sugar over—
> like a syrupy sweet?
>
> Maybe it just sags
> Like a heavy load.
>
> *Or does it explode?*

Langston also tried to use his fame to help people struggling for a better world. He spoke out against lynching, the hanging of black people without trial. He spoke out for people wrongly accused. He spoke out for democracy in the United States and in other countries. Later, Langston became a strong supporter of Martin Luther King Jr.

But Langston sometimes got into trouble for what he spoke and wrote. He often wrote about revolution. He supported the Communist Party, although he was never a member. In 1953, Langston was called before Congress and asked to identify which of his friends were members of the Communist Party. Many others had "named names" to protect their careers, but Langston refused. Many historians today believe Langston Hughes was gay, but he never admitted it. This was probably because there was a lot of discrimination against gay people during his time.

Langston Hughes died in 1967. His poems and writings offered hope and inspiration to the leaders of the civil rights movement. He remains one of the most influential American poets of all time.

**—Jon Van Camp**

## Timeline:

| | |
|---|---|
| 1902 | Born in Joplin, Missouri |
| 1907 | Goes to live with his grandmother when his father leaves and his mother must travel for work |
| 1916 | Named "Class Poet" of his eighth-grade class |
| 1921 | Publishes his first poem in the NAACP's newspaper, the *Crisis* |
| 1925 | As a busboy in Washington, DC, meets Vachel Lindsay, who helps to make Langston's poetry popular |
| 1926 | Publishes *The Weary Blues*, his first book of poetry |
| 1930 | His first novel, *Not Without Laughter,* is published. *and* wins the Harmon Gold Medal for literature |
| 1932 | Publishes *Scottsboro Limited*, a play based on the nine black men who were wrongly accused of attacking a white woman; visits the Soviet Union for the first time and starts writing about revolution |
| 1937 | Travels to Spain to support the democratic government there, which is being attacked by Hitler and his friends |
| 1942 | Begins writing columns for the *Chicago Defender* |
| 1967 | Publishes *The Panther and the Lash*, a book of poetry about the Black Power movement; dies the same year |

## More you can do:

- **Read some of Langston's books:** *The Dream Keeper and Other Poems, My People, The Ways of White Folks: Stories*, and *Not Without Laughter*
- **Write your own poem about someone you know or have read about who has had a hard life. Does this person have hope for change?**

## What do you think?

- **What do you think Langston means by "a dream deferred"? Why would it "explode"?**
- **Do you think you would have "named names" in front of Congress if you were Langston? Why did so many people do it?**

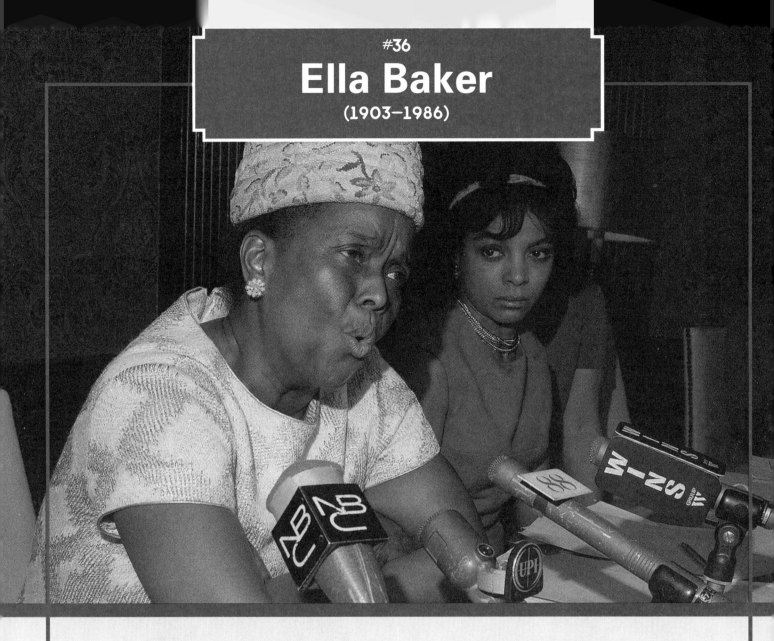

**Ella Josephine Baker was a civil rights organizer. At the age of six, headstrong and courageous, she punched a white boy for calling her "n-----r." Her mother, an activist, taught Ella that women could be leaders.**

Ella excelled as a student, studying about African Americans such as Frederick Douglass and Sojourner Truth and writing for and editing the campus newspaper. In 1927 Ella moved to New York City, drawn to the cultural blossoming known as the Harlem Renaissance.

Ella began writing for many publications including the NAACP's (National Association for the Advancement of Colored People) *Crisis*. After starting a handful of Negro his-

tory and cooperative groups, Ella was hired as a consumer education teacher for the Workers' Education Project. This project was part of a New Deal program aimed at providing relief during the economic crisis of the Great Depression.

Ella became an assistant field secretary for the NAACP in 1941. She was a gifted and natural organizer. Ella's style would become a crucial model for civil rights activists in the South.

Ella's vision was to expand the NAACP, enabling branches to conduct direct action at the local level. This was somewhat at odds with the NAACP's focus on legal and policy struggles at the federal level. After leaving the NAACP in 1946 she worked with friend and fellow activist Bayard Rustin on the Journey of Reconciliation, a bus ride through the South to challenge segregated busing.

When states failed to desegregate after the *Brown v. Board of Education* decision, many civil rights activists began efforts to press the issue. The arrest of Rosa Parks and the Montgomery bus boycott marked a turning point in the civil rights struggle. In the Southern Christian Leadership Conference (SCLC) leaders of various civil rights organizations came together to discuss how to build on the success of the bus boycott. Ella served for a time as executive director of SCLC.

On February 1, 1960, college students in Greensboro, North Carolina, refused to leave the whites-only section of a lunch counter after they had been denied service. They lit a spark that spread like wildfire. Within weeks sit-ins were happening all over North Carolina. Ella convinced the SCLC to fund a conference for young activists on direct action.

At the conference, various civil rights groups tried to convince the students to be part of their organizations. Ella's view, however, was: "Most of the youngsters had been trained . . . to follow adults. I felt they ought to have a chance to learn to think things through and make the decisions." With Ella's help, the Student Nonviolent Coordinating Committee (SNCC, pronounced "snick") was born. SNCC organized more sit-ins, brought students from the North on Freedom Rides through the South to oppose segregated busing, and helped thousands of African Americans to vote.

At age sixty-five, unable to continue life on the road, Ella moved back to Harlem. She became the president of the New York chapter of the NAACP. Ella was a nonstop advocate of civil and human rights until her death.

—**Dan Troccoli**

## Timeline:

| | |
|---|---|
| 1903 | Born in Virginia on December 13 |
| 1918 | Attends Shaw University |
| 1930 | Joins Young Negroes' Cooperative League |
| 1940 | Begins working for NAACP |
| 1957 | Works with the Southern Christian Leadership Conference |
| 1960 | Helps found the Student Nonviolent Coordinating Committee |
| 1961 | Freedom Rides begin |
| 1962 | Works with the Southern Conference Education Fund |
| 1986 | Dies in New York City December 13 |

## More you can do:

- Ella noticed many issues in her community that she worked hard to change. Choose something important to you in your school or neighborhood that you want to change and use some of Ella's methods to address the issue

## What do you think?

- Think about Ella's experience when a white child called her a "n———r." In what ways do hateful words have power? Is there any other way to view this word besides as a term of hate? Why or why not? How can people challenge words and actions they believe are wrong?
- Ella said, "If you somehow talk down to people, they can sense it. They can feel it. And they know whether you are talking *with* them or talking *at* them or talking *about* them." What does this quote tell you about Ella's approach to organizing?
- How was Ella's style of organizing different from traditional civil rights organizations such as the NAACP?

# 37

# Clifford Odets
## (1906–1963)

**Clifford Odets is best remembered for writing plays about the struggles of working people and the need for the working class to join together to improve its members' lives.**

Clifford was born in 1906, and grew up in Philadelphia and the Bronx, New York. His parents were Jewish immigrants from Eastern Europe. It bothered Clifford that many people in America—especially immigrants and blacks—worked very hard but remained poor.

Clifford dropped out of school to become an actor. Later, he wrote plays. In 1931, he joined the Group Theater, which presented plays written by and starring its own members. It also told stories about poverty and injustice.

When Clifford started writing, the Great Depression had begun. Millions of people had lost their jobs and homes. Clifford joined the Communist Party. He believed that capitalism, the system of having people compete to make profits, should be replaced by a system that made sure the needs of everyone in society were met. The plays he wrote were about how people suffer under capitalism. In most of his plays, the characters realize that the only way for the working class to change things for themselves is to join together to demand justice and equality.

*Waiting for Lefty*, a play about cab drivers who decide to go on strike, made Clifford famous. He continued to tell stories about working people in his plays. In 1936, Clifford began writing for movies in addition to plays.

After World War II, many people were frightened of Communism. Some Communists were put in prison for their beliefs. There were people who wanted to make sure they couldn't present their ideas in movies, television, or plays, or even work as actors, directors, or writers. The House Un-American Activities Committee (HUAC) held hearings in Congress to ask people about their political beliefs. Some answered HUAC's questions and apologized for their political activities. Others refused to talk because the Constitution says a person doesn't have to answer questions that might result in their being charged with a crime. They were then "blacklisted," meaning they couldn't work in Hollywood. Some went to jail for refusing to answer because they didn't think HUAC had any right to ask about their political beliefs.

Clifford didn't like the idea of doing any of those things. He answered questions, and told HUAC that he didn't regret joining the Communist Party. He said he had left the party because it tried to tell him what to write, but defended its beliefs. He also criticized HUAC and capitalism.

Many of Clifford's friends felt he had made the wrong decision by answering HUAC's questions. They were angry because he had "named names" by talking about other people who were Communists. Some people who supported HUAC were angry over his attacks on capitalism. This was a difficult time for Clifford, and he did much less writing afterward.

Clifford died of cancer in 1963. His plays are still read and produced today.
—Don Lash

## Timeline:

| 1906 | Born in Philadelphia, Pennsylvania |
|---|---|
| 1923 | Leaves high school to work as an actor in New York City |
| 1923–1931 | Works as a stage and radio actor, ticket-taker, stagehand, and drama critic |
| 1931 | Begins working with Group Theater |
| 1934 | Joins Communist Party |
| 1935 | Writes four of his most famous plays: *Waiting for Lefty*, *Awake and Sing!*, *Till the Day I Die*, and *Paradise Lost*; quits Communist Party over disagreement with party attempts to influence his writing |
| 1936 | Moves to Hollywood to begin writing for films |
| 1937 | Writes *Golden Boy* |
| 1938 | Writes *Rocket to the Moon* |
| 1940 | Ends membership in Group Theater |
| 1952 | Testifies before HUAC |
| 1954 | Writes *The Flowering Peach*; Clifford's third wife, actress Betty Grayson, dies, leaving him to raise their two children alone |
| 1955 | Selected to win Pulitzer Prize for *The Flowering Peach*, but judges were pressured to award prize to another playwright |
| 1963 | Dies of colon cancer at age fifty-seven |

## More you can do:

- **Read Clifford Odets's *Waiting for Lefty and Other Plays***
- **Watch the 1972 performance *Awake and Sing!* and the 1974 performance of *Paradise Lost***

## What do you think?

- **Why did Clifford write in the slang that working-class people used at the time?**
- **In the last scene of *Waiting for Lefty*, actors throughout the theater lead the audience in chanting for a strike. Why did Clifford want the audience to participate in the performance?**

# 38

# Rachel Carson
## (1907–1964)

**Rachel Carson was a writer, scientist, and crusader. Her writing and advocacy inspired the founding of the modern environmental movement.**

Her scientific research, begun in the 1940s, is not only still relevant but in many ways mirrors the same environmental issues that we are facing today.

Rachel was born in Springdale, Pennsylvania. She was very concerned with ecology and the natural world. She became controversial when she researched and wrote about the negative impact that humans were having on the natural world.

As a young girl Rachel lived close to and loved nature. Like many children, Rachel wrote and read stories about animals and nature. As an adult she wrote several essays about the wonders of the ocean, and was known as an expert in her field. But 1945 was a turning point when she learned about a new pesticide called DDT. A pesticide is a chemical that is used to kill insects or other pests. DDT was used on crops like cotton and tobacco to control the amount of pests in the fields. DDT was so effective that it was called the "atomic bomb" of insects. DDT is poisonous not just for pests but for humans and other animals. It also can stay in the environment for a long time, making it a serious health threat.

Rachel studied the way that DDT and other pesticides affected the people and the environments

> "The road we have long been traveling is deceptively easy, a smooth superhighway on which we progress with great speed, but at its end lies disaster. The other fork of the road . . . offers our last, our only chance to reach a destination that assures the preservation of the earth.
>
> —*Rachel Carson*, Silent Spring, *1962*

in which they were sprayed. This research would eventually lead to her most famous—and controversial—book, *Silent Spring*, in 1962. What she found was frightening. DDT is toxic to fish and other marine species. It causes the eggshells of birds to thin and break, making reproduction impossible. The title of the book refers to a future time in which there is so much pollution that there are no sounds of spring, like those of the birds and insects that greet the season.

Her book took on a powerful and wealthy chemical industry, that put profits before health and environmental concerns. She was attacked in the press and her scientific credibility was questioned. Some critics dismissed her writing as "emotional" and lacking scientific merit.

One example appeared in the *New Yorker*: "Miss Carson's reference to the selfishness of insecticide manufacturers probably reflects her communist sympathies. . . . As for insects, isn't it just like a woman to be scared to death of a few little bugs! As long as we have the H-bomb, everything will be OK. PS, she's probably a peace nut too." These attacks did not keep people from reading *Silent Spring*. Instead, it became a very influential book. Rachel testified about DDT in front of Congress. People began to protest and organize to defend the environment because of her book.

Tragically, Rachel Carson developed breast cancer during this time. She had surgery and underwent radiation treatment. In 1964, two years after *Silent Spring* was published, Rachel Carson died of her illness. The Environmental Protection Agency banned most uses of DDT in the United States in 1972.

*Silent Spring* rings true for us as we watch the destruction of forests, wildlife habitats, and the polar ice caps. The situation is much worse now, making Rachel's words even more fitting than they were fifty years ago.

—**Jessie Muldoon**

## Timeline:

|  |  |
|------|-------|
| 1907 | Born in Springdale, Pennsylvania, on May 27 |
| 1925–29 | Studies biology at the Pennsylvania College for Women |
| 1932 | Receives a master's degree in zoology from Johns Hopkins University |
| 1937 | Publishes her first essay in the *Atlantic Monthly* |
| 1941 | Publishes her first book, *Under the Sea Wind* |
| 1945 | Learns of DDT and its dangers |
| 1962 | Publishes *Silent Spring* |
| 1963 | Testifies about DDT before Congress |
| 1964 | Dies of breast cancer |

## More you can do:

- Using descriptive and figurative language, write a poem or short story about your favorite aspect of nature
- Write a letter to the president expressing your three main concerns about the state of the environment today
- Check out a great interactive website: www.rachelcarson.org
- Visit the Rachel Carson Homestead in Springdale, Pennsylvania

## What do you think?

- If Rachel were alive today, what do you think you she would say about the environmental crisis that we are facing?
- Why did Rachel's critics use her gender to attack her scientific arguments? Does this still happen to female scientists?

# 39

# Anita Andrade Castro
## (1907–1980)

**Anita Andrade Castro was a union organizer in Los Angeles from the 1930s through the 1960s. She helped organize Spanish-speaking women in the garment industry.**

Anita was born in Croatia in 1907 and her family moved to Argentina when she was three. She came to the United States in 1922 and moved to Los Angeles in 1934. At that time, Los Angeles was booming. It grew from fifty thousand people in 1890 to 1.2 million people in 1930. People were streaming in from other states and from Latin America, especially Mexico, because business was expanding and there were lots of jobs.

The garment industry had hundreds of small shops locked in competition. To compete, shop owners kept labor costs as low as possible. This meant long hours and miserable conditions for the workers.

In Los Angeles, Anita went to work in a garment shop and joined the International Ladies' Garment Workers Union, known as the ILGWU. She quickly got involved in a general strike. There she had her first nasty encounters with cops and strikebreakers (known as *scabs*). The cops beat up the strikers, and the strikers and scabs went after each other.

Anita soon became an organizer. She organized dozens of shops in Los Angeles and surrounding communities. She spent almost all her time on union activities, often visiting workers in the evening to get them to join the union. She was involved in many strikes. Her husband and son sometimes resented her devotion to the union. She was never afraid to get arrested or to confront scabs. By her count, she was arrested thirty-seven times.

Even after workers won strikes, shop owners found ways to evade the union and labor laws. For example, owners would sign contracts with the union and then close their shops and move somewhere else. They often cheated workers out of their minimum hourly wage by illegally paying them by the piece instead of by the hour. They found ways to get rid of troublemakers like Anita without firing them. Anita's boss once forced her to work behind a barricade, in the hope that she would be so miserable that she would want to leave. Another owner threatened to throw her out of a tenth-floor window.

Anita led the way in organizing Spanish-speaking workers, especially Mexican women. She was elected as a delegate to the union convention year after year because of her popularity with these workers. Workers took their troubles to her because she listened to them. She also fought to get the same pay for women and men doing the same work for the union. She was disappointed that the union did not start a women's Spanish-speaking local. She felt that the union could have recruited many more workers in the 1940s if it had tried a little harder.

Anita was not very interested in politics beyond the union. She did, however, appreciate the Communists in the union because they were not content to just go along with the union leadership.
**—Wally Showman**

## Timeline:

| | |
|---|---|
| 1900 | Founding of International Ladies' Garment Workers Union |
| 1907 | Born in Croatia |
| 1916 | Family moves to Argentina |
| 1922 | Moves with mother to United States |
| 1930 | Moves to California |
| 1934 | Moves to Los Angeles, joins the union, and joins the general strike |
| 1934 | Becomes a union organizer and organizes dozens of shops over the next decade |
| 1942 | Elected as union business agent |
| 1970 | Retires |

## More you can do:

- Listen to the interviews of Anita Andrade Castro by Sherna Berger Gluck in the Virtual Oral/Aural History Archive of California State University, Long Beach
- Learn what languages people speak in your area and find out what issues are important to those immigrant communities

## What do you think?

- Why do workers form unions? Why do they go on strike?
- Why did police beat up striking workers?
- Why do you think the union paid men more than women for the same work?
- Why do you think Anita was successful at organizing Spanish-speaking women garment workers?
- Why were workers who broke strikes called "scabs"? Why would someone want to cross a picket line?

# 40

# Richard Wright
## (1908–1960)

**Richard Wright was an African American writer. He used his talent to highlight the unfairness of racism and inequality in the United States.**

Richard was born on a plantation near Natchez, Mississippi. His childhood was very rough. His father left the family when Richard was five. When he was ten, his mother became sick. Richard lived with one relative after another. He often had to work in order to help provide for his family.

Richard was born in the South during the era of Jim Crow. That system legally discriminated against black people and kept them apart from whites. Richard only went to school through ninth grade. But he developed an

interest in literature. He checked out dozens of books from the library. He used a white man's library card and forged notes in his name. The more he read, the more he became interested in writing.

Like many other African Americans, when Richard turned eighteen, he moved north, hoping to escape racism and poverty. However, his experience changed little. His mother and brother joined him in Chicago. The three of them shared a single windowless room in his aunt's apartment.

Richard got a job as a postal worker. But soon the stock market crashed and the Great Depression began. Like millions of others, he became unemployed. Richard had to wait in line with hundreds of others seeking help from the government. He began to think about the power that the poor could have if they united. Alone, people could feel hopeless. But he thought that perhaps together they could challenge injustice.

Richard joined the John Reed Club, a literary club sponsored by the Communist Party (CP). He wanted to develop as a writer in this club. He also was drawn to the CP's antiracism and the goal of a world without inequalities.

Unlike some writers who made life for African Americans seem better than it was, he showed how black people really lived, without any sugarcoating. He understood that big changes were needed to improve the lives of African Americans.

In his early writings, Richard also showed that such change was possible through protest. For example, "Fire and Cloud," a story in *Uncle Tom's Children*, has a hopeful ending. Blacks and poor whites come together to demand help for people who are hungry.

Richard is best known for his novel *Native Son*, published in 1940. *Native Son* shows the terrible living conditions African Americans faced in Chicago. There was no legal segregation like in the South. But *Native Son* made it clear that racism and discrimination in the North also meant that black people were commonly treated as less than human.

In 1947 Richard left the United States for France with his family because he did not want to raise his children in a country that was so racist. By shining a light on the reality of racism, Richard inspired many other writers and activists, including activists in the civil rights movement.

—Bill Linville

## Timeline:

| | |
|---|---|
| 1908 | Born on September 4 on a plantation east of Natchez, Mississippi |
| 1913 | Father leaves family to be with another woman |
| 1916 | Mother falls ill; Richard spends a month in an orphanage before moving in with grandparents |
| 1917 | Uncle Hoskins murdered by racist whites |
| 1925 | May 29, graduates from junior high school as a valedictorian; refuses to give a speech that was written for him by the principal |
| 1927 | Moves to Chicago |
| 1933 | Joins the Chicago branch of the John Reed club; has poetry published |
| 1934 | Joins the CP |
| 1937 | Moves to New York City to focus on writing; becomes Harlem editor of *Daily Worker* |
| 1938 | *Uncle Tom's Children* is published |
| 1940 | *Native Son* is published and sells 215,000 copies in first three weeks |
| 1941 | *12 Million Black Voices* published |
| 1942 | Leaves the CP |
| 1945 | *Black Boy* published to enthusiastic reviews |
| 1947 | Moves family to France permanently |
| 1953 | *The Outsider* published |
| 1954 | *Black Power*, about trip to Africa, published |
| 1960 | November 28, dies of a heart attack in Paris |

## More you can do:

- **Read *Black Boy*, *Native Son*, and *Uncle Tom's Children***

## What do you think?

- **Do you think racism is as bad today as it was when Richard was alive? Why or why not?**
- **How did Richard's childhood influence his career as a writer?**
- **What do you think about Richard's decision to leave the country?**
- **What were the differences between racism in the South and the North?**

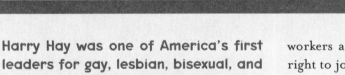

# 41

# Harry Hay, Jr.

## (1912–2002)

Harry Hay was one of America's first leaders for gay, lesbian, bisexual, and transgender (LGBT) rights. During his life, prejudice against LGBT people was vicious. Not only did Harry "come out of the closet" (live openly), but he was one of the first people to organize for equal rights for gays and lesbians.

Harry was born in England and moved to California with his family as a child. He became an activist during the Great Depression. The Great Depression was an economic crisis that threw millions of people into desperate poverty. Harry was drawn to the Communist Party because of its commitment to social justice and its active role in struggle in the 1930s. He became a labor organizer, as

workers around the country fought for the right to join unions.

During the 1948 presidential election, Harry became involved in the campaign for Progressive Party candidate Henry Wallace. Harry and others formed the group "Bachelors for Wallace." The enthusiasm for this group motivated Harry to take steps to establish the first gay rights organization in the United States. Harry and his co-organizers called their group the Mattachine Society. The name of the group came from a secret society in medieval France whose members wore masks so they could criticize royalty without fear of getting caught.

Thousands of people in California became

> "The original [Mattachine] society was based upon . . . a great transcendent dream of what being Gay was all about. I had proposed from the very beginning that it would be [our] job to find out who we Gays were (and had been over the millennia) and what we were for."
>
> —*Harry Hay, 1974*

involved with the Mattachine Society within the next few years. The group—which was open to all, regardless of ethnicity or color—created ways to support LGBT people. One important focus of their activism was to challenge police harassment of gay men. They also started a magazine called *ONE* that shared information, news, and advice with gay audiences for the first time.

Despite its growth, the Mattachine Society had to operate in secret because of the deep prejudice against LGBT people at the time. In addition, some feared the Mattachine Society would become a victim of McCarthyism in the 1950s. McCarthyism was an era when politicians—led by Republican senator Joseph McCarthy—unfairly targeted people for their political beliefs.

Harry opposed McCarthyism and joined protests against it. As the Mattachine members debated ways to deal with these challenges, Harry resigned from the group. The Mattachine Society and its sister organization, the Daughters of Bilitis, were the leading national organizations for gays and lesbians until the 1969 Stonewall Rebellion in New York launched a new generation of activism.

Through the years that followed, Harry continued his activism by participating in many struggles for social justice and radical politics. In the 1960s, he protested the military's treatment of gay men. He opposed the war in Vietnam and the draft. Later, he advocated for AIDS awareness and began the Radical Faeries, a group that promoted an alternative lifestyle for LGBT people.

Like many gay men, he was at first married to a woman, whom he later divorced. He lived with his beloved partner, John Burnside, for forty years until his death in 2002.

—**Michele Bollinger**

## Timeline:

| | |
|---|---|
| 1912 | Born Henry Hay Jr. in Worthing, England |
| 1934 | Becomes active in labor activism and politics in California; joins the Communist Party |
| 1948 | Works on the presidential campaign for Progressive Party candidate Henry Wallace; creates "Bachelors for Wallace" |
| 1950 | Helps found the Mattachine Society |
| 1953 | The Mattachine Society begins publishing its magazine, *ONE*; leaves the Mattachine Society |
| 1963 | Meets his lifelong partner John Burnside |
| 1965 | Protests military exclusion of homosexuals |
| 1969 | Stonewall Rebellion: police raid a gay bar in New York City, and thousands of gay people fight back in angry demonstrations |
| 1977 | Speaks at the first New Mexico Gay Pride march |
| 1979 | Organizes Radical Faeries conference |
| 2002 | Passes away at age 90 |

## More you can do:

- Design a leaflet for the Mattachine Society in the 1950s. How would you encourage people to not live their lives in secret, but to come out?
- View the PBS documentary *Stonewall Uprising*

## What do you think?

- In what ways have LGBT people been discriminated against historically?
- How was Harry's experience as a union organizer helpful when he founded the Mattachine Society?
- For Harry, why was creating an organization for gay people necessary?
- What are the key issues that LGBT people have faced in recent years?

# 42

# Bayard Rustin

## (1912–1987)

**Bayard (pronounced to rhyme with "hired") Rustin was a grassroots organizer for many social movements in the late twentieth century.**

As a gay African American man, he experienced firsthand many of the injustices he fought. Bayard was key to building the famous March on Washington for Jobs and Justice in 1963. Yet he is often left out of mainstream history because he was gay and had radical socialist views.

Bayard was born in West Chester, Pennsylvania, and raised by his grandmother. Julia Rustin introduced Bayard to activism and pacifist tactics. His first political actions included protesting Jim Crow laws in his home

state. He later moved to New York for college. There, he joined the Communist Party (CP). The CP was actively fighting against racism. Bayard connected his struggle for equality to the larger struggles of oppressed people through his work with the CP.

At the beginning of World War II in 1941, the CP shifted its resources away from winning civil rights in the United States. It began to focus on protecting the Soviet Union from German invasion. Partly in response to this, Bayard left the CP and joined A. Philip Randolph in the Socialist Party. The pair worked together to organize a march on Washington in June 1941 against racism in the military. Bayard helped form the Congress on Racial Equality (CORE), whose goal was to struggle

> " What is the value of winning access to public accomodations for those who lack money to use them? The minute the movement faced this question, it was compelled to expand its vision beyond race relations to economic relations, including the role of education in modern society. "
>
> —Bayard Rustin, "From Protest to Politics: The Future of the Civil Rights Movement," Commentary, February 1965

against racism using nonviolent direct action.

During World War II Bayard refused to serve in the military when he was drafted. He was arrested in 1944 and served three years in prison. Even in jail Bayard actively fought for integrated dining halls.

In 1947 he joined with CORE in the Journey of Reconciliation. These bus rides throughout the South tested a law that ruled segregation on interstate transportation was illegal. The riders were arrested and beaten several times on their trips. But they gained much attention for their actions. This model was later used in the Freedom Rides of 1961.

At a time when being gay was a crime, Bayard didn't hide his orientation. But in 1953 he was arrested and his being gay became public knowledge. He had been "outed." Bayard began working with Martin Luther King Jr. on the Montgomery Bus Boycott in 1955. Due to his fame as an organizer as well as his arrest, his friends had to sneak him into the city in the trunk of a car. He later became Martin's main advisor. They formed the Southern Christian Leadership Conference together and organized the March on Washington in 1963.

Bayard endured political attacks, including a campaign that spread lies of a gay relationship between him and Martin. But despite these personal and political assaults, the march was a great success. About a quarter million people came to Washington, DC, to promote civil rights and economic equality for African Americans.

Bayard continued to be an activist, opposing the war in Vietnam and building the gay rights movement until his death. His life was remembered in the 2003 documentary film *Brother Outsider*.

—Nicholas Klinovsky

## Timeline:

| | |
|---|---|
| 1912 | Born in West Chester, Pennsylvania |
| 1932 | Attends Wilberforce University in Ohio |
| 1936 | Joins Young Communist League; trains in community activism and passive resistance |
| 1937 | Attends City College |
| 1941 | Meets A. Philip Randolph; leaves CP and joins Socialist Party |
| 1941 | Becomes field secretary of CORE; helps organize the March on Washington for equality in the military |
| 1944 | Claims conscientious objector status; serves three years in prison |
| 1947 | Helps to organize and participates in Journey of Reconciliation bus rides through the South |
| 1953 | Outed after being arrested; fired from FOR and CORE; becomes leader of War Resisters League |
| 1956 | Assists in the Montgomery Bus Boycott |
| 1957 | Works with MLK to found the SCLC |
| 1960 | Forced to resign from SCLC |
| 1963 | Helps organize the March on Washington for Jobs and Justice |
| 1964 | Founds Asa Phillip Randolph Institute |
| 1977 | Meets Walter Naegle, his life partner |
| 1987 | Dies of a perforated appendix on August 24 |

## More you can do:

- Watch the documentaries *Brother Outsider* and *Eyes on the Prize*
- Read *Time on Two Crosses: The Collected Writings of Bayard Rustin*

## What do you think?

- How do you think Bayard's experience shaped his goal of achieving equality for all people, not just African Americans?
- Do you think a public "outing" would affect Bayard's success as an activist today?

# #43
# Studs Terkel
## (1912–2008)

**Studs Terkel was the world's greatest listener. He was born Louis Terkel on May 16, 1912, to Samuel Terkel and Anna Finkelin in New York City. He had two brothers, Ben and Meyer.**

When Louis was eight his family moved to Chicago. His parents ran a rooming house that was a meeting place for people from all walks of life. Young Louis observed the interactions of the tenants and visitors who gathered in the lobby and stayed in the house. He credited this with helping him develop his interest in oral history, a journalistic technique he innovated and relied on to elicit stories from everyday people.

As a young man, Louis gained his nickname

while acting in a play with another Louis. To keep the two straight, the director nicknamed Louis "Studs" after another Chicago character, the fictional Studs Lonigan from the James T. Farrell book.

Studs became an actor, author, radio DJ, television host, historian, and rabble-rouser. He received a law degree in 1934, but instead of practicing law, he worked as a concierge at a hotel, and soon joined a theater group. In 1939, he married Ida Goldberg and the couple had one son, Dan.

In the 1930s, Studs joined the Works Progress Administration (WPA)'s Federal Writers' Project. He worked in radio, did voiceovers for soap operas, and announced news and

" The thing I'm able to do, I guess, is break down walls. "

—*Studs Terkel, as told to the* Los Angeles Times, *April 2, 1987*

sports. In 1950 he became the host of *Studs' Place*, a television variety show set in a diner. Studs interviewed people and chatted with the staff.

In January 1952, Senator Joseph McCarthy went on a witch-hunt for liberals and leftists. Because of Studs's political leanings, NBC canceled his show and he was blackballed from commercial radio and television.

Fortunately, Studs was able to find work in the theater and one day, in October 1952, after hearing Woody Guthrie on the radio, he called the local radio station, 98.7 WFMT, and pitched an interview and music show. It was a partnership that would last forty-five years. The *Studs Terkel Program* aired in Chicago between 1952 and 1997. The one-hour program was broadcast each weekday. Studs played music and interviewed guests like James Baldwin and Bob Dylan.

But Studs made his name and legacy by talking to ordinary people, too. In the 1960s he went into Chicago's working-class neighborhoods with a tape recorder and produced *Division Street*, the first of his many best-selling books of oral history. He called oral history "guerrilla journalism." He relied on his excited but gentle interviewing style to have people explain, in rich detail, their life experiences and thoughts. In doing so, Studs helped give voice to the American worker and ensured that history would be told from the perspective of all the people. He believed that interesting stories are all around us and that to tell the real story of a place, you have to ask the people who work hard to build it and keep it running.

Studs said, "If I did one thing I'm proud of, it's to make people feel that together they count." And Studs believed that everybody counts.

—**Kevin Coval**

## Timeline:

| | |
|---|---|
| 1912 | Born on May 16 |
| 1920 | Moves with his family to Chicago |
| 1934 | Earns law degree from the University of Chicago |
| 1952 | NBC cancels *Studs' Place*; Studs begins broadcasting the *Studs Terkel Program* in Chicago |
| 1957 | *Giants of Jazz* |
| 1967 | *Division Street: America* |
| 1970 | *Hard Times: An Oral History of the Great Depression* |
| 1974 | *Working: People Talk About What They Do All Day and How They Feel About What They Do* |
| 1977 | *Talking to Myself: A Memoir of My Times* |
| 1983 | *American Dreams: Lost and Found* |
| 1984 | *The Good War* wins the Pulitzer Prize |
| 1986 | *Chicago* |
| 1992 | *Race: What Blacks and Whites Think and Feel About the American Obsession* |
| 2003 | *Hope Dies Last: Keeping the Faith in Difficult Times* |
| 2007 | *Touch and Go* |
| 2008 | Dies on October 31 in Chicago |

## More you can do:

- Read Stud's collections *Working, Hard Times*, and *Race*
- Think about what stories you know of your own family history. Prepare an interview with someone in your family. What questions will you ask them?
- Come up with some questions and strategies for interviewing your classmates, team up, and conduct interviews with each other

## What do you think?

- Why did Studs think that oral history helped to "break down walls"? Do you agree or disagree?
- Why do you think Studs was "blackballed" in the aftermath of McCarthyism?
- Why does Studs call oral history "guerrilla journalism"?

**#44**
# Rosa Parks
(1913–2005)

**7053**

**In 1955, Rosa Parks was arrested for refusing to give up her seat on a crowded bus in Montgomery, Alabama.**

According to the racist rules of segregation, when the white section was full, black people had to give up their seats in the middle section so that whites could sit down. Rosa stayed in her seat and was arrested. Activists in Montgomery organized a boycott against the bus company. For 381 days, no African Americans used the buses. They walked or hitched rides to get to work and back. Some whites supported the boycott, but others were angry. Many black people who boycotted the buses were fired from their jobs, including Rosa. In the end, the movement claimed victory when the Supreme Court ruled in 1956 that segregation on buses was illegal.

Some say Rosa refused to give up her seat because she was tired from working all day. Rosa worked at a department store, but she was also a lifelong activist and organizer, not a "tired old lady." She was only forty-two at the time of her arrest. Rosa had refused to follow the segregation laws on the buses long before 1955. In fact, she had done this so many times that bus drivers in Montgomery often recognized her and refused to stop and pick her up.

She married Raymond Parks, one of the first activists she had ever met. In 1943 she became the second woman to join the Montgomery branch of the National Association for the

Advancement of Colored People (NAACP). She was trained by Ella Baker, attended workshops at the Highlander School in Tennessee, and was a member of the Montgomery Women's Political Caucus, the group that helped to organize the Montgomery Bus Boycott.

The boycott's success put Martin Luther King Jr. and Rosa in the national spotlight. Rosa was invited to speak at civil rights rallies and meetings across the country. She became an inspiration to people everywhere who wanted to stand up to segregation. She was a symbol of the movement, but it was difficult to be female and a leader in those days. Many people thought that men should lead the movement. For example, Rosa was invited to be on stage at the famous 1963 March on Washington but was not asked to speak. "Nowadays women wouldn't stand for being kept so much in the background," she later wrote, "but back then women's rights hadn't become a popular cause yet."

Death threats eventually caused her to move from Montgomery to Detroit. Rosa continued to stay involved in political issues. She began working for Michigan congressman John Conyers in 1965. Rosa never tried to use her fame to become rich. At the time of her death, she was able to get by only because her landlord stopped charging her rent. Rosa received many honorary degrees and awards, including the Congressional Gold Medal of Honor. Up to her death in 2005, she continued speaking out about racism. Even when she was attacked and robbed outside her home, she asked the public not to blame all black youth in response.

Rosa Parks had, in her own words, "a life history of being rebellious."

—Brian Jones

## Timeline:

|  |  |
|------|-------|
| 1913 | Born in Tuskegee, Alabama |
| 1932 | Marries Raymond Parks |
| 1943 | Joins the NAACP |
| 1955 | Refuses to give up her seat on the Cleveland Avenue bus |
| 1956 | Supreme Court rules that bus segregation is illegal |
| 1957 | Moves to Detroit, Michigan |
| 1963 | Appears at the March on Washington |
| 1965 | Begins working for Congressman John Conyers |
| 1987 | Cofounds the Rosa and Raymond Parks Institute for Self-Development |
| 1992 | Publishes *Rosa Parks: My Story* |
| 1996 | Awarded the Presidential Medal of Freedom |
| 1999 | Awarded the Congressional Gold Medal |
| 2000 | The Rosa Parks Library and Museum opens in Montgomery, Alabama |
| 2005 | Dies in Detroit, Michigan |

## More you can do:

- Act it out! Imagine what it was like to try to organize against segregation laws. Improvise a scene in which one of you (Rosa) wants to boycott the buses. Your friend says she does not want to join the boycott. What would Rosa say to convince her to boycott?

## What do you think?

- Rosa said she refused to give up her seat not because she was physically tired but because she was "tired of giving in." What do you think that means?
- The boycott lasted 381 days. Why do you think it took so long to end segregation on the buses?
- When Rosa refused to give up her seat for a white person, she was breaking the law. Are there any laws today that you think are unfair?

# 45

# Genora Dollinger

## (1913–1995)

**Genora Dollinger helped to win one of the most important strikes in US history and to found the United Auto Workers (UAW) in 1937. She was a pioneer in the fight for women's equality because she organized women to play a decisive role in the workers' victory.**

Genora grew up in Flint, Michigan, where both Ford and General Motors (GM) had huge auto plants. The conditions in the factories were dangerous and degrading for the workers. Most regularly worked twelve-hour days and had many physical problems. Black workers were given the most dangerous jobs, pushing metal through furnaces that baked the skin on their backs. Supervisors often sexually harassed the women who worked in the factories.

Genora's first husband, Kermit Johnson, was among a group of workers that was trying to organize the UAW union. They wanted to be able to bargain with the boss as one group, so that no one would be discriminated against. They also wanted higher wages and to stop GM from making them work faster every year. But what they wanted more than anything, according to one female worker, was "to be treated like human beings." They wanted basic human dignity and they thought that a union could help them. GM refused to recognize the UAW.

To win a union, the workers had to strike in the winter of 1936–37. Rather than holding picket signs and standing outside the factory in the freezing cold, Kermit and the other

> **Following the strike, the autoworker became a different human being.**
> **The women that had participated actively became . . . a different type from any we had ever**
> **known anywhere in the labor movement. . . . They carried themselves with a different walk,**
> **their heads were high, and they had confidence in themselves.**
>
> *—Genora Dollinger, as told to Susan Rosenthal in* Striking Flint, *1996*

men decided to occupy the factory, to stop the company from hiring replacement workers. The women—both workers and supporters—were asked to wait outside. Genora organized the Women's Emergency Brigade to picket outside the factory.

At one particular battle called "Bull Run," the fate of the strike hung in the balance. The police were almost successful in violently removing the strikers from the factory. But Genora organized women to break through police lines and defend the men in the building. The actions of the women helped turn the tide in the strike. GM had to recognize the union. The men inside the factory also had newfound respect for women and they began to treat their wives more equally.

Genora was a socialist. After the Flint sit-down strike, she became active in many other causes. She organized to stop evictions and helped evicted families win relief by camping out in front of the mayor's office. She organized chapters of the NAACP (National Association for the Advancement of Colored People) in Flint and Detroit, and fought against the way that the criminal justice system treated black people unfairly.

In California she was involved in the fights for civil rights and quality schools, and provided support for the 1970 strike that founded the teachers' union. One of her most important contributions was fighting for a voice for women. She supported the Equal Rights Amendment, which would have made it illegal to pay female workers less than males. It never passed. But she helped women and all workers to find the courage to stand up for their rights.

—Sarah Knopp

## Timeline:

| | |
|---|---|
| 1913 | Born in Kalamazoo, Michigan |
| 1930 | Marries Kermit Johnson |
| 1929 | Joins Young People's Socialist League in Flint; becomes active with the Socialist Party |
| 1936–1937 | Wintertime Flint sit-down strikes at General Motors |
| 1938 | Organizes successful "Death Watch" encampment of evicted families in Flint; joins Socialist Workers Party (SWP) |
| 1941 | Is blacklisted from all Flint factories but works at Budd Wheel and is a union shop steward |
| 1942 | Marries Sol Dollinger |
| 1960 | Works as organizer with the NAACP in Detroit |
| 1963–64 | Organizes against the wars in Southeast Asia |
| 1966 | Moves to Los Angeles |
| 1970 | Supports teachers in Los Angeles |
| 1970s | Strongly supports the Equal Rights Amendment |
| 1994 | Inducted into Michigan Women's Hall of Fame; involved in trying to form a labor party |
| 1995 | Dies in Los Angeles |

## More you can do:

- Watch *With Babies and Banners: Story of the Women's Emergency Brigade*
- Listen to an interview with Genora at the History Matters website

## What do you think?

- How could a strike change the women who were involved into "a different type of woman?" What does that mean?
- What was the connection between organizing for a union among autoworkers and fighting racism and sexism in Detroit?
- One of the things that Genora was most proud of is the way that the women in the Women's Emergency Brigade stood up to the police. Why did they have to stand up to the police? Were they justified in doing so?

# 46

# Carlos Bulosan

## (1913–1956)

**Carlos Bulosan was a poet and playwright. He came to the United States from the Philippines, a country made up of thousands of beautiful islands.**

There, in the village of Mangusmana, Carlos was raised with four brothers and two sisters. His parents were loving but very poor. So when Carlos was thirteen, he left school. He liked learning, but he needed to work full time to help his family.

Young Carlos farmed with his father and sold fish with his mother. He was often exhausted and hungry. Yet Carlos had some fond memories of his youth. He loved his water buffalo, who was both a pet and trusted coworker. He enjoyed learning from his older brothers. Carlos loved camping and fishing in the jungle with his father. But it became very hard to survive. At sixteen, Carlos decided he had to leave his homeland and his family. He began saving money to set sail for the United States.

Carlos was sad to leave, but he was also excited. In school, he had learned about our Declaration of Independence and Bill of Rights. He also learned about President Abraham Lincoln, his hero. Filipinos learned about the United States because our government ran their country. In 1898, many Filipinos fought Spain to form their own government. But President McKinley ordered the US military to step in. He often said Americans needed to help their "little brown brothers."

> **America is not a land of one race or one class. . . . We are all Americans that have toiled and suffered and known oppression and defeat, from the first Indian that offered peace in Manhattan to the last Filipino pea pickers.**
>
> —*Carlos Bulosan,* America Is in the Heart

Carlos imagined arriving in a land of equality among all people. He dreamed of being able to find a job, send money to his parents, and enjoy life. But when Carlos arrived, he was heartbroken. He saw that Filipinos were not treated equally, in Seattle or anywhere. Across the country, Filipinos earned a living by picking fruits and vegetables. They cleaned fish in Alaska and cut sugarcane in Hawaii. Everywhere, Filipinos worked hard for very little money. But many people despised them. Stores and other businesses put up signs that read "No Filipinos or dogs." There were laws that forbade Filipinos to marry white Americans, even if they were in love. Oftentimes, Filipinos were attacked and their homes were burned.

Carlos refused to let this injustice be ignored. He decided to begin writing to tell his people's story. Carlos wrote poetry, put together newspapers, and created plays. One play called *The Romance of Magno Rubio* is still performed today. Carlos and his friends also built farmworkers' unions and schools. They wanted immigrants from various countries to be able to work and learn together.

Carlos is best known for his lyrical and moving memoir, *America Is in the Heart*. In it, he shared many stories about the suffering of Filipino Americans. He also wrote about solidarity and imagined how things might change. In everything he did, Carlos worked to create an America more like the one in his heart: a country of equality for all people.
—**Sarah Macaraeg**

## Timeline:

| | |
|---|---|
| 1913 | Born on island of Luzon, Philippines |
| 1927–30 | Anti-Filipino riots in Washington and California |
| 1930 | Arrives in Seattle, Washington |
| 1930–36 | Works in an Alaskan fishery, as a farmworker, and dishwasher before editing the *New Tide*, a worker's magazine; becomes involved in the multiracial United Cannery and Packing House Workers of America union |
| 1936–38 | Is hospitalized for tuberculosis, loses right side of ribs and lungs in surgery; begins to write |
| 1936–44 | Publishes in *Poetry*, the *New Republic*, the *New Yorker*, and the *Saturday Evening Post*; sets up workers' schools |
| 1942–46 | Edits poetry collections *Letter from America* and *Chorus for America*; writes *Laughter of My Father*, and *America Is in the Heart* |
| 1956 | Dies of bronchopneumonia; buried in Seattle |

## More you can do:

- **Visit the Carlos Bulosan Memorial Exhibit at the historic Eastern Hotel in Seattle**
- **Farmworkers are still fighting for just wages and working conditions—learn more about their struggles at the Coalition of Immokalee Workers website**

## What do you think?

- **Why did McKinley call Filipinos "little brown brothers"?**
- **Carlos came to America speaking little English, but he became a popular writer. What do you think this means?**
- **Is America now more like the America in Carlos's heart? Is it a country of equality for immigrants?**

# 47

# Grace Lee Boggs

## (1915—)

**When Grace Lee Boggs was young, if she cried, the waiters at her father's restaurant would say, "Leave her on the hillside to die. She's only a girl." Grace later wrote in her autobiography that this "gave [her] an inkling that all is not right with this world."**

Grace, who is Chinese-American, earned an advanced degree in philosophy in 1940 but couldn't get a job because universities wouldn't hire Asians to be professors. Grace became an author, speaker, and lifelong activist for social justice. When World War II began, blacks threatened to march on Washington to demand jobs in the factories. This forced President Franklin Roosevelt to issue an order to end racial discrimination in the defense industry. Grace explained that this showed "the power that the black community has within itself to change this country when it begins to move. As a result, I decided . . . to become a movement activist in the black community."

Grace took part in struggles for tenants' rights, and joined the Workers Party in 1940. She worked with the Trinidadian socialist C. L. R. James to develop ideas around black freedom and socialism. They believed black struggles against racism would lead to questions about capitalist society. Grace thought that workers should run society for themselves. She wrote many articles encouraging workers to run their workplaces without owners. During the war, she distributed leaflets and newspapers about the high profits in the defense industry. She also called for an end to the unions' no-strike pledge. On the day World War II ended, Grace tried to organize a sit-in. The demand was that workers stay employed while the plant changed to peacetime production. The action failed because other members of the Workers Party met with management to get her to leave.

Grace moved to Detroit in 1952. There she became involved in civil rights and labor struggles. She married black revolutionary autoworker James Boggs in 1953. With local preachers and Dr. Martin Luther King, they helped organize a march of more than 250,000 people. They also built a conference with the black revolutionary Malcolm X. Malcolm X often stayed at their house when he spoke in Detroit. Together, they trained others who would become leaders in the Dodge Revolutionary Union Movement and the League of Revolutionary Black Workers. These groups fought against racist abuse and for equal pay and job opportunities in the Detroit auto plants.

In 1967 racial tensions erupted in Detroit. While some called this a "riot," Grace called it a rebellion against the racism people faced every day. But this rebellion and other uprisings at the end of the 1960s caused Grace to rethink her ideas about revolution. She still saw capitalism as the problem, but she also began to focus on how "you cannot change any society unless you take responsibility for it, unless you see yourself as belonging to it and responsible for changing it."

She also helped to start the Beloved Communities Initiative and programs like Detroit Summer. Focusing on rebuilding Detroit from the ground up, Grace and her fellow activists renovate houses, plant community gardens in vacant lots, and create community murals. To this day, Grace continues to write and remains active in Detroit.

—Nick Chin

## Timeline:

| 1915 | Born in Providence, Rhode Island |
|------|-----|
| 1940 | Graduates with PhD in philosophy from Bryn Mawr College and moves to Chicago; becomes involved in political activism |
| 1942 | Moves to New York to work with C. L. R. James and other socialists |
| 1953 | Moves to Detroit and marries Jimmy Boggs |
| 1956 | Becomes editor of *Correspondence* |
| 1967 | Detroit Rebellion |
| 1970 | Grace and Jimmy's lectures are collected and published in 1974 as *Revolution and Evolution in the Twentieth Century* |
| 1976 | Helps found the National Organization for an American Revolution |
| 1984 | Visits China for the first time |
| 1986 | Begins working with SOSAD to prevent gun violence in Detroit |
| 1992 | Starts the youth program Detroit Summer |
| 1993 | James Boggs dies |
| 1995 | Boggs Center founded |
| 1998 | Writes autobiography *Living for Change* |
| 2005 | Helps create Beloved Communities Initiative |
| 2011 | Writes *The Next American Revolution* |

## More you can do:

- Watch videos of Grace at americanrevolutionaryfilm.com
- Check out the Boggs Blog, which includes Grace's latest video/audio interviews and the work of the Boggs Center, at conversationsthatyouwillneverfinish.wordpress.com

## What do you think?

- Why did Grace think that struggles for black freedom would lead to questions about capitalist inequality?
- Why did Grace get involved with the black struggle instead of the Asian American one?
- How have Grace's views on social change evolved since the height of the movements of the sixties and seventies?

# Billie Holiday
## (1915–1959)

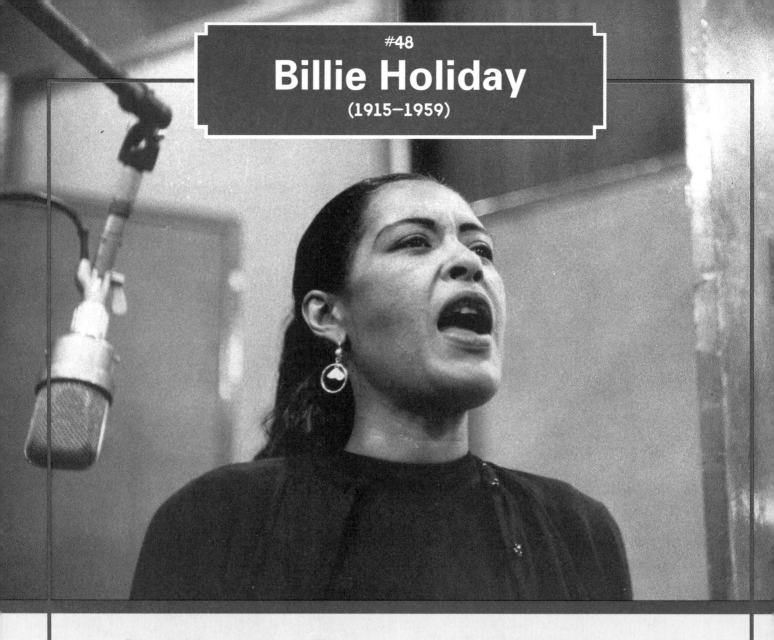

**Billie Holiday once said, "The whole basis for my singing is feeling. Unless I feel something I can't sing it." The feelings Billie experienced throughout her life were sometimes painful.**

But her ability to express these feelings in a totally original way made her one of the greatest jazz singers of all time.

She was born Eleanora Fagan in 1915 and spent much of her childhood in Baltimore, Maryland. Her mother mostly raised Billie because her father was often traveling as a guitar player in a popular swing band. Billie faced a series of difficult events growing up. Her father died of pneumonia in 1937 after being exposed to poison gas as a soldier during World War I.

When Billie was only ten years old, she had a very traumatic experience. A neighbor attacked her. The judge on her case failed to protect Billie. He forced her to leave her mother and go to a reformatory school for girls. After leaving the school, Billie joined her mother in New York and started working as a prostitute. When the police raided the brothel where she was working, she was arrested and spent several months in jail.

After Billie got out of jail, she moved to Harlem and got her first job singing at a nightclub. Great jazz musicians soon knew of her talent. By age eighteen, Billie had played with legendary saxophonist Lester Young and with Benny Goodman's swing music band. She went on tour with the famous Count Basie and Artie Shaw jazz orchestras.

Before Billie, female jazz singers were often in bands mainly to sing a chorus. But her sense of timing and amazing ability to change the way she sang to fit the mood made her an equal to the other musicians in the band. Billie also changed music in another way. When she joined Artie Shaw's band it was one of the first times a black woman had ever joined an orchestra of white musicians. When they played shows in the South, some white people would yell racial slurs at Billie while she was singing. And sometimes she would yell right back at them.

Billie's long personal struggles against racism led her to launch her solo career with perhaps her most famous song, "Strange Fruit." The "strange fruit" she sang about was the bodies of African Americans who had been hung from trees by white racists. This practice was known as lynching. Between 1889 and 1940, at least 3,446 black people were lynched. Billie sang "Strange Fruit" to tell people how horrible lynching was and help stop it. Drummer Max Roach said, "When she recorded it, it was more than revolutionary. . . . No one was speaking out. She became one of the fighters. . . . She became a voice of black people and they loved this woman."

Billie died much too young on June 17, 1959. She was addicted to drugs and they took a toll on her body. But even in her short life, she forever changed popular music and jazz singing. And when Billie raised her voice against racism, she helped inspire struggles against white supremacy.

—Jesse Hagopian

## Timeline:

| | |
|---|---|
| 1915 | April 7, born in Philadelphia, Pennsylvania |
| 1930 | Appears in various Harlem clubs |
| 1933 | Records her first album at eighteen |
| 1935 | Stars alongside Duke Ellington in the film *Symphony in Black* |
| 1937 | Receives the nickname "Lady Day" from sax player Lester Young and joins the Count Basie Orchestra |
| 1938 | Teams up with Artie Shaw |
| 1939 | Becomes one of the first artists to perform at Café Society, where she introduces the songs "Strange Fruit" and "God Bless the Child"; records her first major session at Commodore |
| 1944 | Records her second major session at Commodore; signs with Decca Records |
| 1946 | Stars in the film *New Orleans*; headlines at New York's Town Hall |
| 1954 | Tours Europe |
| 1959 | July 17, dies in New York City |

## More you can do:

- Read the lyrics to "Strange Fruit" and watch a video of Billie performing it, then write a protest song of your own about a problem you see in your community
- Watch the PBS documentary *Jazz*—episode 5, "Swing: Pure Pleasure," and episode 6, "Swing: The Velocity of Celebration"; both feature Billie

## What do you think?

- What impact do you think a song can have in changing the way people think about an issue?
- If you ever became very well known, would you use fame to address a cause you believed in?
- What singers today do you think Billie may have influenced? In what way?

# 49

# Jacob Lawrence

## (1917—2000)

**Jacob Lawrence was an African American artist who used his creative talent to fight against racism. After World War I, millions of African Americans left the rural South for Northern cities in search of jobs and a better life. Jacob's family was among them.**

Jacob was born in Atlantic City. His family later moved to Philadelphia and then Harlem, New York City. In 1930, Harlem was a place of intense poverty and racism. But the previous decade had also known the Harlem Renaissance, a heyday for black music, arts, and literature.

When Jacob was thirteen, his mother put him in art classes at the Utopia Children's Center. There his talents were nurtured by the thriving artistic community. Jacob remembered, "I started painting street scenes. I painted peddlers, parades, fire escapes, apartment houses—all that was new to me."

At sixteen, Jacob dropped out of school and worked in a laundry and a printing plant. During the Great Depression, he joined the Federal Artists Project, a jobs program for artists sponsored by the government. It put thousands of artists to work creating public murals, sculptures, and paintings, and teaching art classes in newly established community centers across the country.

Jacob became friends with artists and writers such as Langston Hughes, Richard Wright,

> **If at times my productions do not express the conventionally beautiful, there is always an effort to express the universal beauty of man's continuous struggle to lift his social position and to add dimension to his spiritual being.**
>
> *—Jacob Lawrence, speech to the NAACP on winning the Spingarn Medal*

Alain Locke, and the great sculptor Augusta Savage. Radical ideas about the need for social change and the role of artists in this process were discussed constantly. "Eventually teachers, friends, even actors on street corners helped me understand how my own experiences fit into a much larger story—the history of African Americans in this country. It seemed almost inevitable that I would tell this story in my art."

Jacob painted in a style often called social realism, in which artists portrayed the issues they saw on the streets—poverty, racism, injustice, and police brutality. His signature style was to paint in simple shapes and bright blocks of color.

Jacob wanted young people to learn about history from his paintings and take pride. In 1937, Jacob made a series of forty-one small paintings about the leader of the Haitian revolution, Toussaint L'Ouverture. Jacob also painted series on the lives of the great abolitionists Frederick Douglass, Harriet Tubman, and John Brown.

In 1940, Jacob made sixty paintings called "Migration of the American Negro." The Migration series showed the journey from the South to the North that millions of African Americans made. "Uprooting yourself from one way of life to make your way in another involves conflict and struggle. But out of struggle comes a kind of power, and even beauty. I tried to convey this in the rhythm of the pictures, and in the repetition of certain images," Jacob said.

During the 1950s and 1960s, as the civil rights movement spread across the country, Jacob painted marches, church meetings, interracial marriages, and battles with the police in the streets. He continued to paint and teach until his death in 2000. The *New York Times* called him "among the most impassioned visual chroniclers of the African-American experience."
**—Annie Zirin**

## Timeline:

| | |
|---|---|
| 1917 | Born on September 7 in Atlantic City, New Jersey |
| 1930 | Family moves to Harlem, New York, and discovers his love of art at the Utopia Children's house |
| 1932 | Studies at the WPA Harlem Art Workshop |
| 1937–38 | Paints "Touissant L'Ouverture" series |
| 1940 | "Migration of the American Negro" series makes him nationally famous when *Fortune* magazine publishes part of it in 1941 |
| 1941 | Marries the painter Gwendolyn Knight |
| 1943 | During World War II, Lawrence enlists in the US Coast Guard and serves in the first racially integrated crew |
| 1970 | Becomes a professor of art at the University of Washington in Seattle |
| 1983 | Paints "Hiroshima" series, which imagined what ordinary people were doing in the moment just before the United States dropped the atomic bomb on Hiroshima, Japan, in 1945 |
| 2000 | June 9, dies in Seattle |

## More you can do:

- **View Jacob's art and read more about him at www.jacobandgwenlawrence.org**
- **Check out *The Choice Is Yours: An Art Activity Handbook for Young Artists***
- **Paint a picture of someone from history who inspires you**

## What do you think?

- **Jacob painted in a style called "social realism." Can you think of examples of this style in other art forms today?**
- **Why do you think Jacob felt that it was important to paint about events from African American history?**
- **If you were to paint a series, what topics would you focus on and why?**

# 50

# Fannie Lou Hamer

## (1917–1977)

**The 1964 Democratic Party convention in Atlantic City was supposed to be the usual good ol' boys' gathering.**

Instead, a black woman from Mississippi named Fannie Lou Hamer challenged the party on national television. She showed America the courage and dignity of the civil rights movement.

Like many poor Mississippians, Fannie Lou's parents were sharecroppers. They worked hard growing cotton on a large plantation but were never paid enough to own their land. Fannie Lou was a bright student. But she started picking cotton when she was only six years old and had to drop out of school after eighth grade to work.

At age twenty-seven, Fannie Lou married Perry Hamer and moved to a plantation in Sunflower County in West Mississippi. Throughout the South, blacks could not vote or demand other rights without risk of losing their jobs, their homes, and even their lives.

Fannie Lou tried to register to vote in 1962. Not only was she rejected, but when her boss found out, he kicked her family off his plantation. From that day on, she devoted her life to the fight for equality. Many civil rights workers were killed in those years. In June 1963, Fannie Lou almost became one of them. Police in Winona, Mississippi, threw her in jail for three days. There they forced other African American inmates to beat her with nightsticks. Fannie Lou's health was never the same. Yet she not only found the strength to keep fighting, she gave others courage, too.

At this time, the Democratic Party didn't allow African Americans to vote at its conventions. Fannie Lou and others created the Mississippi Freedom Democratic Party. The Freedom Party was open to all people no matter what race, class, or gender. Farmers, teachers, and housecleaners all participated in making decisions. The Freedom Party demanded that its members help choose the Democratic candidate for the next election for president. It organized its own elections and traveled to Atlantic City as the only Mississippi delegation open to all voters.

At the convention, Fannie Lou shocked a national audience with her story. She described losing her job, death threats, and the beating in Winona. The Democrats, led by President Lyndon Johnson, were embarrassed, but they only offered two out of sixty-eight seats to Freedom Party members. "We didn't come for no two seats when all of us is tired," declared Fannie Lou as her group angrily left the convention. By the next election the Democratic Party was integrated in Mississippi and across the South.

For the last ten years of her life, Fannie Lou kept organizing for equality. She helped to found the National Women's Political Caucus in 1971. In Sunflower County, she created education and antipoverty programs. In 1977 Fannie Lou's tremendous heart finally failed and she passed away. In the end, death proved to be the only force that could stop Fannie Lou Hamer.

**—Danny Katch and Laura Lising**

## Timeline:

| | |
|---|---|
| 1917 | Born in Montgomery County, Mississippi |
| 1923 | Starts working in the fields at age six |
| 1944 | Marries Perry Hamer and moves to Sunflower County, Mississippi |
| 1962 | Attends first civil rights meeting; becomes a field organizer for the Student Nonviolent Coordinating Committee |
| 1963 | Succeeds at registering to vote; suffers major police beating in a Winona, Mississippi, jail |
| 1964 | Testifies at Democratic Party convention in Atlantic City, New Jersey |
| 1968 | Selected as delegate to Democratic Party convention in Chicago |
| 1969 | Founds the Freedom Farm Cooperative |
| 1971 | Attends the founding conference of the National Women's Political Caucus |
| 1977 | Dies in Ruleville, Mississippi |

## More you can do:

- **Watch Fannie Lou's 1964 "Speech to the Democratic National Convention"**
- **Visit the Fannie Lou Hamer Memorial Garden in Ruleville, Mississippi**
- **Listen to the song "Fannie Lou Hamer" by Sweet Honey in the Rock**

## What do you think?

- **Why do you think the rich white men who controlled Mississippi did not want blacks to vote?**
- **In what ways was the Mississippi Democratic Freedom Party much more democratic than the regular Democratic Party?**
- **Why did Fannie Lou fight on other issues besides voting rights? Do you agree or disagree with her about this?**

# 51

# Fred Korematsu

## (1919–2005)

THE WHITE HOUSE
WASHINGTON

**Fred Korematsu resisted the forced detention of Japanese Americans during World War II. He tried, unsuccessfully, to get the Supreme Court to declare the internment camps unconstitutional.**

He continued to speak out until Congress apologized—forty years after the war.

On December 7, 1941, the Japanese military bombed a US Navy base at Pearl Harbor in Hawaii. The United States entered World War II the next day.

In 1942, when Fred was twenty-three years old, President Franklin Roosevelt issued Executive Order 9066 to place all Japanese Americans in "internment" camps. Roosevelt stated that any person of Japanese ancestry, citizen or not, could be a threat to the United States because they might spy for the Japanese government.

Fred had been drafted into the military in 1940, but couldn't serve because he had stomach ulcers. He had just lost several jobs due to anti-Japanese racism. He went into hiding in the San Francisco Bay Area, and even tried to alter his face so that he didn't look Japanese. He was caught and taken to jail.

Japanese people had three choices when sent to detention centers. They could cooperate, which many did to prove their good citizenship. They could join the military instead of going to

> ## "If you have the feeling that something is wrong, don't be afraid to speak up."
> —*Fred Korematsu*

camps. Or they could resist. Fred was in a minority of people who resisted. The military tried to draft detainees. A group of four hundred people in the camps who refused to be drafted formed the Fair Play Committee.

The ACLU of Northern California used Fred's case to challenge Executive Order 9066 and Public Law No. 503. Fred lost his first case and was convicted. He and his family were sent to the Tanforan Assembly Center in Utah. They lived in a horse stall and did backbreaking labor for twelve dollars a month.

On December 18, 1944, the Supreme Court upheld Fred's conviction. They claimed that the government had the right to take away civil liberties in a time of war. According to the Supreme Court in earlier cases, citizens who were a "clear and present danger" during wartime could have free speech and other civil rights taken from them.

In 1983 a San Francisco court symbolically overturned his conviction. He said, "If anyone should do any pardoning, I should be the one pardoning the government for what they did to Japanese-American people." In 1988, Congress apologized for the action and each citizen who had been interned was awarded $20,000.

When Fred was young, many states did not allow people of different races to get married. Fred and his wife Kathryn got married in Michigan, where mixed-race marriage was legal, because they could not marry in California.

For the rest of his life, Fred fought against violations of civil rights in the name of war. He spoke out on the cases of Shafiq Rasul and Al Odah in 2003. These men were accused of being terrorists and were detained indefinitely without trial at Guantánamo Bay. Fred warned the government about the damage done when people of certain ethnicities, in this case Arabs, are racially profiled and detained.

—Sarah Knopp

## Timeline:

| | |
|---|---|
| 1919 | Born in Oakland, California |
| 1941 | Loses his welding job and is unemployed because of discrimination |
| | May, refuses order to report to internment camp in; is imprisoned until the end of the war |
| 1944 | Fred's conviction is upheld by the Supreme Court |
| 1946 | Marries Kathryn Pearson in Detroit |
| 1988 | Congress apologizes and grants each survivor of the internment camps $20,000 |
| 1998 | Awarded the Presidential Medal of Freedom by Bill Clinton |
| 2001–2005 | Serves on the Constitution Project's Liberty and Security Project, speaking out against racial profiling |
| 2003 | Speaks out on behalf of prisoners in Guantánamo Bay prison camp and files papers comparing their cases to his |
| 2005 | Dies in Marin County |

## More you can do:

- Explore the US government archives on Japanese American internment: www.archives.gov/education/lessons/japanese-relocation
- Read the Fair Play Committee Bulletin #1 "One for All—All for One" from 1944 and design a leaflet for its first organizing meeting
- Read Jeanne Wakatsuki Houston and James D. Houston's *Farewell to Manzanar*

## What do you think?

- Many historians point out that all people of Japanese ancestry in Hawaii were allowed to continue to work in the fields and were not detained. The island could not operate without Japanese labor. How does this fact contradict the stated reason for Japanese internment in California?
- Compare and contrast racism against Japanese Americans during World War II and the treatment of Arab Americans during the War on Terror

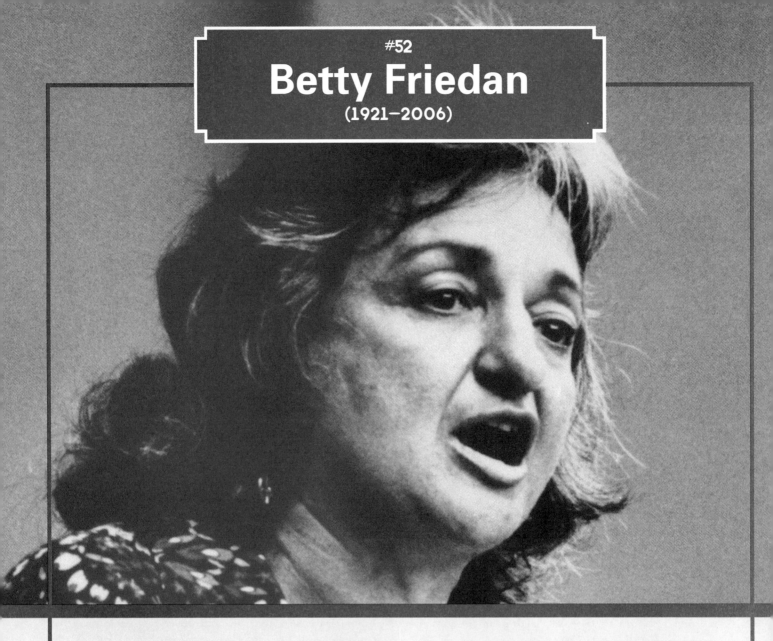

# 52

# Betty Friedan
## (1921–2006)

**Betty Friedan was an American feminist who helped start the women's liberation movement of the 1960s and 1970s. She is most famous for her book *The Feminine Mystique.***

She was also one of the founders of the National Organization for Women (NOW).

Bettye Naomi Goldstein was born in Peoria, Illinois. Being a smart, outspoken Jewish girl made Betty unpopular in her school. In 1938, Betty began studying at Smith College and became interested in radical ideas. She was also the editor of a weekly newspaper. After graduating in 1942, she moved to Berkeley, California, to continue her studies in psychology.

In 1943, Betty moved to Greenwich Village in New York City. She began working as a journalist for the *Federated Press*, a left-wing newspaper. In 1946 she took a job as a reporter for *U. E. News*, the newspaper of the United Electrical, Radio and Machine Workers of America union. During these years, she wrote many articles promoting unions and discussing the inequalities faced by working-class and African American women.

In 1947, she married Carl Friedan, with whom she had three children before divorcing in 1969. At first she continued working as a journalist, but was fired from her job in 1952 after asking for maternity leave for her second pregnancy. She moved to Rockland County, New York, with her family. Her experiences during this time living in a suburban community helped to inspire *The Feminine Mystique*.

For this book, Betty interviewed hundreds of women who were stay-at-home wives and mothers. The 1950s American housewife of TV shows was someone whose happiness was based entirely on the home. Women were told by the media, their doctors, and others that if they weren't happy as housewives, there must be something wrong with them. Betty showed that the unhappiness many women felt was *because* they were forced to spend their lives doing boring work in the home without using their minds or pursuing their own interests. In *The Feminine Mystique*, Betty called this unhappiness "the problem with no name."

The book was hugely popular. By 1970 it had sold more than five million copies. But the book did more than just educate people. It helped to start a movement for women's liberation. Betty was an active member of this movement from the very beginning. In 1966, she helped form NOW. She was the president of NOW until 1970. That year, she led a march of tens of thousands of women down Fifth Avenue in New York City as part of the National Women's Strike for Equality.

Betty was often criticized for her focus on white, middle-class, educated women and their issues. Many people felt that she ignored other voices, especially African American women and poor white women. She also refused to support the rights of lesbians within the movement, arguing that it might make fewer people support women's rights. She referred to activists fighting for lesbian rights as "the lavender menace." Because of her comments, many lesbians, including the activist and writer Rita Mae Brown, left NOW. Despite this, Betty fought hard for women to attain many advances in society that today might be taken for granted.

—**Megan Behrent**

## Timeline:

| | |
|---|---|
| 1921 | Is born in Peoria, Ill |
| 1938–1942 | Studies at Smith College |
| 1942–1943 | Studies psychology at the University of California, Berkeley |
| 1946 | Begins working as journalist for *UE News* |
| 1947 | Marries Carl Friedan |
| 1952 | Is fired from *UE News* |
| 1963 | Publishes *The Feminine Mystique* |
| 1966 | Helps found the National Organization of Women |
| 1969 | Helps found the National Association for the Repeal of Abortion Laws, now known as NARAL Pro-Choice America |
| 1970 | Participates in the Women's Strike for Equality |
| 2006 | Dies on her eighty-fifth birthday |

## More you can do:

- **Read Betty Friedan's book, *The Feminine Mystique***
- **Betty helped women organize "consciousness-raising" groups to talk about their problems. Think of a problem you want to discuss and organize your own consciousness-raising group**

## What do you think?

- **Why were many women not satisfied with being housewives?**
- **Why do you think *The Feminine Mystique* was so popular? Do you think the book is still important today? Why or why not?**
- **What is "the problem with no name"? Do you think this "problem" still exists today?**
- **Why do you think Betty saw women's rights and lesbian rights as separate? Do you think she was right or wrong?**

# 53

# Del Martin and Phyllis Lyon

## (1921–2008; 1924–)

**In an era when it was illegal for a woman to love another woman, Del Martin and Phyllis Lyon lived openly as lesbians.**

They helped found the first national lesbian organization, the Daughters of Bilitis (DOB), and its magazine, the *Ladder*.

Del grew up in San Francisco. Phyllis grew up in Oklahoma. They both went to college in Berkeley, California, but they did not meet until 1950, when they worked for the same magazine in Seattle.

Del and Phyllis became lovers in 1952, a time when men and women who were physically attracted to people of the same gender were considered mentally ill. Lesbians and gays were often fired from jobs and shunned by their families. It was difficult for lesbians to meet each other. Even bars for lesbians were against the law and police sometimes arrested women who went to them.

In 1955, Del and Phyllis, along with six other lesbians, organized the DOB in San Francisco. The group became a social space for lesbians to meet. It also worked to challenge society's discrimination and the laws that criminalized their love.

Phyllis was the first editor of the DOB's literary magazine, the *Ladder*, which published fiction, poetry, and research that showed that women who love women are perfectly normal and could be happy if society's laws would change.

Phyllis earned a doctoral degree in human sexuality so that she could lecture and write to help mobilize a movement to change the laws. Del also spoke publicly and wrote widely to explore and speak out against the false idea that women are weaker and less intelligent than men. And Del organized, wrote, and spoke out to win justice for women who were physically abused by their husbands and boyfriends.

During the 1960s the African American civil rights movement influenced Del and Phyllis. They believed fighting for the freedom to love a person of the same gender was also a civil rights struggle, which was a radical idea at that time. Despite the racism that dominated in the fifties and early sixties, the DOB was open to all women. It also did not bar people for their political beliefs. One of the founding members was a Latina, another was a Filipina, and the group's president from 1963 to 1966 was a black woman, Cleo Bonner.

In part because of their efforts to fight for equality, laws and ideas in society about lesbians changed. After fifty-five years together as a couple, Del and Phyllis were among the first lesbians to legally marry on June 16, 2008, two months before Del passed away.

The movements they helped launch have made it possible for millions of lesbian women in the United States to be who they are openly and be accepted by their families, friends, and coworkers.

Del and Phyllis wrote two books together: *Lesbian/Woman* (1972) and *Lesbian Love and Liberation* (1973). Many of their ideas about gender and sexuality are useful to a new generation who are continuing the struggles they helped start.

—Sherry Wolf

## Timeline:

| | |
|---|---|
| 1921 | May 5, Del born Dorothy Louise Taliaferro in San Francisco, California |
| 1924 | November 10, Phyllis born in Tulsa, Oklahoma |
| 1955 | Four female couples, including Del and Phyllis, form the Daughters of Bilitis, the first national lesbian organization in the United States |
| 1956 | Phyllis becomes the first editor of the new organization's newsletter, *The Ladder*. Until 1957, she uses a false name, Ann Ferguson, to protect her privacy |
| 1965 | Members of the Daughters of Bilitis join gay men and picket outside the White House for the first time to demand equal rights for lesbians and gays |
| 1972 | Del and Phyllis cowrite the award-winning book *Lesbian/Woman*; in 1973 they write *Lesbian Love and Liberation* |
| 2008 | Married on June 16 in the first same-sex wedding ever to take place in San Francisco<br><br>August 27, Del dies at age 87 with Phyllis by her side |

## More you can do:

- Watch the 2003 documentary film *No Secret Anymore: The Times of Del Martin and Phyllis Lyon. Last Call at Maud's*, about a San Francisco lesbian bar, also features Del and Phyllis

## What do you think?

- Why was it so important that Phyllis and Del created an organization for lesbians in 1955?
- In what ways are *lesbian rights* the same as *civil rights*?
- Why do many people believe that two women or two men who love each other should be allowed to marry?
- What has changed for lesbians in the United States since the 1950s, when Del and Phyllis first met?

# 54

# Philip and Daniel Berrigan

## (1923–2002; 1921–)

**Philip and Daniel Berrigan were radical Catholic peace activists. They bridged the gap between antiwar activism, Catholic faith, teaching, and writing for decades.**

They have written many books about the connection between nonviolence and their Christian faith. They have also been important in showing how direct action can be effective against war.

Philip and Daniel were born in Minnesota into an Irish Catholic family. They were active in their church. Philip went to college at Holy Cross and later joined a seminary. Daniel went directly to Jesuit seminary from high school.

After a short time at college, Philip was drafted to fight in World War II. This experience pushed him to confront war and injustice upon his return to the United States. African Americans were expected to fight for their country in the war. But they were treated as second-class citizens at home. Philip saw that as a double standard. As Daniel began seminary, he also participated in sit-ins, boycotts, and marches. He gained a hands-on understanding of civil disobedience and its usefulness in confronting injustice.

During the late 1960s the brothers began to engage in radical protests against the war in Vietnam. They often vandalized and destroyed military property. In October 1967,

Philip organized an action in Baltimore in which participants poured blood onto draft board files. Philip explained his actions: "This sacrificial and constructive act is meant to protest the pitiful waste of American and Vietnamese blood in Indochina." He was sentenced to six years in prison but did not serve the sentence until 1970.

The brothers took part in another action that put them on the front lines in the struggle against the war. On May 17, 1968, Daniel, Philip, and seven other peace activists went into a draft office in Catonsville, Maryland, took 378 draft board files out into the parking lot, and burned them with homemade napalm. Again, they waited for police arrest. For the rest of their lives, both Daniel and Philip would be in and out of prison for radical actions. The brothers were unwilling to compromise their morals. They gave up material comforts and safety to ally themselves with a greater struggle.

In 1980, Daniel and Philip, along with six other activists, illegally entered a GE missile plant in Pennsylvania. They vandalized several nuclear weapons. Again they poured their own blood on files. This action, which they called the "Plowshares" movement, inspired many other actions that were based on the Bible verse about true peacemakers: "They will beat their swords into plowshares and their spears into pruning hooks. Nation will not take up sword against nation, nor will they train for war anymore."

Philip was arrested again in 1999 for vandalizing a warplane to protest war and spent two years in jail. He died of cancer in 2002. Today Daniel is still active as an activist and a poet.
—Nicholas Klinovsky

## Timeline:

| | |
|---|---|
| 1921 | Daniel born in Virginia, Minnesota, on May 9 |
| 1923 | Philip born in Two Harbors, Minnesota, on October 5 |
| 1939 | Daniel joins the Society of Jesus (Jesuit order) |
| 1943 | Philip spends one semester at Holy Cross before being drafted into World War II |
| 1945 | Upon returning from the war, Phillip joins the Josephite order |
| 1952 | Daniel ordained as a Jesuit priest, travels to France, and becomes familiar with the worker-priest movement |
| 1954 | Daniel begins teaching theology |
| 1964 | Daniel helps found the Catholic Peace Fellowship |
| 1968 | January, Daniel accompanies Howard Zinn to Hanoi, Vietnam; he later writes *Night Flight to Hanoi* |
| | May 17, Daniel and Philip participate in a direct action against a Catonsville, Maryland, recruitment center |
| 1973 | Philip is excommunicated from the Catholic Church for marrying a nun |
| 1980 | First "Plowshares" action |
| 2002 | December 6, Philip dies of cancer in Maryland |
| Present | Daniel resides in New York City, where he teaches at Fordham University and serves as its poet in residence |

## More you can do:

- **Read Daniel's *To Dwell in Peace: An Autobiography* and Philip's *Fighting the Lambs War: Skirmishes with the American Empire***

## What do you think?

- **How do you think Philip and Daniel's upbringing and education shaped their actions and beliefs?**
- **Why do you think their interpretation of Catholicism brought new people into the Catholic church?**
- **What was the significance of pouring blood on draft records? What did this direct action say on American foreign policy?**

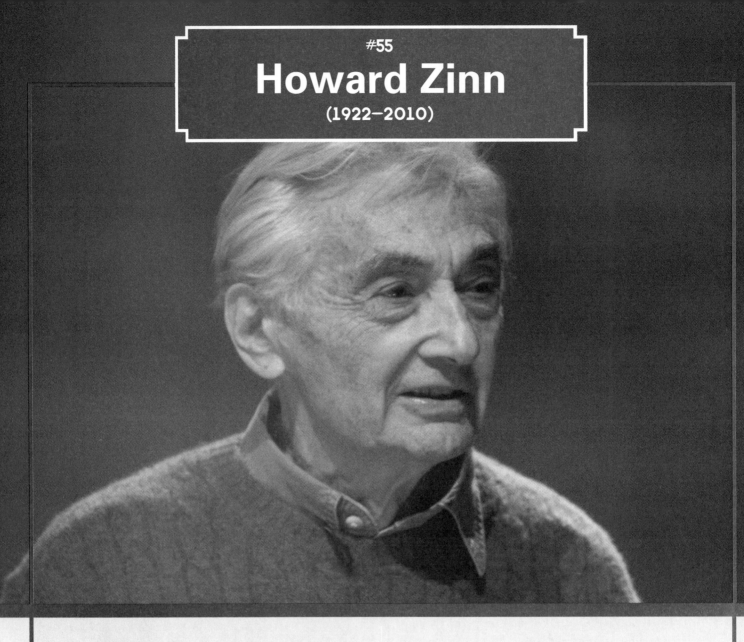

# 55

# Howard Zinn
## (1922–2010)

**Howard Zinn was a historian, playwright, and activist who told the stories of ordinary people. Howard believed that every story had more than one side, and he told the stories that didn't always make it into the history books.**

Howard grew up in Brooklyn in a working-class, immigrant household. At eighteen he became a shipyard worker. He then flew bomber missions during World War II. These experiences helped shape his lifelong opposition to war and passion for history.

Howard went to college under the GI Bill and studied history at New York University and Columbia. He then taught at Spelman College, a black women's college in Atlanta, where he became active in the civil rights movement. Howard decided that the point of studying history was not to write papers and attend lectures but to make history, to help inform struggles to change the world.

Among Howard's students at Spelman were Alice Walker, the novelist and poet who wrote *The Color Purple*; Marian Wright Edelman, who later became head of the Children's Defense Fund; and Bernice Johnson Reagon, who formed the band Sweet Honey in the Rock.

Howard wrote the book *A People's History of the United States*, "a brilliant and moving history of the American people from the point of view of those . . . whose plight has been largely omitted from most histories."

> Think for yourself. Don't believe what the people up there tell you. Live your own life. Think your own ideas. And don't depend on saviors. Don't depend on the Founding Fathers, on Andrew Jackson, on Theodore Roosevelt, on Lyndon Johnson, on Obama. Don't depend on our leaders to do what needs to be done.
>
> —*Howard Zinn, asked what the characters in* The People Speak *would say to us today, 2009*

The book, which has sold more than two million copies, has been featured on television shows such as *The Simpsons* and in the film *Good Will Hunting*.

In the beginning of the book, Howard explained his approach to history this way:

> I prefer to try to tell the story of the discovery of America from the viewpoint of the Arawaks, of the Constitution from the standpoint of the slaves, of Andrew Jackson as seen by the Cherokees, of the Civil War as seen by the New York Irish, of the Mexican war as seen by the deserting soldiers of Scott's army, of the rise of industrialism as seen by the young women in the Lowell textile, of the Spanish-American war as seen by the Cubans, the conquest of the Philippines as seen by black soldiers on Luzon, the Gilded Age as seen by southern farmers, the First World War as seen by socialists, the Second World War as seen by pacifists, the New Deal as seen by blacks in Harlem.

After being fired by Spelman for his support for student protesters, Howard became a professor of political science at Boston University, where he taught until his retirement in 1988.

Howard was the author of many books, including an autobiography, *You Can't Be Neutral on a Moving Train*, and the plays *Marx in Soho* and *Emma*.

In 2009, the History Channel aired *The People Speak*, a documentary codirected by Howard, based on *A People's History* and a collection of primary sources, *Voices of a People's History of the United States*.

Through his writing, his great sense of humor, and his own example, Howard changed the way millions of people teach and learn about history—and inspired many others to see that they and other ordinary people have a role in making the world a better place.
—**Anthony Arnove**

## Timeline:

| | |
|---|---|
| 1922 | Born in New York |
| 1943 | Joins Army Air Corps and fights in World War II |
| 1956 | Begins teaching at Spelman College |
| 1958 | Receives PhD in history from Columbia University |
| 1959 | Publishes his first book, *La Guardia in Congress* |
| 1963 | Fired from Spelman for supporting student protests |
| 1964 | Begins teaching at Boston University |
| 1967 | Publishes *Vietnam: The Logic of Withdrawal* |
| 1980 | Publishes *A People's History of the United States* |
| 1988 | Retires from Boston University |
| 2009 | Releases *The People Speak* |
| 2010 | Dies at age 87 |

## More you can do:

- **Read Howard's *You Can't Be Neutral on a Moving Train: A Personal History of Our Times* or watch the film of the same title**
- **Check out some resources online at www.howardzinn.org**
- **Watch the documentary *The People Speak***
- **Act out a scene from one of Howard's plays *Marx in Soho* or *Emma***

## What do you think?

- **How does a point of view shape our ideas of historical events? Does it matter how history is taught and learned?**
- **What does the title *You Can't Be Neutral on a Moving Train* mean to you? How might sitting still be worse than taking action? Can you think of any instances in history that have shown this to be true?**

# 56

# Mary and Carrie Dann
## (1923–2005; 1932–)

**Carrie Dann is a Western Shoshone (Newe) elder. Her sister, Mary, was an elder as well. Together, they led struggles against the US government to protect their land, culture, and way of life.**

In 1863, the Western Shoshone tribe signed the Treaty of Ruby Valley with the United States. This land included most of modern-day Nevada. The treaty allowed for safe passage for the United States to the West Coast. It gave up no land—it was a treaty of peace and friendship.

Western Shoshone land sits on top of one of the richest gold deposits in the country. Corporations have wanted access to this gold for some time. But the Western Shoshone believe the land, water, air, and sun were given to them by the creator. As Carrie once said, "each one represents life and if you don't have one of those you don't have life." Mary and Carrie were also ranchers who were dependent on the land their animals grazed upon. Like other Western Shoshone, they viewed the land as sacred and not as an object that could be bought and sold.

In 1973, the US Bureau of Land Management (BLM) informed Mary and Carrie that their animals were trespassing on US public land without a permit. The sisters refused to pay for the permit, stating that the land was Western Shoshone land as outlined in the Treaty of Ruby Valley. The United States sued them for trespassing. So their battle with the BLM continued.

In 1979, the federal government determined that the Western Shoshone had lost their land in 1872. The United States said they would pay for the land that they stole, but the Western Shoshone voted overwhelmingly to refuse the money. They believed the land was not for sale. The Supreme Court determined that Mary and Carrie no longer had a claim because of the money the United States had offered.

In 1992, the sisters stopped the BLM from taking their livestock. Later that year, the BLM came back with more force and took their livestock. The BLM returned to Mary and Carrie's land again in 2002 and 2003 to round up more than two hundred horses and cattle. Mary and Carrie were left with no way to make a living. And once the animals were out of the way, corporations rushed in to mine for gold. The mining operations required the use of twenty thousand gallons of water per minute. The mining was not only wasteful but polluting as well.

In the midst of their struggle, Mary passed away after a ranching accident in 2005. Carrie was determined to carry on the fight. She took the case to the United Nations Committee on the Elimination of Racial Discrimination. The committee urged the United States to stop the mining and negotiate with Carrie and the Western Shoshone. But three weeks later, the United States decided they would perform the largest open-air test bombing in history, on Western Shoshone land. After many protests by the Western Shoshone and their allies, the test was canceled.

Today, Carrie is still vigilantly fighting the US government for Western Shoshone land rights and in defense of Mother Earth.

—Brian Ward

## Timeline:

| | |
|---|---|
| 1863 | Treaty of Ruby Valley signed |
| 1923 | Mary born in Nevada |
| 1932 | Carrie born in Nevada |
| 1973 | Bureau of Land Management tells Mary and Carrie that their ranch is on US public land and demands they pay for a permit |
| 1974 | US sues Mary and Carrie for trespassing |
| 1979 | Indian Claims Court (ICC) decides that the Western Shoshone lost their land in 1872 and offers $26 million for 24 million acres of land |
| 1983 | Court decides in favor of Mary and Carrie |
| 1985 | *US v. Dann* rules that the Danns have no right to the land because the US offered money |
| 1992 | Mary and Carrie stop the BLM from taking their livestock; later that year the BLM takes the animals |
| 1993 | Honored with the Right Livelihood Award |
| 2003 | BLM takes Mary and Carrie's livestock and gold corporations start mining their land |
| 2006 | United Nations Committee on the Elimination of Racial Discrimination urges the United States to stop mining and engage in dialogue with the Western Shoshone |
| 2006 | United States plans the largest open-air bomb test on Western Shoshone land |
| 2007 | Western Shoshone and allies protest and force the cancellation of the test |

## More you can do:

- Watch the documentary *American Outrage*
- Read Carrie's acceptance speech for the Right Livelihood Award in 1993
- Explore the Western Shoshone Defense Project website: www.wsdp.org

## What do you think?

- Why did the US government fight so hard against Mary and Carrie and the Western Shoshone?
- How is Mary and Carrie's experience with the US government similar to those of Native Americans in the past?

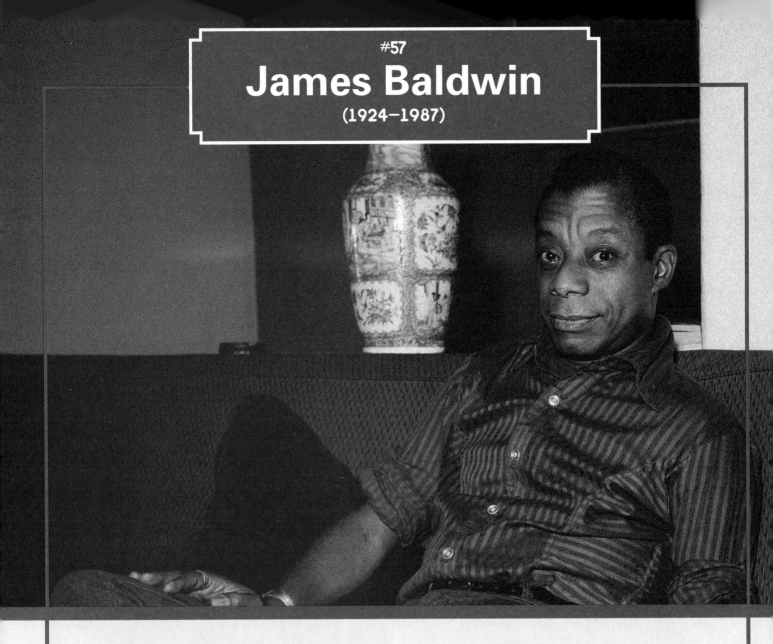

# 57

# James Baldwin

## (1924–1987)

James Baldwin was a novelist, play-wright, poet, and essayist who wrote more than twenty books. James saw himself not as a spokesman for African Americans but a witness to social wrongs.

James was born in the Harlem neighborhood of New York City. He never knew his father. He was raised by his mother, Emma Berdis Joynes, and stepfather, David Baldwin. His mother worked as a maid. His stepfather worked in a factory and was a part-time preacher. His family was very poor and struggled to make ends meet. When James was not taking care of his siblings, he spent most of his time reading at the Schomburg Library. James knew he wanted to be a writer. He re-

called: "I read everything. I read my way out of the two libraries in Harlem by the time I was thirteen." James said, "I knew I was black, of course, but I also knew I was smart. I didn't know how I would use my mind, or even if I could, but that was the only thing that I had to use."

In 1938, he started high school at DeWitt Clinton in the Bronx. He was also active in his church. In fact, he became a teenage preacher at the Fireside Pentecostal Assembly. He became known for being a fine orator. "I would improvise from the texts, like a jazz musician improvises from a theme."

By James's telling, his stepfather "was a pious, very religious and in some ways a very beautiful man, and in some ways a terrible man." Their relationship was filled with conflict. At eighteen James left home to work at a defense plant and later, at a meatpacking factory in Manhattan. After a brief time, he moved to Greenwich Village, where he met and became friends with Richard Wright, Marlon Brando, and other writers and artists. He worked as a waiter and wrote reviews until Richard helped him get a grant to write full time. In 1948, James moved to Paris, France. He wrote while living in and traveling across Europe and the Near East for the next few decades.

His most well-known books include the novels *Go Tell It on the Mountain* and *Giovanni's Room* and the essays collected in *Notes of a Native Son.* The poet Langston Hughes once said that James used words "as the sea uses waves." Most of James's writings explored African American life and racism in the United States. James spoke out for civil rights before the civil rights movement was formed. And when that movement arose, James threw himself into it. "There was something very beautiful about that period, something life-giving for me to be there, to march, to be a part of a sit-in, to see it through my own eyes." He was also gay and wrote about gay and bisexual characters before there was a movement for gay rights.

Although James lived abroad for many years, he remained focused on key issues and challenges for the United States. His essays reflected on racial tensions, stereotypical representations of blacks in film, and the impact of poverty on everyday life. James pointed out that if people's rights were ignored and social needs (like housing, jobs, and food) went unmet, then the result would be "chaos for everybody in society." He warned that the words of an old spiritual sung by enslaved people might come true: "God gave Noah the rainbow sign / No more water, the fire next time!"

**—Dao X. Tran**

## Timeline:

1924   August 2, born in Harlem

1938   Enters DeWitt Clinton High School and becomes a young minister with the Fireside Pentecostal Assembly

1941   Stepfather dies

1942   Works as a waiter

1945   Writes reviews for the *New Leader* and the *Nation*; hangs out with socialists and Trotskyists

1946   Best friend commits suicide

1948   Moves to Paris, France, with $40 in his pocket

1953   Publishes acclaimed first novel, *Go Tell It on the Mountain*

1956   First book of nonfiction, *Notes of a Native Son* is published; also publishes *Giovanni's Room*, which was controversial for its explicit gay content

1963   Gains widespread fame as a "voice" for civil rights; goes on a lecture tour for the Congress of Racial Equality; participates in a voter registration drive in Alabama; appears on the cover of *Time*

1979   Revisits the South as a journalist

1984–87   Speaks and teaches widely

1987   December 1, dies in the South of France from stomach cancer

## More you can do:

- **Read James's novels and essays**
- **Read Jordan Elgrably's interview with James on "The Art of Fiction" in the *Paris Review***

## What do you think?

- **How did James's writing express the difference between being a witness and being a spokesperson for the civil rights movement?**
- **Why did James continue to write about the United States even though he didn't always live there?**
- **What does it say that James considered himself not a gay or African American writer primarily, but an American one?**

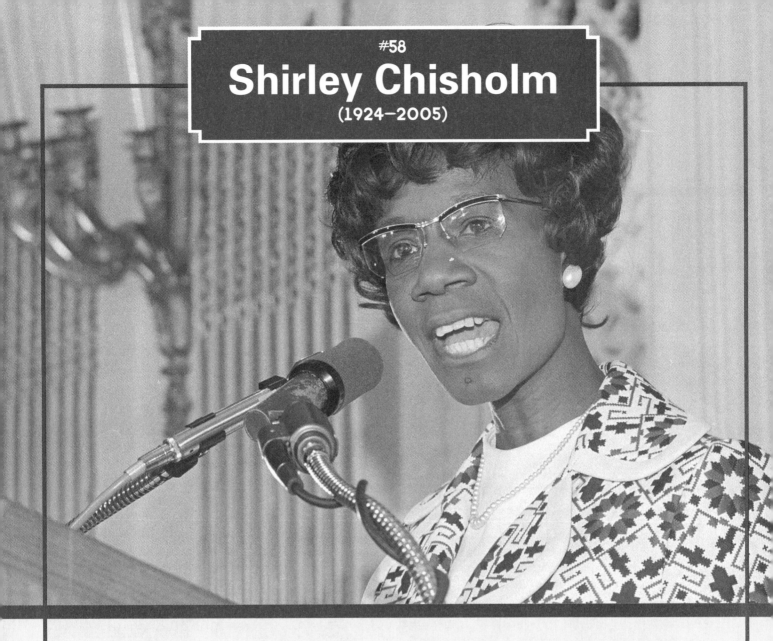

# 58

# Shirley Chisholm
## (1924–2005)

**Shirley Chisholm was an educator and politician. She was the first black woman ever elected to Congress.**

She ran for president as a Democrat, becoming one of the first black women to run for the nomination of a major party.

Shirley was born in Brooklyn in 1924. After graduating from college, she ran a day-care center. She worked to create programs for the education of young children. Shirley was elected to the New York state legislature. She then surprised political "experts" by winning a race for Congress.

Shirley spoke out against white and black male politicians who didn't take women seriously.

She also criticized activists for women's rights who didn't pay attention to poor women of color. She said things other blacks and women in Congress were afraid to say. For example, she was the only member of Congress to call for the black activist Angela Davis to be released when she was facing murder charges.

Shirley ran for president in 1972 even though she knew she couldn't win. She couldn't even raise enough money to run a real campaign with TV ads and paid staff. But she had many supporters across the country. She also thought other black politicians were making a mistake by trying to select a candidate to run as a way to get more power within the Democratic Party. While Shirley agreed blacks should use their voting power to demand more power in

> ❝ When I die, I want to be remembered as a woman . . . who dared to be a catalyst for change. I don't want be remembered as the first black woman who went to Congress. . . . I want to be remembered as a woman who fought for change in the twentieth century. ❞
>
> —*Representative Shirley Chisholm,* Unbought and Unbossed

the party, she didn't believe bosses—whether black or white—should decide how that power should be used.

Shirley didn't campaign as a "black candidate" or a "woman candidate." She was a candidate who fought against the oppression of blacks, Latinos, women, gays, and working-class men and women of all backgrounds. When gay male supporters appeared at a rally in "women's" clothing, she thanked them for coming and for supporting her. She also thanked the Black Panther Party for supporting her. No other candidate wanted to be seen as "radical." Shirley was amused when fellow candidate George Wallace, who was running a campaign that appealed to the fears of white voters, paid her a "compliment." He said Shirley and he were the only two candidates who spoke their minds in front of every audience in every part of the country. She agreed, and felt her liberal opponents were making a mistake when they avoided taking stands on tough issues.

Shirley managed to win more votes than some of the "serious" white, male candidates with big-budget campaigns. She said later that her campaign showed that women, blacks, Latinos, Asians, young voters, and others who favored radical change could work together. They made mistakes and faced many challenges. But the inexperienced volunteers who worked on her campaign were able to unite many people.

Shirley remained in Congress until 1983. She then became a college professor. Shirley remained active in her later life. In 1990 she helped form a group called African-American Women for Reproductive Freedom to fight for black women's right to access birth control and abortion. Shirley died in 2005 at age eighty.

—**Don Lash**

## Timeline:

| | |
|---|---|
| 1924 | Born in Brooklyn, New York |
| 1952 | Awarded master's degree in education at Columbia University |
| 1953–64 | Manages a day-care program in Brooklyn and helps establish child care and early childhood education programs in New York City |
| 1964 | Elected to New York State Assembly |
| 1968 | Becomes first black woman elected to Congress |
| 1969–1983 | Serves as congresswoman |
| 1970 | Writes first book, *Unbought and Unbossed* |
| 1972 | Runs for president, winning about 10 percent of votes in the primaries she entered, while spending a total of about $300,000 on the campaign |
| 1973 | Writes second book, *The Good Fight* |
| 1983 | Leaves Congress and begins new career teaching college |
| 2005 | Dies at age eighty |

## More you can do:

- **Read Shirley's books *Unbought and Unbossed* and *The Good Fight***
- **Watch the PBS documentary *Chisholm '72: Unbought and Unbossed***

## What do you think?

- **In 2008, the Democratic nomination for the presidency became a contest between Barack Obama and Hillary Clinton. Did Shirley's campaign help to make their campaigns possible? In what ways did their campaigns differ from hers?**
- **What was important about Shirley's disagreement with other black leaders about how and why to run for president?**

# 59

# Malcolm X
## (1925–1965)

**"No one man should have that much power." That's what one police officer said about Malcolm X.**

The officer was frightened by Malcolm and the crowd of five hundred people protesting the brutal police beating of an African American man in New York City. On that night of April 20, 1957, Malcolm and his followers forced the police to allow the injured man to see a doctor.

Malcolm was born with the name Malcolm Little, in Omaha, Nebraska, on May 19, 1925. When he was four years old, Ku Klux Klan members burned down his family's home. When Malcolm was just six, his father was found dead on the railroad tracks, most

likely pushed in front of the train by white supremacists.

Malcolm's mother soon had a mental breakdown under the strain of raising seven children by herself. Malcolm was taken away from his mother and put into various state institutions. In his teenage years he moved to Boston and from there to New York City. Then known as "Detroit Red," he soon became involved with criminal activity and at the age of twenty he went to jail for burglary.

In jail, Malcolm made a big change in his life. He became a follower of the Nation of Islam (NOI). Elijah Muhammad was the prophet of the NOI and he preached hard work, self-reliance, and black separation from white

> ## "Our objective is complete freedom, justice, and equality by any means necessary."
>
> *—Malcolm X, spech at the founding of the Organization of Afro American Unity, 1964*

society. When Malcolm got out of jail, he took the last name "X." The "X" represented the unknown name that been taken away from his ancestors when they were kidnapped from Africa in the slave trade.

In part because of Malcolm's great skills, he soon became the national spokesman for the NOI. He told black people they had a right to defend themselves if they were attacked. He urged people to fight racism "by any means necessary." Eventually, Malcolm became impatient with the NOI for not participating more in the civil rights movement. It wasn't easy, but he decided to leave the NOI.

Malcolm then traveled to Africa and the Middle East—a journey that again changed his worldview. He made the spiritual pilgrimage called a *hajj* to Mecca (the holiest place in Islam) and prayed with people of all skin tones. He took the name El-Hajj Malik el-Shabazz. When Malcolm returned home from Africa, he formed the Organization of Afro American Unity. He surprised many when that he said would now work in coalition with "white people who are truly sincere" in their opposition to racism. Tragically, Malcolm was shot and killed while giving a speech in 1965 and never got the chance to find out just how powerful a newly changed movement could have been.

During his life, Malcolm opposed capitalism because he said it was an unfair system that made a few people rich and many people poor. He argued for black people not to join the Democrats or the Republicans because they supported this unfair system. He spoke out against the US war against Vietnam. And he was a leader in the fight against racism. His ideas would live on with the young Black Power activists he inspired in the late 1960s and 1970s.

**—Jesse Hagopian**

## Timeline:

**1925** Born Malcolm Little on May 19 in Omaha, Nebraska

**1929** Home in Lansing, Michigan, is burned to the ground

**1939** Mother is committed to the State Mental Hospital in Kalamazoo, and Malcolm placed in a juvenile home.

**1946** Is sentenced to eight to ten years for armed robbery; serves six years at Charlestown State Prison

**1948–49** Converts to Islam

**1953** Changes name to Malcolm X

**1958** Marries Sister Betty X

**1959** Travels to the Middle East and Africa

**1964** March, leaves the NOI

April, travels to Middle East and Africa and makes the *hajj*

May, starts the OAAU, a secular political group

**1965** February 14, home is firebombed

February 21, is assassinated as he begins his speech at the Audubon Ballroom

## More you can do:

- Watch a video of a reading of Malcolm X's speech, "Message to the Grass Roots." Then write your own speech about something that needs to be changed in your community

## What do you think?

- Describe the ideas Malcolm X had under each of his names: Malcolm Little, Detroit Red, Malcolm X, and El-Hajj Malik el-Shabazz
- If Malcolm were still alive, what would he say about what needs to be done to address racism in the United States today? What movements for justice do you think he would support?

# 60

# Elizabeth Martinez
## (1925–)

Growing up in a mostly white suburb outside of Washington, DC, Elizabeth Sutherland Martinez always felt different. She spoke Spanish at home with her Mexican father and white mother.

When she and her father rode on the segregated buses, they were forced to move to the back. Elizabeth connected this to the racism blacks faced. She saw the possibility and need for building an alliance between blacks and Mexicans to fight racism. This became her lifelong work.

Elizabeth did well in school and became the first Latina to graduate from Swarthmore College. She earned a degree in history and literature in 1946. After graduating with honors, she landed her dream job at the United Nations, where she "hoped to bring about world peace." Unfortunately, she quickly realized that would not be so easy. For five years she worked in an office doing research on former colonies of the world. "The more research I did, the more I understood colonialism and how it interfaced with racism. I wanted to fight that."

In 1963, racists bombed an Alabama church and killed four little girls. This moved Elizabeth to dedicate herself full time to the civil rights movement. She began by leading the New York office of the Student Nonviolent Coordinating Committee. In summer 1964 she traveled to Mississippi with thousands of other people to help register black voters. Upon her return, she edited a volume of letters from young people relaying their experiences fighting racism in Mississippi. The letters were full of stories of the poverty and oppression that the activists saw.

The movement against racism that targeted black people helped start movements to challenge racism against other people of color, including Mexicans and others from Latin America. Elizabeth moved to New Mexico, where she cofounded and published the newspaper *El Grito del Norte/The Cry of the North*. The paper advocated for land rights and against racism. Chicano/as (Mexican Americans) had lost land in the American Southwest when the United States invaded Mexico. Elizabeth's paper advocated for this land to be returned to Chicano/as and for the US government to apologize for their invasion of Mexico.

Elizabeth moved to California and ran for governor in 1982. She campaigned in opposition to what she called "Reagan's war machine." She pointed out that every man, woman, and child would pay a thousand dollars that year in taxes that would go directly to fund war. War spending would drastically increase under Ronald Reagan's presidency. This was money, she argued, that could be spent to take care of people instead of destroying them.

Elizabeth founded the Institute for MultiRacial Justice, which "aims to . . . help build alliances among peoples of color and combat divisions." She also helped start the newspaper *War Times/Tiempo de Guerras* in opposition to the US war on terror. Her best-known work is *500 Años del Pueblo Chicano/500 Years of Chicano History in Pictures*, a bilingual history that also became the basis for a film. She continues to struggle against racism, war, and oppression through her activism, writing, and teaching.

—Erik Wallenberg

## Timeline:

| | |
|---|---|
| 1925 | Born in Washington, DC, on December 12 |
| 1946 | First Latina to graduate from Swarthmore College |
| 1947–53 | Works at the United Nations as a researcher on colonialism |
| 1964 | Works for the Student Nonviolent Coordinating Committee's Summer Program in Mississippi |
| 1965 | Edits *Letters from Mississippi*, a collection of letters home from young people who participated in the Freedom Summer in 1964 |
| 1968–73 | Begins publishing *El Grito del Norte/The Cry of the North*, a Chicano/a land and civil rights newspaper |
| 1982 | First Chicana on the ballot for governor in the state of California; runs as a member of the Peace and Freedom Party |
| 1991 | Writes *500 Años del Pueblo Chicano/500 Years of Chicano History in Pictures* |
| 1997 | Founds the Institute for MultiRacial Justice in San Francisco |
| 2002 | Helps start bilingual newspaper, *War Times/Tiempo de Guerras* |

## More you can do:

- Read *Letters from Mississippi* and think about what you could change in one summer
- Watch *Viva la Causa: 500 Years of Chicano History*

## What do you think?

- How is racism used to justify war?
- Do you agree with Elizabeth that people of different oppressed groups can work together against all kinds of oppression? Why or why not?
- Research how much money is currently spent on war and the military. What else could that money be used for in your community?

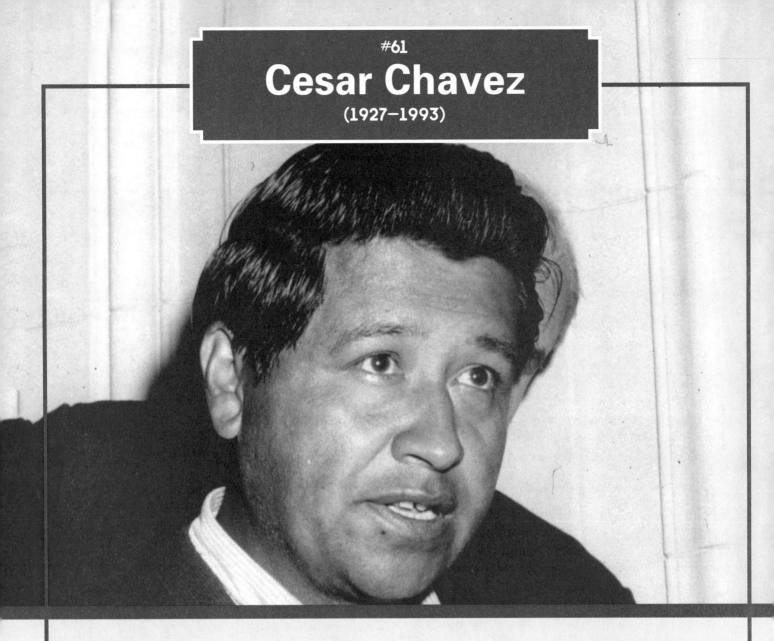

# 61

# Cesar Chavez

## (1927–1993)

**Cesar Chavez was an organizer of migrant farmworkers in California and a civil rights activist.**

Cesar was born in Arizona. When his family's small farm went bankrupt, the Chavezes turned to migratory farmwork to make ends meet, moving from town to town in California.

Though he liked to learn, Cesar had a hard time in school. He was named Cesario, after his grandfather, but his teacher shortened his name to Cesar. In school Cesar and his classmates were forbidden to speak Spanish. He was ridiculed for showing up to school without shoes when his family couldn't afford them. After eighth grade he dropped out of school to work.

When Cesar left the navy after World War II, he married Helen Fabela. He continued to do migratory farmwork and sharecropping. Cesar befriended a priest, Father McDonnell, who introduced him to books about labor leaders like Eugene Debs and John L. Lewis. The teachings of Mahatma Gandhi also had a lasting influence on Cesar. In 1952 he joined the Community Service Organization (CSO), through which he successfully organized many Latinos to vote.

Cesar soon turned to organizing farmworkers. One major problem was competition from the *bracero* (the name is derived from the Spanish word for *arms*) workers. Starting in 1942, a government program brought people from Mexico to do temporary farmwork in

> ❝The fight is never about grapes or lettuce.
> It is always about people.❞
>
> —Cesar Chavez, in a speech at the Commonwealth Club, 1984

the United States. Growers forced braceros to work for much less pay, using the constant threat of returning them to Mexico. Cesar organized workers to pressure the Farm Placement Service to prioritize hiring local farmworkers over the braceros. Cesar eventually left the CSO after the organization refused his many requests to support a farmworkers' union drive. In 1962, he and fellow activist Dolores Huerta founded the National Farm Workers Association (NFWA).

The NFWA recruited a couple hundred workers and had some early strike victories, but the turning point came when the mostly Filipino American workers in the Agricultural Workers Organizing Committee (AWOC) struck against grape growers in California. Cesar spoke at nearby colleges and called for a boycott of the growers. The more growers harassed the strikers and had them arrested, the more their public support grew. The workers organized a march through California to the capitol to draw attention to the strike and pressure the governor to help them. As the march progressed, support for the strike grew dramatically and eventually the growers caved in, increasing workers' pay.

Other growers continued to resist farmworkers' organizing efforts. The NFWA and AWOC merged and later became the United Farm Workers (UFW). Strikes and boycotts spread to all the grape growers in California. In order to keep the strike nonviolent, Cesar began a hunger strike. The fast helped to raise more public support for the strike and drew more workers into the UFW. Soon after, growers signed a contract with the UFW that raised pay and set up a workers' welfare fund.

Cesar's commitment to organizing poor farmworkers and nonviolent tactics made him a civil rights icon. He continued to organize until his death.
—**Dan Troccoli**

## Timeline:

1927   March 31, born in Arizona

1944   Joins the navy

1948   Marries Helen Fabela

1952   Begins organizing with Community Service Organization

1962   Founds the National Farm Workers Association

1965   Delano Grape Strike begins

1966   March from Delano to Sacramento, California; begins first hunger strike

1970   "Salad Bowl" strike in California over representation dispute with the Teamsters Union

1972   Fasts against pesticide use

1993   April 23, dies in Arizona

## More you can do:

- **Find and read Cesar's "Wrath of Grapes Boycott" speech. Think about what themes he used and whether you find them effective**
- **Go to a grocery store or produce market and look at the labels on fruits and vegetables. Where were they grown? Find out more about where your food came from by researching the growers**

## What do you think?

- **Describe some of the influences on Cesar's activism**
- **How did the bracero program make it difficult to organize farmworkers?**
- **Cesar is often seen as a civil rights leader and a union leader. Compare these two aspects of his work**
- **How do you think Cesar's legacy impacts immigrants' rights today?**

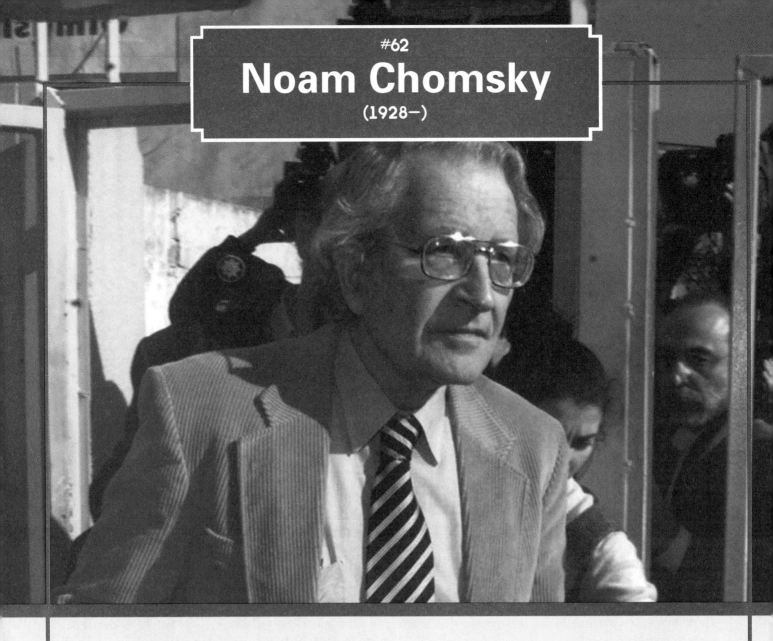

# 62

# Noam Chomsky

## (1928–)

**Avram Noam Chomsky was born in Philadelphia and raised among Jewish immigrants from Eastern Europe. His father fled from Russia in 1913 to escape being forced into the army.**

Noam grew up during the Depression and the rise of fascism around the world. As he later recalled, "Some of my earliest memories, which are very vivid, are of people selling rags at our door, of violent police strikebreaking, and other Depression scenes." While his parents were, as he puts it, "normal Roosevelt Democrats," he had aunts and uncles who were garment workers in trade unions and political organizers. As a child, Noam was immersed in the radical Jewish intellectual culture in New York City. He regularly

visited newsstands and bookstores with anarchist literature. According to Noam, this was a "working-class culture with working-class values, solidarity, socialist values."

From a very young age, Noam was interested in the science of language. He left high school early and studied linguistics, mathematics, and philosophy at the University of Pennsylvania. In 1955, he received his PhD and began teaching at Massachusetts Institute of Technology, where he has taught linguistics and philosophy ever since.

In the mid-1950s, Noam wrote articles and longer works that completely changed how we think about language. In 1988, he received the Kyoto Prize in Basic Science, given "to

> ## "It is the responsibility of intellectuals to speak the truth and expose lies."
>
> —Noam Chomsky, "The Responsibility of Intellectuals," in the New York Review of Books, 1967

honor those who have contributed significantly to the scientific, cultural, and spiritual development of mankind." The prize noted that "Chomsky's theoretical system remains an outstanding monument of 20th century science and thought."

While Noam got international attention for his linguistic work, he began to speak out on political topics and started writing long, detailed essays against the war in Vietnam. He became one of the most important critics of the US war effort, earning a place on President Richard Nixon's "enemies list."

But Noam was not just a critic of the war against the people of Indochina. He participated in direct action to back up his beliefs. Noam was part of one of the first public protests against the war in Boston in October 1965. There, protesters were outnumbered by counterdemonstrators and police. Noam was also involved in the Central American solidarity movement and protest against the 1991 and 2003 US interventions in Iraq and other wars.

Noam has continued to speak out and encourage others to become involved in movements for change. He has published hundreds of books and his work has been translated into dozens of languages. While speaking and writing often about issues of war, the media, and economics, he remains passionately engaged with his students and others in the field of linguistics, an area where he has continued to challenge and revise his own theories and work.

Noam's work has given millions a critical view of how our world works and helped them to better understand how to change it.

—Anthony Arnove

## Timeline:

| 1928 | Born in Philadelphia |
| 1955 | Begins teaching at MIT |
| 1957 | Writes his first linguistics book, *Logical Structure of Linguistic Theory* |
| 1959 | Writes his first political book, *American Power and the New Mandarins* |
| 1965 | Participates in early movement against war in Vietnam |
| 1971 | Added to "enemies list" of President Richard Nixon |
| 1988 | Wins Kyoto Prize |
| 2002 | Speaks at the World Social Forum in Brazil |

## More you can do:

- Check out www.chomsky.info, with many key essays and articles
- Organize a book discussion group around one of Noam's many books. You can find a sample flyer for *Understanding Power* at www.understandingpower.com
- Noam teaches people how to think critically about what they see in the media. Watch the news on TV and see if you can spot anything that tells you how to think. Can you think of other ways to tell the same story?

## What do you think?

- How is direct action important to "a functioning democratic culture"?
- What role has Chomsky played in public life? What effect did he hope to have in the "political arena"?
- What did Chomsky mean by the quote above about the responsibility of intellectuals? What opportunities do US citizens have to speak the truth and expose lies?

# 63

# Martin Luther King Jr.
## (1929–1968)

**Most people remember the Reverend Dr. Martin Luther King Jr. for his "I Have a Dream Speech," which he gave on August 28, 1963, at a march of hundreds of thousands in Washington, DC.**

At the March for Jobs and Justice he imagined a future without racial segregation, saying: "I have a dream that my four little children will one day live in a nation where they will not be judged by the color of their skin but by the content of their character."

He became known years before, in 1955, when he helped to lead a boycott against segregated buses in Montgomery, Alabama. Martin argued that African Americans should remain nonviolent, even when violently attacked. He used this approach to fight racial segregation in many Southern cities.

In 1963 Martin was arrested at a protest in Birmingham, Alabama. Other ministers said that he was wrong to protest. They said that he and other activists should wait for a better time. In his jail cell, Martin wrote a response that reads in part: "Frankly, I have yet to engage in a direct-action campaign that was 'well-timed' in the view of those who have not suffered unduly from the disease of segregation. For years now, I have heard the word 'Wait!' . . . This 'Wait' has almost always meant 'Never.' We must come to see . . . that 'justice too long delayed is justice denied.'"

In 1964 Martin won the Nobel Peace Prize,

and new laws made racial segregation illegal. But Martin wasn't done fighting. There was more to his dream. He dreamed of a world without war. He protested against the war in Vietnam. At the Riverside Church in Harlem in 1967, he put the blame for the war on US leaders. He spoke out against what he called "the greatest purveyor of violence in the world today—my own government."

Martin questioned capitalism. He dreamed of using America's wealth to help the poor:

> You can't talk about solving the economic problem of the Negro without talking about billions of dollars. You can't talk about ending slums without first saying profit must be taken out of the slums. You're really tampering and getting on dangerous ground because you are messing with folk then. You are messing with the captains of industry . . . now this means that we are treading in difficult waters, because it really means that we are saying that something is wrong... with capitalism. . . . There must be a better distribution of wealth and maybe America must move toward a democratic socialism.

In 1968 Martin went to Memphis to support African American garbage workers who went on strike. The workers wanted higher pay, better working conditions, dignity, and to form a union. Martin marched with them and said that everyone should support them.

On April 4, Martin was standing on the balcony of his hotel room in Memphis when he was hit in the face by a bullet. People around the world were very angry about his death. But Martin's dream is not dead. Many people are still fighting for the kinds of changes he wanted. In his book *Where Do We Go from Here?*, Martin encouraged his readers to build a movement to make these dreams a reality.

—Brian Jones

## Timeline:

| | |
|---|---|
| 1929 | Born in Atlanta, Georgia |
| 1948 | Graduates from Morehouse College |
| 1951 | Graduates from Crozer Theological Seminary |
| 1955 | Earns his PhD at Boston University |
| 1955–56 | Helps lead the Montgomery Bus Boycott |
| 1957 | Founds the Southern Christian Leadership Conference |
| 1963 | Gives "I Have a Dream" speech at the March on Washington |
| 1964 | Awarded Nobel Peace Prize |
| 1966 | Moves his family to Chicago to fight segregation and poverty in the northern states |
| 1967 | Speaks out against the war in Vietnam |
| 1968 | Travels to Memphis, Tennessee, to support garbage workers on strike; assassinated on April 4 by James Earl Ray |

## More you can do:

Write your own jailhouse letter!
People who want change are often told to be patient and wait for things to get better. Think about your life, family, school, and your community. What do you think needs to change right away? Pretend that someone is telling you to wait for those changes, and write your own letter about why you need change now

## What do you think?

- Why is it that "justice too long delayed is justice denied"?
- Why do you think Martin said that fighting for economic justice meant "treading in difficult waters"?
- Martin called the war in Vietnam "cruel manipulation of the poor"—what did he mean by that?
- What's the difference between "flinging a coin to a beggar" and "restructuring" the "edifice which produces beggars"?

# 64

# Dolores Huerta

## (1930–)

**Dolores Huerta is a farmworkers' rights activist. She cofounded the United Farm Workers (UFW) with Cesar Chavez.**

The UFW led the way in improving the lives of California migrant farmworkers beginning in the 1960s.

Dolores was born in 1930 in northern New Mexico. Her father was a miner, field worker, union activist, and state official. Her mother owned a seventy-room hotel that often put up farmworkers' families for free.

Dolores became a teacher when she graduated from college. She quickly left that job to become an organizer. In 1955 she met Fred Ross, who founded the Community Service Organization (CSO). The CSO was dedicated to voter registration and better public services for workers. Dolores and Fred founded the Stockton, California, chapter of the CSO.

During 1960–62, Dolores successfully lobbied for fifteen bills in the California legislature. These included public assistance, retirement benefits, and unemployment insurance for farmworkers, regardless of whether they were citizens. In 1962, Dolores met Cesar Chavez and the two founded the National Farm Workers Association (NFWA). They spent the next three years recruiting workers and building the union. By 1965, the NFWA conducted its first strike against a rose nursery. The strike lasted four days and achieved a wage increase.

> "For a long time I was the only woman on the executive board [of the UFW]. And the men would come out and say their stupid little jokes about women. So I started keeping a record. At the end of the meeting, I'd say, 'During the course of this meeting you men have made fifty-eight sexist remarks.' Pretty soon I got them down to twenty-five, then ten, and then five."
>
> —Dolores Huerta, "Woman of the Year," Ms., January/February 1988

The union then joined a strike with mostly Filipino grape pickers in Delano. The owners hired replacement workers, so the union organized a grape boycott. Dolores spent 1966 organizing and publicizing the boycott. The boycott was the most famous and successful workers' boycott in US history. It gave the union the strength to negotiate the first-ever farmworkers' contract with a grape grower. Other contracts made during the five-year strike won a minimum wage, paid vacations, and unemployment insurance, and prohibited toxic pesticides.

In 1972, the NFWA joined the AFL-CIO and named itself the United Farm Workers. The UFW reached 100,000 members in the 1970s. It organized grape pickers and other workers in the agricultural industry. A second boycott, this time of grapes, lettuce, and Gallo Wines, led to the Agricultural Labor Relations Act. The act granted farmworkers the right to organize and bargain for better wages and working conditions.

Later Dolores advocated for women's rights, particularly in a campaign by strawberry workers. She fought against anti–women's rights laws, including the Welfare Reform Act and California's Proposition 209.

Dolores has been arrested twenty-two times because of her union activities. In 1988 she was viciously beaten by a cop while participating in a protest. She suffered a ruptured spleen and broken ribs. She sued the city of San Francisco and won an award and changes in its police crowd-control procedures.

Dolores is known as a very hard worker and has sacrificed much for her union activities, including time with her eleven children. She has received many awards and honorary degrees.

—Wally Showman

## Timeline:

| | |
|---|---|
| 1930 | Born in Dawson, New Mexico |
| 1955 | Meets Fred Ross and began working for the CSO |
| 1962 | Joins Cesar and Helen Chavez to form the NFWA |
| 1965 | Helps organize grape pickers' strike and grape boycott |
| 1966 | Organizes 300-mile march from Delano to Sacramento, California, to publicize boycott |
| 1968 | Directs boycott effort in New York City |
| 1970 | Negotiates union contracts as a result of the boycott |
| 1972 | Elected vice president of UFW |
| 1975 | Second boycott of grapes, lettuce, and Gallo Wines |
| 1988 | Attacked by cop in San Francisco protest |
| 2002 | Participates in 165-mile march to Sacramento for mandatory mediation bill for farmworkers |
| 2010 | Celebrates her eightieth birthday |

## More you can do:

- Watch *A Crushing Love: Chicanas, Motherhood, and Activism*, a film that features Dolores as one of five activists
- Write four interview questions that you would ask Dolores if you had a chance to speak to her

## What do you think?

- Do farmworkers need a union? Why or why not?
- Why is it that women in unions must not only fight against the bosses for workers' rights but also fight within their own unions for women's rights?
- What is the difference between a strike and a boycott? Why do they succeed or fail?
- Why did the farmworkers want their bosses to stop using pesticides?

# 65

# Harvey Milk
## (1930–1978)

**Harvey Milk was a groundbreaking figure in the history of the lesbian, gay, bisexual, and transgender (LGBT) civil rights movement. He was killed in 1978.**

A crowd of thirty to forty thousand mourners marched in a candlelight vigil the night of Harvey's death.

Harvey was born in 1930, at a time when men who loved other men were taught to hate themselves. Homosexuality was considered a mental disease by medical authorities until 1973. LGBT people were discriminated against in every area of public life. Love between two men was a crime. People could be fired from their jobs if they were thought

to be gay. The US government banned gays from the military. Police would beat gay men in the streets and could legally arrest them just for socializing with one another at a bar.

The son of Jewish shopkeepers, Harvey spent his early life in the suburbs of New York City. His wit, charm, and athletic nature made him a popular figure throughout his life. But until he was nearly forty, Harvey kept his gayness a secret from most people. In other words, he was "in the closet."

Harvey was greatly influenced by the social protests in the United States against the war in Vietnam. He also found the fight for equal rights of women and African Americans inspiring. Though he had been a conservative

> "Gay people, we will not win [our] rights by staying quietly in our closets . . . we are coming out! We are coming out to fight the lies, the myths, the distortions! We are coming out to tell the truth about gays! . . . For I'm tired of the conspiracy of silence."
>
> *—Harvey Milk, San Francisco Gay Freedom Day Parade speech, June 25, 1978*

businessman, the movements of the 1960s led him to support economic and social equality.

Harvey left his job, grew his hair long, and headed out west. He settled in San Francisco, a city that drew many gay men and lesbians. Harvey was a dynamic organizer. He was able to unite various ethnic and racial groups. He also won over many "straight" (non-gay) people to the cause of LGBT rights. He became a San Francisco supervisor in 1977. The heart of San Francisco's main gay neighborhood was Castro Street. As one of the first openly gay elected officials in history, Harvey was often referred to as "the mayor of Castro Street."

Harvey played a key role in building struggles that won important victories in the 1970s. Some beer companies tried to prevent workers from earning higher wages and benefits. Harvey worked with unionized truck drivers who delivered beer to gay bars to organize a boycott of those companies. The success of that boycott led the truck drivers' union to start hiring openly gay men as drivers, which had never happened before.

In 1978 the Briggs Initiative, a proposed new law, threatened to fire anyone suspected of being LGBT from teaching in California's public schools. Harvey helped build street protests and a media campaign to stop the bigoted initiative from becoming a law.

His ability to bring people together led some to despise him. Dan White, a politician who was jealous of Harvey, murdered him, along with the mayor of San Francisco, in City Hall on November 27, 1978. Out of respect for Harvey and disgust with bigotry, thousands participated in a riot when Harvey's murderer was given a light jail sentence in 1979.
**—Sherry Wolf**

## Timeline:

**1930** Born in Woodmere, New York

**1972** At the age of forty-two, turns his back on his conservative politics and lifestyle, grows his hair long, and moves to San Francisco

**1973** Opens the Castro Camera shop, which becomes a neighborhood gathering spot for progressive politics and organizing for gay rights; he and other gay activists help Teamster delivery drivers win a fight against Coors beer

**1977** Wins election to the San Francisco Board of Supervisors, becomes one of the city's (and nation's) first openly gay elected officials

**1978** June, rides on a float in the Gay Freedom Day Parade and calls for lesbians and gays to "come out of the closet"

November 7, succeeds, along with other activists, in stopping the antigay Briggs Initiative

November 27, assassinated at City Hall along with Mayor George Moscone; more than 30,000 people peacefully march from the Castro neighborhood to City Hall and hold a candlelight vigil

**1979** May 21, in response to a very light prison sentence for Milk's killer, thousands of people riot around San Francisco's City Hall to express their outrage; becomes known as the White Nights Riot

## More you can do:

- **Watch the films *The Life and Times of Harvey Milk* and *Milk***
- **Read Randy Shilts's *The Mayor of Castro Street***

## What do you think?

- **Why is it important for LGBT people to come out of the closet? Why was this hard for people to do? Is it still hard?**
- **Harvey Milk did not start out as a political activist; why did he change?**
- **What is the importance of Harvey Milk's efforts to unite truck drivers, teachers, and non-gays in the struggle for LGBT rights?**

# 66

# Lorraine Hansberry

## (1930–1965)

Lorraine Hansberry was an African American playwright. Her play *A Raisin in the Sun* took its title from the famous Langston Hughes poem "Harlem." She is known for her impact on politics and culture in the civil rights era.

Lorraine was born in Chicago. Her father was a businessman and her parents were leaders in their community. When she was eight years old, her parents bought a new home in Woodlawn, which was segregated. African Americans were banned from renting or buying homes in areas where whites lived.

The Hansberry family faced violence and harassment. One night, Lorraine was nearly killed by a piece of concrete thrown through the window. However, the family stood their ground. Lorraine remembered her "desperate and courageous mother," who stayed awake all night guarding her children.

White residents, led by Anna M. Lee, sued to evict the Hansberrys. Carl Hansberry lost the case, but he appealed it. *Hansberry v. Lee* went all the way to the Supreme Court, which finally ruled in favor of Lorraine's father.

Lorraine's parents influenced her views on civil rights and led her into activism. Growing up, Lorraine was surrounded by activists like singer Paul Robeson and poet Langston Hughes. After leaving college to become a writer, she worked for Paul Robeson's newspaper *Freedom*. She participated in struggles for social justice.

> **"I think, then, that Negroes must concern themselves with every single means of struggle: legal, illegal, passive, active, violent and nonviolent."**
>
> —*Lorraine Hansberry,* To Be Young, Gifted and Black

Around this time, Lorraine joined the Daughters of Bilitis, an organization for lesbian women. She wrote about civil rights, women's rights, and gay rights. Later, she worked with the Student Nonviolent Coordinating Committee, which was leading campaigns against segregation in the South.

Lorraine's play *A Raisin in the Sun* was based on her family's experiences when she was a child. In it, a working-class black family, the Youngers, confronts economic hardship. The groundbreaking characters of Mama Younger and her children, Walter and Beneatha, share a common experience of racism. However, they each represent a different perspective about how to respond to it.

*A Raisin in the Sun* was produced in New York City in 1959. It was the first play performed on Broadway that was written by an African American and the fifth Broadway play to be written by a woman. Lorraine's work was a critical and a popular success. It attracted black theater-goers in large numbers. As writer James Baldwin explained, "Never before, in the entire history of the American theater, has so much of the truth of black people's lives been seen on the stage." The play also opened the eyes of many white theater-goers to the racism and hatred that blacks faced in their quest for political freedom and economic security.

Lorraine continued to write plays and essays. In *To Be Young, Gifted and Black*, she wrote about black writers, artists, musicians, and educators who became adults during the civil rights movement. She hoped they would set an example for future generations of young African Americans.

**—Melissa Pouridas and Michele Bollinger**

## Timeline:

| | |
|---|---|
| 1930 | Born in Chicago |
| 1938 | Family moves to a segregated neighborhood in Chicago |
| 1940 | The United States Supreme Court decides *Hansberry v. Lee* |
| 1953 | Marries Robert Nemiroff |
| 1959 | *A Raisin in the Sun* appears on Broadway |
| | Wins the New York Drama Critic's Circle Award for Best Play |
| 1961 | *A Raisin in the Sun* film produced, starring Sidney Poitier, Ruby Dee, and Claudia McNeil |
| 1962 | Divorces Robert Nemiroff; they continue to work together professionally |
| 1964 | Writes *The Movement: Documentary of a Struggle for Equality* |
| | *The Sign in Sidney Brustein's Window* is produced |
| 1965 | Dies from cancer at age 34 |
| 1968 | The Fair Housing Act is passed as part of the Civil Rights Act |
| 1969 | *To Be Young, Gifted and Black: Lorraine Hansberry in Her Own Words* is published |

## More you can do:

- Read *A Raisin in the Sun* by Lorraine Hansberry and write a skit that shows a family dealing with modern-day problems related to where they live
- Listen to the song "To Be Young, Gifted and Black" by Nina Simone. Think about the message of the song and why it was written

## What do you think?

- How did Lorraine's experiences as a child influence her later in life?
- Read "Harlem" by Langston Hughes. What is the difference between a dream that "dries up" and one that "explodes"? What causes these two different outcomes?
- In what ways can drama—plays, movies, and theater—make statements or tell stories that are not seen in the news or popularly known?

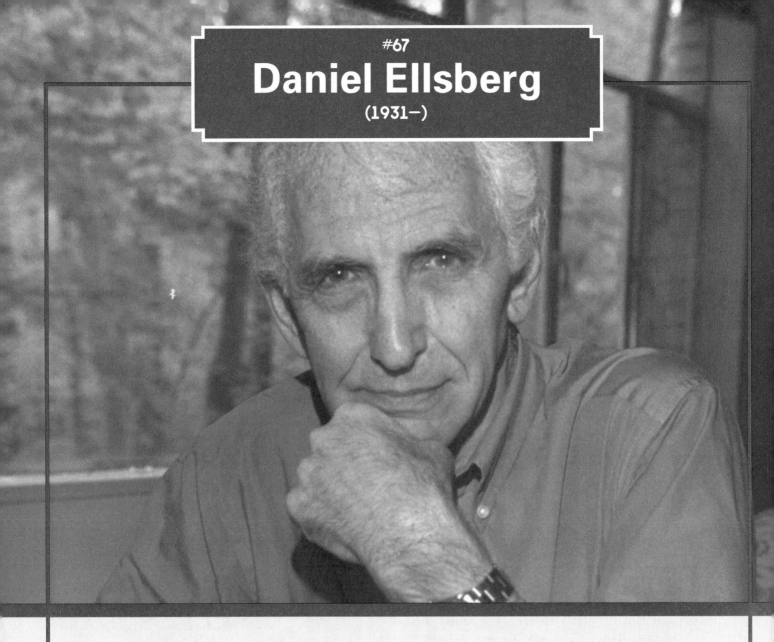

# 67

# Daniel Ellsberg
(1931–)

**Daniel Ellsberg is one of the most important whistleblowers (people who expose wrongdoing) in US history. He helped expose US government lies and war crimes during the war in Vietnam.**

In the process, he helped build the movement to end the war.

In 1967, Daniel, then a strategic analyst at the RAND Corporation and a former government official, began work on a secret study authorized by the secretary of defense, Robert McNamara, titled "U.S. Decision-making in Vietnam, 1945–68." But Daniel was outraged by the lies being told to support the war. He secretly began to copy thousands

of pages of the document. In 1969 he gave seven thousand copied pages to the Senate Foreign Relations Committee.

In 1971, he leaked the Pentagon Papers, as they came to be known, to the *New York Times*, the *Washington Post*, and seventeen other newspapers. Those newspapers published excerpts, or portions, of the papers despite the government's attempt to stop them. In fact, the government's challenge to the newspapers went to the Supreme Court, which upheld the right of the *Times* and other publications to print them. This was a landmark case for the freedom of the press. As a result of their publication, millions of people were able to see the gap between the public discussion about Vietnam and the reality.

I felt that as an American citizen, as a responsible citizen, I could no longer cooperate in concealing this information from the American public. I did this clearly at my own jeopardy and I am prepared to answer to all the consequences of this decision. "

—Daniel Ellsberg, statement to the press, 1971

Daniel paid a very high price for his actions. As Daniel wrote in his memoir, he copied and leaked the documents despite the potential personal costs. "I believed this course . . . would probably put me in prison for the rest of my life."

In 1971, officials working for President Richard Nixon plotted to break into the office of Daniel's psychiatrist. They were looking for information in Daniel's files that would discredit him. But an investigation into their criminal misconduct was begun. It also became clear that Daniel's conversations had been recorded secretly without any court approval and that the government had tried to illegally influence the outcome of the trial. The judge hearing the case dismissed all the charges against Daniel in May 1973. Nixon resigned in disgrace on August 9, 1974, to avoid his almost-certain impeachment for the crimes associated with what is known as the Watergate scandal.

After his trial, Daniel spoke out widely against the war. But Daniel had not always opposed the war against the people of Vietnam. He actually had for years been part of what President Dwight D. Eisenhower famously called "the military-industrial complex."

As a result of changing his mind, and leaking the papers, Daniel risked his privileges and comfort to stand for what is right.

Daniel has since spent years defending other whistle-blowers and encouraging government and corporate officials to expose wrongdoing whenever they are aware of it.

—Anthony Arnove

## Timeline:

| | |
|---|---|
| 1931 | Born in Chicago |
| 1952 | Graduates from Harvard University |
| 1954–57 | Serves in US Marine Corps |
| 1957–59 | Is a junior fellow in the Society of Fellows at Harvard University |
| 1959 | Becomes a strategic analyst at the RAND Corporation |
| 1962 | Earns PhD in economics at Harvard |
| 1964 | Joins the Pentagon |
| 1965–67 | Joins the State Department and works at the US Embassy in Vietnam |
| 1967 | Returns to RAND Corporation |
| 1969 | Photocopies the Pentagon Papers secretly and gives them to the Senate Foreign Relations Committee |
| 1971 | Gives the Pentagon Papers to the *New York Times*, the *Washington Post*, and seventeen other newspapers |
| 1971 | Break-in at office of Ellsberg's psychiatrist |
| 1973 | Judge dismisses all charges against Ellsberg |
| 2002 | Publishes *Secrets: A Memoir of Vietnam and the Pentagon Papers* |
| 2006 | Wins Right Livelihood Award |

## More you can do:

- Watch *The Most Dangerous Man in America* and see the companion website: www.mostdangerousman.org
- Check out Daniel's website at www.ellsberg.net and the National Security website at www.gwu.edu/nsarchiv

## What do you think?

- Why was this a "landmark case for the freedom of the press"?
- Do you think Ellsberg was being a "responsible citizen" when he decided to copy pages of a secret government document? Why or why not?
- What do you think would have happened if Ellsberg had not leaked the Pentagon Papers?

# 68

# Richard and Mildred Loving

## (1933–1975; 1939–2008)

When Mildred Jeter was a young girl growing up in the small town of Central Point, Virginia, she met a boy named Richard Loving.

Richard loved bluegrass music and had gone out to see Mildred's seven brothers play a farmhouse concert. She thought he was arrogant at first and didn't like him very much. But as they grew up, Mildred saw that Richard was actually very nice—so nice that they started dating and got married!

They loved each other very much, and also loved their country life with family and friends. Every Saturday, on Richard's day off from construction work, he and Mildred went to the local car races. Built with his two best friends, Richard's racecar won ninety-nine trophies. Everyone in their neighborhood—American Indians, whites, and blacks—would farm the land together whenever anyone needed help. One neighbor explained, "We just grew up all as a family together . . . there was no difference. They was all working, just trying to make a living."

The Lovings looked forward to raising children in Central Point. But only a month after they were married, three police officers broke into their house in the middle of the night. The police took them from their bed to jail. Because she was Native American and black and he was white, Mildred and Richard's marriage was against the law.

In 1958 twenty-four states had "miscegenation" laws that made interracial marriages illegal. Richard and Mildred were each sentenced to a year in jail, to be suspended only if they left the state of Virginia. In order to be together, the Lovings moved to Washington, D.C., and had three children, Donald, Peggy, and Sidney. But they were very homesick, and on one trip home, they were arrested again.

The Lovings decided enough was enough and found two young lawyers, Bernard Cohen and Philip J. Hirschkop, who were with the American Civil Liberties Union (ACLU). They fought for the Lovings' freedom to be married and live together as a family, taking the case *Loving vs. Virginia* all the way to the Supreme Court. There, Cohen shared Richard's words: "Tell the court I love my wife and it is just unfair that I can't live with her." On June 12, 1967, the court declared Virginia's miscegenation laws unconstitutional. It was a historic ruling that paved the way for interracial couples everywhere to be married and live together without fear of going to prison.

Mildred and Richard were "overjoyed" and moved back to Central Point. Richard built a new home for his family, where they both lived out the rest of their days. On the fortieth anniversary of *Loving vs. Virginia*, in 2007, Mildred Loving released a statement: "I am proud that Richard's and my name is on a court case that can help reinforce the love, the commitment, the fairness, and the family that so many people, black or white, young or old, gay or straight, seek in life. I support the freedom to marry for all. That's what *Loving*, and loving, are all about."

**—Sarah Macaraeg**

## Timeline:

**1933**   Richard born in Central Point, Virginia

**1939**   Mildred Jeter born, just a few miles from Richard

**1958**   Marry in Washington, DC, and arrested five weeks later in their home

**1958–62**   The Lovings live in exile in DC (but secretly return home to Central Point often), where they raise their three children, Donald, Peggy, and Sidney

**1963**   Mildred writes a letter to Robert F. Kennedy, who directs her to the ACLU

**1965**   The State of Virginia rules against the Lovings' appeal; Judge Bazile concludes: "The Almighty God created the races . . . and he placed them on separate continents. . . . The fact that he separated the races shows he did not intend for the races to mix."

**1967**   The Supreme Court hears *Loving vs. Virginia* and rules Virginia's miscegenation laws unconstitutional, paving the way for all remaining miscegenation laws across the country to fall

**1975**   Richard Loving dies in a car accident. Mildred later says, "I married the only man I ever loved, and I'm happy for the time we had together."

**2000**   Alabama is the last state to remove its miscegenation law from the state constitution

**2008**   Mildred dies of pneumonia in her home a year after releasing a statement in support of gay marriage

## More you can do:

- **Watch the documentary *The Loving Story***
- **Organize or attend a Loving Day event honoring the Lovings and mixed-race families on the anniversary of the court ruling, June 12**

## What do you think?

- **What do you think of Judge Bazile's statement in the timeline?**
- **What else was happening in this era, connected to the Lovings' struggle?**
- **How are families separated today? Do you think marriage and immigration laws should change?**

# 69

# Audre Lorde
## (1934–1992)

"Black, lesbian, mother, warrior, poet." These were the words Audre Lorde used to describe herself. She was born in Harlem, New York, to immigrant parents from Grenada in 1934.

Audre changed her name from Audrey Geraldine Lorde because she liked the way her new name looked more. Like many black immigrants in the United States at the time, her family faced racism and hard economic times. Even though she had two older sisters, Audre always felt like an outsider. She was more comfortable with books and poetry. She often used poetry to understand her own emotions and society.

Audre's poetry spoke of the toll that racism, sexism, and homophobia took on her life and the lives of others. In 1948 on a family trip to Washington, DC, she encountered racism firsthand when her family was refused service in an ice cream parlor. She was active in the movements for civil rights and women's rights in the 1960s. She was critical of the feminist movement for its focus on white, middle-class women while ignoring the needs of black women, who also faced racism and poverty. At the same time, Audre criticized the civil rights movement for its sexism.

Some people felt that Audre was too harsh and critical. And they thought she focused too much on defining personal identities. But she wasn't just interested in defining people. Her main goal was to challenge oppression and injustice. She felt that understanding different parts of their identity could help people understand their oppression better. She wanted people to see themselves as black or lesbian, for example, to clarify how being white and lesbian meant one didn't suffer from both racism and homophobia. She also felt that people couldn't challenge oppression alone as individuals but needed to be part of a collective effort. Some of her later work was focused on writing critical essays to challenge oppression.

She was diagnosed with breast cancer in 1978 and lived with the disease for another fourteen years. Audre's poetry after this period reflects a new anger. In fact, it was only after her diagnosis that she began to also define herself as a "warrior." Audre had one breast surgically removed when she got cancer. She saw herself as being like one of the legendary warrior-women of the Amazon who removed one breast so that they could be better archers and do battle. Audre began to not just publish poetry but also speak to people and hold workshops on oppression.

In 1983 the United States invaded Audre's family's home, Grenada. She flew to the island and was horrified at the destruction she saw. She returned to this country angry about injustice abroad as well. She moved to Berlin, Germany, in disgust. There she was involved in organizing discussions against oppression. She worked in an Afro-German community of women and helped to develop new poets, writers, and thinkers. She also became part of the world movement against apartheid in South Africa. That system forced black South Africans to be second-class citizens while giving all privileges to whites.

Although racism and sexism remain challenges today, Audre's writing played an important part in deepening struggles against them.

—Alpana Mehta

## Timeline:

| | |
|---|---|
| 1934 | Born to immigrant parents from Grenada on February 18 in New York City |
| 1948 | Enrolls at Hunter College in New York |
| 1951 | Publishes first poem |
| 1961 | Enrolls at Columbia University in New York |
| 1968 | Publishes first book of poetry, *First Cities* |
| 1968 | Begins teaching at Tougaloo College in Mississippi and encounters Jim Crow racism in the American South |
| 1978 | Diagnosed with breast cancer |
| 1978 | Publishes *The Black Unicorn*, featuring one of her most famous poems, "A Litany for Survival" |
| 1979 | Addresses the first national march for gay and lesbian rights |
| 1983 | The United States invades Grenada, prompting Audre to become active against US empire |
| 1984 | Moves to Berlin, Germany |
| 1992 | Dies November 17 in St. Croix |

## More you can do:

- Watch *A Litany for Survival: The Life and Work of Audre Lorde*
- Read *The Collected Poems of Audre Lorde*
- Read Audre's poem "Coal" out loud and talk about what you think it means

## What do you think?

- Do you think black and white women face different types of discrimination? What if we factor in sexuality?
- Can poetry be a vehicle for social change?
- Do you think political and social events contribute to art?

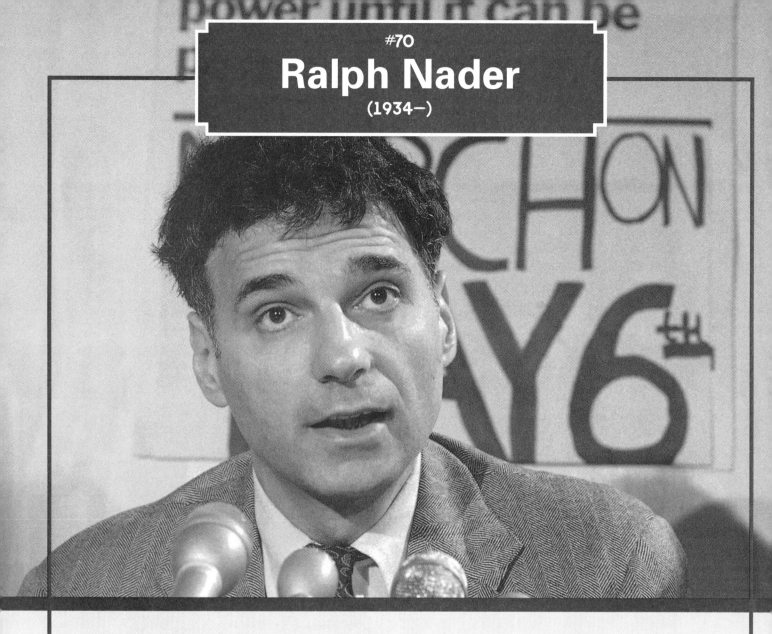

# 70

# Ralph Nader

## (1934—)

In the 2000 presidential election, more than two and a half million Americans voted for someone other than the candidate of the Republican or Democratic Parties: Ralph Nader, the presidential candidate of the Green Party.

Ralph was born in Connecticut in 1934, the child of Lebanese immigrants who owned a bakery. He spoke Arabic at home with his family. He was a good student and went to law school at Harvard, where he began to write articles about consumer safety. Ralph thought that companies should be held responsible for making sure that the products they made didn't hurt people.

In 1966 he wrote *Unsafe at Any Speed*, which exposed greed in the auto industry. He said car companies should be required to build cars with seatbelts and other safety features. General Motors, one of the country's biggest carmakers, was so upset by the book that it hired spies to try to find out something about Ralph to turn into a scandal. The plan backfired, however, when Ralph sued GM and won $425,000.

Ralph used that money to found the first Public Interest Research Group. He then inspired and started dozens of groups working on issues ranging from environmentalism and consumer protection to democracy in government. He also crusaded against corporate greed. As the years went by, he saw the

Democratic Party become just as committed to corporate profits as the Republicans. He decided to run for president in 2000.

Ralph did not have as much money to spend on his campaign as the Democrats or Republicans because his campaign did not accept donations from corporations. Only individuals could contribute to his campaign. Also, Ralph was not allowed to be in the televised debates between George W. Bush and Al Gore.

So Ralph's campaign was a grassroots effort. Volunteers held meetings in their homes, at schools, and in other public places across the country to talk about Ralph's candidacy and his positions on the issues. The campaign also organized huge political meetings, called "super rallies," in sports arenas in several big cities.

Ralph always knew he would not come close to winning the election. He ran to educate people about issues like war, racism, women's rights, and corporate greed. He also hoped to build grassroots movements for justice and equality. Ralph described the civil rights movement as "ordinary people producing extraordinary history." He saw his campaign as part of a long history of people's movements in the United States.

After the election, some blamed Ralph for helping Republican George W. Bush win by taking votes away from Al Gore. They said if Ralph had not run, most of his votes would have gone to the Democrat instead. Ralph said that many who voted for him would not have voted at all because they were fed up with politics as usual. He also said that if Al Gore had promised to do more for poor and working people, he would have gotten more votes than George W. Bush.

Ralph felt the voice of working people had been drowned out within presidential elections. He ran for president to be that voice.

**—Ben Dalbey**

## Timeline:

1934 Born in Connecticut to parents who were immigrants from Lebanon

1955 Graduates from Princeton University and later Harvard Law School

1965 Publishes *Unsafe at Any Speed*

1966 March, CEO of General Motors apologizes to Ralph for hiring spies in an attempt to discredit him

May, National Traffic and Motor Vehicle Safety Act, requiring automakers to install seat belts in new automobiles, is signed into law

1970 Settles invasion of privacy lawsuit with GM for $425,000 and founds the Public Interest Research Group (PIRG) law firm

1970s–1990s Builds a decentralized network of PIRGs and founds the organization Public Citizen (1971)

1996 Drafted as a presidential candidate for the Green Party, but does not run a true campaign

2000 Campaigns in all fifty states for president, winning more than 2.5 million votes

2004 Runs again for president as an independent candidate

## More you can do:

- Watch the documentary *An Unreasonable Man*
- Read Ralph Nader's *Crashing the Party: How to Tell the Truth and Still Run for President*

## What do you think?

- Can you imagine a time when cars did not have seat belts? Do you think any companies today are selling products that they know to be dangerous? Why or why not?
- In what ways do you agree or disagree with Ralph that corporate greed is a problem?
- Does the United States need more than two political parties?

# 71

# Gloria Steinem

**(1934–)**

**Gloria Steinem is a leading feminist, writer, and activist who played an important role in the women's rights movement of the 1960s and 1970s.**

Gloria was born in Toledo, Ohio. When she was young, her family moved a lot and struggled to make ends meet. Eventually her parents divorced. Gloria's mother had a mental illness, which meant Gloria had to take care of her even though she was only a child. Eventually, Gloria was able to move away and attend Smith College.

Gloria became an adult at a time when American society did not treat women as being equal to men. Sexism—discrimination against women—was widespread throughout society.

Women in abusive relationships had few rights or resources to help them. They were pressured to find fulfillment through marriage and motherhood only. Women who worked were not paid equally to men and were expected to do all the housework. Some women defied these expectations, but they were often targets of harassment or abuse.

During the late 1950s and 1960s people began to speak out for social change. The civil rights movement brought hundreds of thousands of people into activism. Students began to organize campaigns for civil rights and to protest against the US war in Vietnam.

Women, including Gloria, were part of these movements from the beginning. However,

> Most important to me, I have been denied a society in which women are encouraged, or even allowed, to think of themselves as first-class citizens and responsible human beings.
>
> —*Gloria Steinem, testimony before the Senate Judiciary Committee on the ERA, 1970*

even within movements for social justice, women were not treated equally. A new movement for women's rights began to grow.

Gloria became a leading voice of that movement by researching and writing about sexism. She went undercover to expose how women were mistreated in certain jobs. Gloria and others marched against beauty contests, for equal pay, affordable child care, and reproductive rights. Gloria helped start *Ms.* magazine, which many male writers joked would never last.

As women protested, many became feminists. They claimed that radical change was necessary to improve the lives of women. Radical women advocated for liberation (full freedom) for women. Many argued that everyone in society—men included—would be better off if the status of women improved.

Gloria led a campaign to ban discrimination of women through the Equal Rights Amendment. The ERA failed, but several groundbreaking laws were passed because of the feminist movement. Title IX banned discrimination in any educational program or activity receiving federal funding, including school sports.

Since then, the mainstream women's movement has stepped back from protest. Leaders like Gloria continue their work in different forms but have not returned to the level of protest of the 1960s and 1970s. Gloria has written many books, started many groups like Choice USA, won many awards, and continues to speak publicly.

—**Michele Bollinger**

## Timeline:

| | |
|---|---|
| 1934 | Born in Toledo, Ohio |
| 1956 | Graduates from Smith College in Northampton, Massachusetts |
| 1963 | Works undercover as a journalist to expose sexism |
| 1964 | The Civil Rights Act becomes law |
| 1966 | The National Organization for Women (NOW) is founded |
| 1972 | Cofounds *Ms.* magazine |
| | Title IX passes, banning discrimination in educational programs |
| | Equal Rights Amendment (ERA) passes |
| 1973 | US Supreme Court decides *Roe v. Wade* |
| 1974 | Cofounds Coalition of Labor Union Women |
| 1982 | ERA expires because not enough states ratify it |

## More you can do:

- Explore the resources on www.gloriasteinem.com
- Gloria went "undercover" to expose sexism by working at a nightclub where women had to wear demeaning outfits. Think about where you could go if you wanted to expose sexism in a workplace today

## What do you think?

- Today, many women use the title "Ms." in their names instead of "Miss" or "Mrs." What is the difference between these terms? Why would some women prefer this term?
- In what ways were women treated unfairly before the rise of the 1960s women's movement? In what ways are women still not treated equally? Why would many people think that women need to fight for more rights today?
- Why were some of the laws passed in the wake of the women's movement—such as Title IX—"groundbreaking"?

142

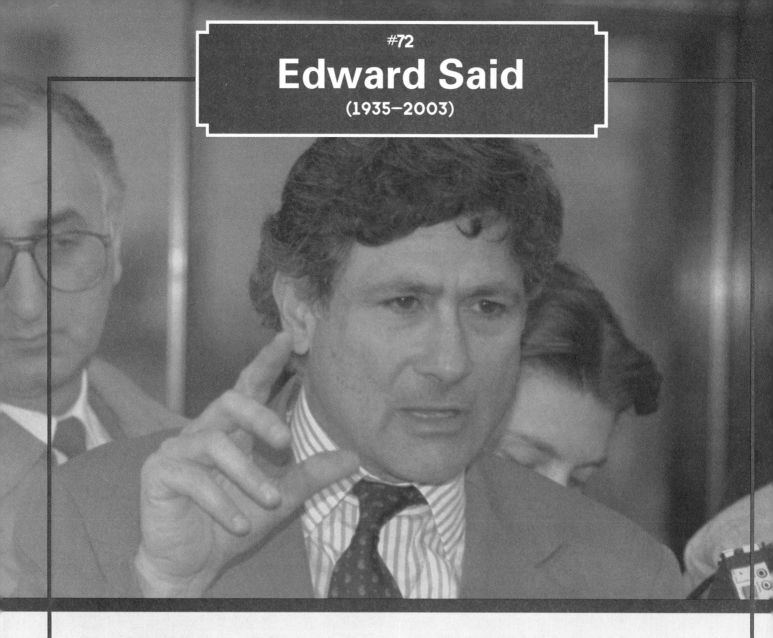

# 72

# Edward Said

## (1935–2003)

**Edward Said was a Palestinian American writer and cultural critic. He became the best-known spokesperson in the United States for the Palestinians.**

Edward was born in Palestine in 1935 when it was occupied by Britain. In 1948 the state of Israel was founded on Palestinian land, against the wishes of the Palestinian majority. Israel pushed out hundreds of thousands of Palestinian Arabs and took their property. Arabs who stayed in Israel became second-class citizens. Palestinians outside of Israel had no state of their own.

Edward's family fled to Egypt. In the 1950s he came to the United States as a student. From the mid-1960s he taught at Columbia

University in New York City. Edward's book *Orientalism* was very influential. It analyzed the racist ideas that the West has about the Middle East and Asia.

In 1967 Israel invaded and occupied more Palestinian land. Edward called for an end to the Israeli occupation and began to speak out for Palestinian rights. The FBI spied on him. He became a target of pro-Israel extremists. He got death threats and his office at Columbia was set on fire.

Edward was a member of the Palestinian National Council (PNC), which was created by the Palestine Liberation Organization (PLO), a group that fought for the rights of the Palestinian people. But he became critical

"This isn't a battle between two states. It's a battle between a state [Israel] with basically a colonial army attacking a colonized population, using all forms of collective punishment."

—Edward Said, 2001

of the PLO's strategy and plans and the undemocratic style of its leader, Yasser Arafat. The PLO wanted the major world powers and Arab governments to make a deal. But Edward argued for an international campaign against Israel, like the one that helped defeat the racist system of apartheid in South Africa.

Edward resigned from the PNC in 1991. Two years later, with US support, Arafat signed the Oslo accords with Israel. The media praised this as a step toward peace, but Edward thought the agreement was a sell-out. The Oslo agreement offered the newly created Palestinian Authority (PA) future control over only a small part of historic Palestine. The land would be broken into hundreds of pieces that would remain under Israeli military and economic domination. It also ignored the rights of Palestinian refugees around the world. In particular, the "right of return" for refugees to go back to their homes has not been addressed.

Edward argued that the Oslo accords allowed Israel to take more Palestinian land and build more illegal settlements in the West Bank. He said the PA was corrupt and that its leaders had "become willing collaborators with the [Israeli] military occupation." Arafat responded by banning Edward's books.

For a time, Edward accepted the PLO's call for a separate Palestinian state to exist side by side with Israel. He later believed this "two-state solution" would never offer Palestinians true freedom. He supported one state with equal rights for all its citizens, Jews and Arabs.

In his last years, Edward opposed the US wars in Kosovo, Afghanistan, and Iraq, and criticized the "brutal imperial arrogance" of the US government.
—Phil Gasper

## Timeline:

| 1935 | Born in Jerusalem; grows up between Jerusalem and Cairo, Egypt |
| 1948 | Flees Jerusalem for Cairo at the beginning of the war that would establish the state of Israel |
| 1951 | Sent to school in the United States |
| 1960 | Earns his PhD in English literature from Harvard |
| 1962 | Marries Maire Jaanus |
| 1963 | Begins teaching at Columbia University |
| 1967 | The "Six-Day War" begins and Israel takes over more Palestinian land. Edward becomes an activist for Palestinian rights. He receives death threats and is investigated by the FBI |
| | Divorces Maire |
| 1970 | Marries Mariam Cortas; they have two children |
| 1977 | Appointed to Palestinian National Committee |
| 1978 | Publishes *Orientalism* |
| 1985 | Someone sets Edward's office on fire to try to stop him from speaking out for Palestinians' rights. |
| 1991 | Resigns from PNC |
| 1998 | Makes a documentary film called *In Search of Palestine* |
| 1999 | Cofounds the West-Eastern Divan Orchestra with Daniel Barenboim |
| 2003 | Dies of leukemia in New York City |

## More you can do:

- **Explore the Edward Said Archive: www.edwardsaid.org/**
- **Watch Edward's film *In Search of Palestine* on YouTube**

## What do you think?

- **Why did the FBI spy on Edward?**
- **Do you agree with Edward that Jews and Arabs in Israel and Palestine can overcome their differences and live together peacefully?**
- **Research the apartheid conditions in South Africa and the treatment of Palestinians today. Was Edward correct to draw this comparison? Why or why not?**

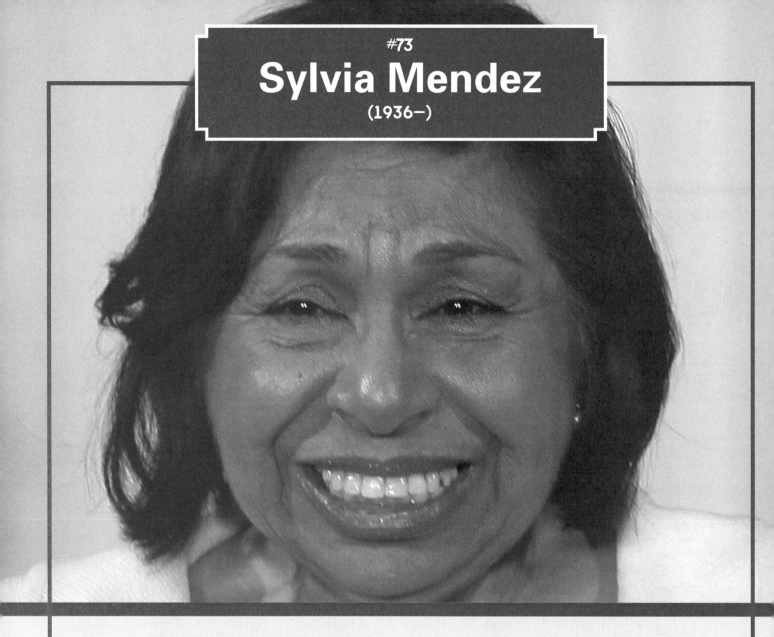

In 1944, eight-year-old Sylvia Mendez arrived at the 17th Street School in Westminster, California, to enroll for the fall semester. She came with her aunt, her two brothers, and her two cousins.

A school administrator looked at the family and told Sylvia and her brothers that they were "too dark" to attend 17th Street School and had to go instead to Hoover, the "Mexican school" down the street. Sylvia's cousins were light-skinned enough to attend the "white" school. Like many California towns at the time, Westminster was divided: one world for whites with better schools, housing, and jobs and another with run-down schools, poor housing, and hard farm labor for Mexican immigrants.

Sylvia's family was furious that she was denied the right to attend the better school in her neighborhood. They decided to take the fight to the school board and eventually all the way to the US District Court. Some of the most important people in Sylvia's corner were her parents, Gonzalo and Felicitas, who believed that their children had a right to an education and hoped for them to become anything they wanted. Sylvia's parents organized other Mexican families and sent a letter of protest to the Westminster School Board. They argued that their children should have the right to be able to attend any public school in the district. They were denied, but they did not give up.

On March 2, 1945, the Mendezes and four other Mexican American families filed a class action lawsuit against several Orange County school boards on behalf of more than five thousand children who were attending segregated schools. Sylvia and her family became organizers and activists. They went around and knocked on neighbors' doors, held protests, and wrote about their fight. They even got the attention of a young African American attorney named Thurgood Marshall who would later win an important case against school segregation of black children in the South. He and several others from the National Association for the Advancement of Colored People (NAACP) wrote letters to the courts supporting the Mendez family and asking for justice.

In court, Superintendent James L. Kent said that "Mexicans should be segregated like pigs in pigpens," because they carried lice and diseases. Despite racist testimony like this, Judge Paul McCormick ruled in favor of Sylvia and the other children on February 18, 1946. The Orange County school boards filed an appeal, but the decision was upheld. Sylvia and her family had proven in court that public schools cannot deny students access on the basis of race or ethnicity. In September 1947 Sylvia and her two brothers, Gonzalo Jr. and Geronimo, enrolled in the 17th Street School. In several other Orange County school districts that fall, many Mexican children also enrolled in previously white-only schools.

Sylvia and her family were pioneers in the fight for equal rights in education. Sylvia grew up and became a nurse, but she never stopped talking to students and families about how to fight for civil rights and equality. On February 15, 2011, Sylvia Mendez was awarded the Presidential Medal of Freedom by President Barack Obama. She continues to fight for all children to have access to a quality education.

**—Dana Blanchard**

## Timeline:

| | |
|---|---|
| 1936 | Born in Westminster, California |
| 1944 | Tries to enroll in 17th Street School and is told she must go a "Mexican" school instead |
| 1945 | The Mendez family and families from other Orange County school districts file charges of discrimination against Westminster School District and others |
| 1946 | Judge Paul McCormick rules in favor of Sylvia's family in the US District Court |
| 1947 | Judges in the United States Court of Appeals, Ninth Circuit, deny the school districts' appeal and rule again in favor of the Mendez family |
| 1947 | Sylvia and her brothers attend 17th Street School for the first time |
| 1954 | *Brown vs. Board of Education* outlaws racial segregation in public schools nationally |
| 2011 | Receives the Presidential Medal of Freedom |

## More you can do:

- **Watch *Mendez vs. Westminster: For All the Children/ Para Todos los Niños***
- **Read the decisions in *Mendez vs. Westminster School District* and *Westminster School District et al. vs. Mendez et al.***

## What do you think?

- **Why were education and the right to attend good schools important to Mexican families in Westminster?**
- **Sylvia's family played an important role in winning justice for Mexican Americans. Have you and your family and friends ever organized around something important to you?**
- **What is similar and different about public education today compared to 1945?**

# Claudette Colvin
## (1939–)

Claudette Colvin grew up outside Montgomery, Alabama, with her great-aunt Mary Ann, great-uncle Q. P., and sister Delphine. The family moved there when Claudette was eight.

Claudette attended Booker T. Washington High School, where she first became an activist against racism. Her first campaign was around Jeremiah Reeves, a fellow student sentenced to death by an all-white jury for an alleged attack on a white woman. Claudette and other students rallied, wrote letters, and collected money on his behalf. Although Reeves claimed he was forced to confess to the crime, he was executed.

On March 2, 1955, fifteen-year-old Claudette refused to give up her seat on the bus for a white woman—nine months before Rosa Parks's similar action sparked the Montgomery bus boycott. Claudette remembers: "My head was just too full of black history . . . the oppression that we went through. It felt like Sojourner Truth was on one side pushing me down, and Harriet Tubman was on the other side of me pushing me down. I couldn't get up." She was dragged off the bus by two cops, arrested, and charged with violating segregation law, disturbing the peace, and assaulting the officers.

Important civil rights activists came to Claudette's aid. They included Dr. Martin Luther King Jr.; Jo Ann Robinson, a leader in the local Women's Political Council; E. D. Nixon, a leader in the NAACP; and Rosa Parks.

" As a teenager, I kept thinking, Why don't the adults around here just say something? Say it so that they know we don't accept segregation? I knew then and I know now that, when it comes to justice, there is no easy way to get it. You can't sugarcoat it. You have to take a stand and say, 'This is not right.' And I did. "

—*Claudette Colvin, as quoted in* Twice Toward Justice

Fred Gray, Claudette's lawyer, hoped to use the case to end segregation on the buses. But Claudette was found guilty on all three charges. Later, through an appeal, all charges were dropped except the assault charge. She was put on probation under the custody of her parents. Support for Claudette's case soon decreased. To some she seemed too "rebellious." Movement leaders stepped back from Claudette as well, seeing her youth as a barrier to winning changes on the buses. Claudette also became pregnant that year. At that time, people thought it was very shocking for an unmarried teenager to have a baby. Some in the movement thought that Claudette's pregnancy would make them look bad. She felt further shunned by her community.

In December 1955, Rosa Parks was arrested for refusing to give up her seat on the bus to a white person. This time, a boycott of the buses in Montgomery was organized through mass weekly meetings. Claudette had moved to Birmingham after learning she was pregnant, but returned to Montgomery to help organize the boycott.

In May 1956, Fred Gray filed a lawsuit, *Bowder v. Gayle*, against the state of Alabama, challenging segregation on buses based on the *Brown v. Board of Education* ruling against segregation in public schools. Gray called on Claudette and four other black women to be plaintiffs in the case. Their strong testimonies and the ongoing boycott pushed the Alabama court to find segregation on the Montgomery buses unconstitutional. Though Claudette is not well known, her courageous stance was one necessary spark of this victorious movement.

—Akunna Eneh

## Timeline:

1939   Born Claudette Austin in Birmingham, Alabama

1947   Moves to Montgomery with great-aunt, great-uncle, and sister

1952   Sister Delphine dies of polio

1952   Begins high school at Booker T. Washington High

1954   *Brown vs. Board of Education* outlaws racial segregation in public schools

1955   March, refuses to give up her seat to a white woman on the bus, is arrested and charged with violating segregation law, disturbing the peace, and assaulting an officer; later found guilty on all three charges

  May, two charges are dropped at her hearing; she is placed under probation

  December, Rosa Parks arrested after refusing to move for a white person on the bus; Montgomery bus boycott begins

1956   June, court rules segregation on buses in Montgomery is unconstitutional

  December, federal marshals impose *Bowder v. Gayle* ruling in Montgomery, forcing integration of the buses, and the boycott ends

## More you can do:

- Read the chapter "Claudette Colvin Goes to Work," in *On the Bus with Rosa*
- Go see the play *Rage Is Not a One Day Thing* by Awele Makeba, about Claudette Colvin and the Montgomery Bus Boycott
- Read Phillip Hoose's book *Claudette Colvin: Twice Toward Justice*

## What do you think?

- Why do you think Claudette is not as well known as Rosa Parks?
- What experiences may have influenced Claudette to refuse to give up her seat?
- Claudette remembers thinking the day she refused to get up: "My head was just too full of black history . . ." What do you think she meant?

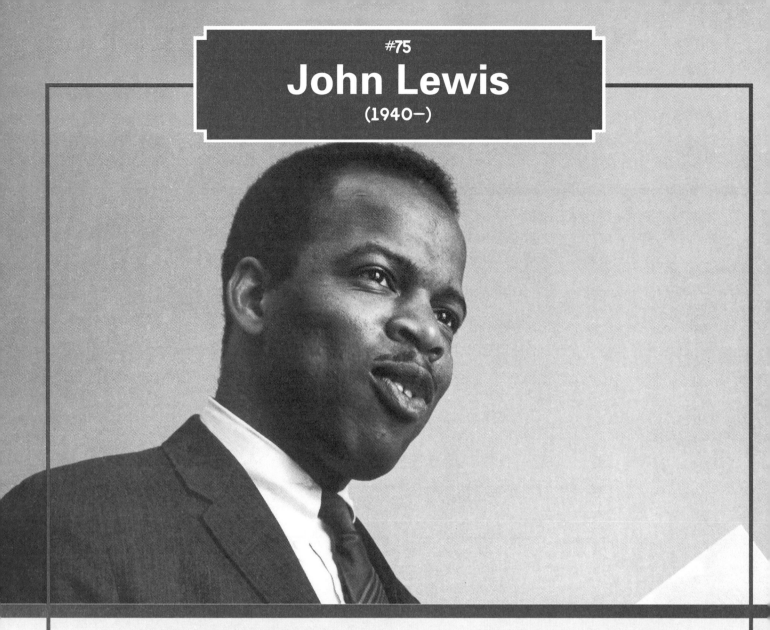

# #75
# John Lewis
## (1940–)

**The son of Alabama sharecroppers, John Lewis was a central figure in the civil rights movement.**

Although he was only a child at the time of *Brown v. Board of Education* and the Montgomery bus boycott, John was deeply involved in most of the significant civil rights events that followed. He often played a leadership role. In 1960, John emerged as a leader of a group of college students who sat down at a segregated Nashville lunch counter and refused to leave. The "sit-ins" were protests that sparked similar actions throughout the South. They also led to the creation of the Student Nonviolent Coordinating Committee (SNCC, pronounced "snick"). John was one of the founders of SNCC and also a participant in

the 1961 Freedom Rides sponsored by the Congress of Racial Equality (CORE). The purpose of the Freedom Rides was to test the 1960 *Boynton v. Virginia* decision that banned segregation on buses and in bus stations. John was beaten up in Rock Hill, South Carolina, in the first of many violent episodes that marked the Freedom Rides. After a bus was firebombed, CORE wanted to call off the Freedom Rides. John and other members of SNCC chose to continue the rides in spite of the danger. Like other Freedom Riders, John was badly beaten in Montgomery, Alabama, and jailed in Mississippi.

John was the youngest person to speak at the 1963 March on Washington and is the only speaker from that day who is still alive. He had

**We, the men, women, and children of the civil rights movement . . . wanted to realize . . . the Beloved Community, an all-inclusive, truly interracial democracy based on simple justice, which respects the dignity and worth of every human being.**

*—Representative John Lewis*

written a speech accusing President Kennedy of not doing nearly enough to help the civil rights movement and claiming that black people might "burn Jim Crow to the ground—non-violently." Older civil rights leaders persuaded John to tone down his speech and, reluctantly, he did so. John was also an organizer of Mississippi Freedom Summer in 1964. Like other young people, both black and white, he risked his life to help African Americans learn about their rights and register to vote.

In 1965 John led the march over the Edmund Pettus Bridge in Selma, Alabama, on the day that came to be known as Bloody Sunday. Martin Luther King Jr., as head of the Southern Christian Leadership Conference, was supposed to lead the march. But King chose not to come to Selma that day. Other members of SNCC, believing that the march was too dangerous, also did not participate. When protesters stopped on the bridge to pray, Alabama state troopers attacked them with nightsticks and tear gas. John's skull was badly fractured that day. Before he was taken to the hospital, he stopped to talk to reporters. On camera, he asked President Lyndon Johnson to send troops to Alabama. But he was out of the hospital in time to walk with Dr. King several weeks later when the march actually made it all the way from Selma to Montgomery. John stood alongside King and Rosa Parks when Lyndon Johnson signed the landmark 1965 Voting Rights Act.

Since 1987, John has represented Georgia's 5th District in Congress where he continues to fight on behalf of people who lack power throughout the nation and the world.

**—Amy Cohen**

## Timeline:

**1940**    Born in Troy, Alabama

**1960**    As a seminary student at Fisk University in Nashville, John is trained in nonviolent tactics and becomes a leader of the lunch counter sit-ins

**1961**    Is one of the original thirteen Freedom Riders; is beaten several times but continues the ride until jailed in Mississippi

**1963**    As president of SNCC, meets with President Kennedy and leaders of other four major civil rights organizations to plan the March on Washington

**1965**    Leads the march that becomes known as "Bloody Sunday"; participates in the successful march from Selma to Montgomery and witnesses the signing of the Voting Rights Act

**1987–Present** As a representative from an Atlanta, Georgia, district, Lewis is known as "the conscience of the Congress" for his consistently liberal positions and his willingness to speak out against war and in favor of social programs

## More you can do:

- **Find and compare the original and revised versions of John's March on Washington speech**
- **Watch footage of the police attacking the march on the Pettus Bridge on YouTube**

## What do you think?

- **Under pressure from more conservative black leaders like A. Philip Randolph, John edited his March on Washington speech, blunting his criticism of the Kennedy administration. Do you think he "chickened out" or was it the right thing to do given the circumstances?**
- **When John Lewis led marchers over the Edmund Pettus Bridge in Selma, Alabama, he knew that he might get arrested (he carried a backpack with a toothbrush and other necessities during the march) and that violence was highly probable. Was it courageous or foolhardy to lead others into such a perilous situation?**

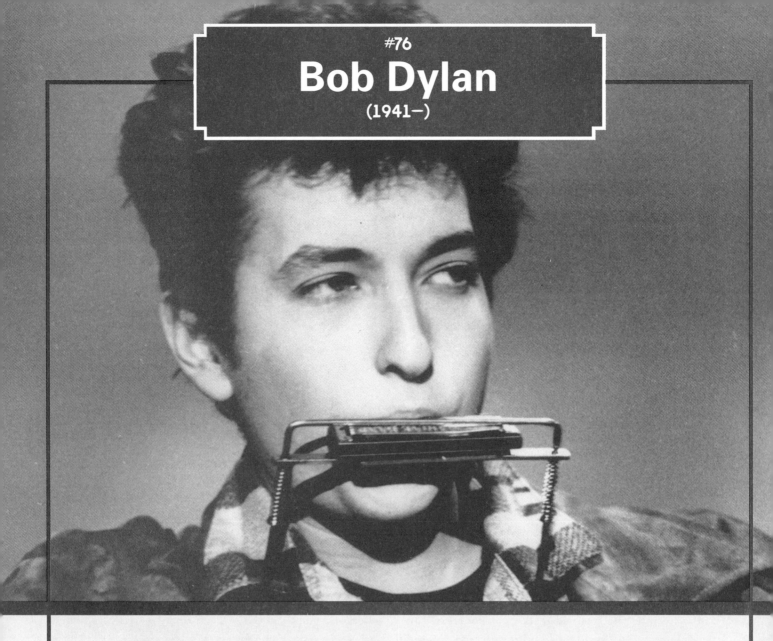

# 76

# Bob Dylan
## (1941–)

On a cold day early in 1961, a scruffy young man from northern Minnesota named Bob Dylan stepped out of a friend's car onto the streets of New York City.

He had just hitchhiked across half the country carrying no more than a suitcase and a guitar. He had come to Greenwich Village, which was the place to go if you did not fit in anywhere else. For Bob, it was a road to a home he had yet to find.

Bob was born Robert Allen Zimmerman. His grandparents were Jewish immigrants who came to the United States from Eastern Europe in the early 1900s. He played in several bands as a teenager.

Early in his career, Bob became known among musicians for his strong commitment to folk music and his skills as a performer. Most of all, Bob became known for writing his own songs. At that time, most popular musicians sang songs written by other people. Many folk musicians were not interested in songs by commercial songwriters. Instead, they sang traditional music and it was unusual for them to write their own songs.

Bob's songs were different from what anyone else was writing. For example, just weeks before the Cuban missile crisis, when the United States and Soviet Union came as close as they ever got to nuclear war, Bob began performing his song "A Hard Rain's A-Gonna Fall." The structure of the song combines modern

> ## "You better start swimmin' or you'll sink like a stone
> ## For the times they are a-changin'
>
> *—Bob Dylan, "The Times They Are A-Changin'," 1964*

poetry with the form of an old English ballad. The song's lyrics combine images of ruin with a determination to find purpose in a world of violence. The song was very popular during the "hottest" days of the Cold War.

Similarly, one of Bob's most famous compositions, "Blowin' in the Wind," captured the sentiments of many people involved in the civil rights movement. It served as a call to action for some early antiwar activists.

In 1965, Dylan plugged in. His hit single of that year, "Like a Rolling Stone," featured electric guitars and keyboards. It was more than six minutes long—twice as long as any pop single playing on the radio at that time. Columbia Records almost did not release the song as a single because it was so long. When it was finally released, it rose to number two on the Billboard charts, right behind the Beatles' "Help!"

Most pop songs on the radio in 1965 were love songs. "Like a Rolling Stone" was thematically, lyrically, and melodically more complex than anything else on the charts. The song talks about feeling alienated, or isolated and standing apart from life. In the song, Bob searches for something real in a society of meaningless glamour. He asks in every chorus: "How does it feel/To be without a home/Like a complete unknown/Like a rolling stone?"

Some of Bob's fans were outraged at his new style, booing and heckling him at his concerts. They felt he had abandoned folk music for commercial rock and roll. In fact, Bob had dramatically expanded the artistic horizons for a new generation of singers and songwriters who would give voice to the hopes and fears of a generation. Decades later, his songs are just as vital and life-affirming as they were when they were recorded.

**—Ben Dalbey**

## Timeline:

**1941**    Born Robert Allen Zimmerman in Duluth, Minnesota

**1961**    Arrives in New York City; meets Woody Guthrie; signs record deal with Columbia Records

**1963**    Releases *The Freewheelin' Bob Dylan*, including the songs "Blowin' in the Wind," "A Hard Rain's A-Gonna Fall," and "Masters of War"

**1964**    Releases two albums in the same year: *The Times They Are A-Changin'* and *Another Side of Bob Dylan*

**1965**    Again releases two albums in the same year: *Bringing It All Back Home* and *Highway 61 Revisited*, including the hit single "Like a Rolling Stone"

**1965**    Is booed after his electric set at the Newport Folk Festival

**1966–2011**    Releases an additional twenty-seven studio albums, and in 1988 begins his *Never Ending Tour*, playing approximately a hundred live shows every year

## More you can do:

- Listen to the studio albums and live recordings of Bob Dylan's music
- Watch Martin Scorsese's film *No Direction Home: Bob Dylan*
- Think about an issue that is important to you and write a song about it

## What do you think?

- Why do you think protest music was so prominent in the 1960s?
- What is folk music?
- Why were people so upset when Bob began playing his electric guitar?
- What fears did people have about nuclear war in 1963? Why did Bob's song "A Hard Rain's A-Gonna Fall" become so popular?

# 77

# Jesse Jackson
## (1941–)

**Jesse Jackson is a civil rights activist, Baptist minister, and founder of Operation PUSH and the National Rainbow Coalition. He ran twice for the Democratic Party presidential nomination.**

Jesse was born in Greenville, South Carolina. He was such a good athlete at his segregated high school that several colleges recruited him to play both baseball and football. When he found out that some white baseball players signed contracts worth more than ten times what he was offered, Jesse accepted a scholarship to play football for the integrated University of Illinois. He later transferred to North Carolina Agricultural & Technical College, a historically black college in Greensboro. It was there that he began his involvement in the civil rights movement.

Working with the Congress of Racial Equality, the star quarterback began organizing sit-ins and demonstrations. In 1963, Jesse enrolled in Chicago Theology Seminary, honing his gifts as an effective public speaker to become a minister. He began working for the Southern Christian Leadership Council (SCLC), which had dramatic successes integrating areas in the South. In 1965, the leaders of the SCLC, James Bevel and Martin Luther King Jr., called for marches from Selma to Montgomery, Alabama, to peacefully demonstrate for African Americans to have the right to vote. Jesse heard the call and brought half the seminary's student body to participate.

> "America is not like a blanket—one piece of unbroken cloth, the same color, the same texture, the same size. America is more like a quilt: many patches, many pieces, many colors, many sizes, all woven and held together by a common thread."
>
> —*Jesse Jackson, address before the Democratic National Convention, 1984*

The following year, Jesse welcomed Martin to Chicago, paving the way for civil rights tactics from the South to be used in the North. They became part of the struggle for fair housing practices and better jobs.

After Martin was assassinated in 1968, Jesse created a new civil rights organization called Operation PUSH (People United to Save Humanity) in 1971. Through Operation PUSH, Jesse led boycotts of major companies such as Nike, Coca-Cola, Kentucky Fried Chicken, and CBS, seeking better jobs for blacks. Operation PUSH also gave awards to prominent blacks, promoted youth education, and tried to protect homeowners, businesses, and workers.

In 1984, Jesse moved to Washington, DC He ran for office, aiming to win the Democratic presidential nomination. He created the National Rainbow Coalition to build support for his campaign. While he did not get the nomination, he led an impressive campaign that would serve as a foundation for him to try again four years later. In 1988, Jesse gained enough support to lead the race for the Democratic nomination for a period of time. Ultimately, though, he finished second to Michael Dukakis.

In 1996, Jesse merged Operation PUSH and the National Rainbow Organization to form the Rainbow/PUSH Coalition, which continues to fight for economic and political equality. To this day, Jesse continues to take up causes in which people are harmed but lack the resources to represent themselves. He is an outspoken activist promoting the continued advancement of civil rights in the United States and around the world.

—Dave Zirin

## Timeline:

| 1941 | October 8, born in Greenville, South Carolina |
| 1959–64 | Graduates from high school and attends the University of Illinois and then North Carolina A&T; becomes a leader of civil rights demonstrations in the student desegregation sit-in movement. |
| 1964–71 | Enters the Chicago Theological Seminary; joins thousands of protestors responding to MLK's call for a march on Selma and Montgomery; asks MLK for a job and begins organizing with the SCLC |
| 1968 | April 4, MLK assassinated in Memphis, TN |
| 1971 | Resigns from the SCLC and founds Operation PUSH |
| 1983 | Enters the 1984 Democratic presidential race |
| 1984 | Founds the National Rainbow Coalition |
| 1988 | For a while, leads in popular votes and delegates for the 1988 Democratic presidential nominee |
| 1992–96 | Returns to Operation PUSH in Chicago and merges it with the Rainbow Coalition |
| 1997–present | Acts as a highly respected and trusted world leader, serving as a diplomat around the globe; receives numerous awards and citations from international governments and organizations |

## More you can do:

- As a student activist, Jesse organized civil disobediences and mass protests. As an adult, he organized an election campaign for president. Compare and contrast the tactics of the young Jackson and the older Jackson

## What do you think?

- Jesse entered politics as a student angry at the racial injustice around him and ended up fighting for much more than just racial equality. Why do you think some people become such ardent fighters for social justice and not others?
- Why do you think Jesse left the SCLC to form Operation PUSH?

# 78

# Joan Baez
## (1941–)

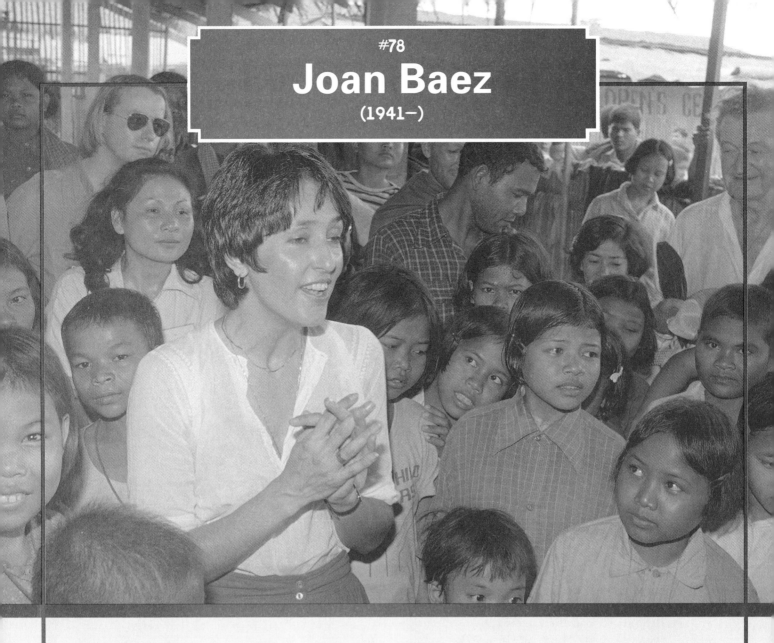

In 1963, Joan Baez sang the civil rights anthem "We Shall Overcome" at the March on Washington. It was the same march where Dr. Martin Luther King Jr. gave his famous "I Have a Dream" speech.

At the time, Joan was twenty-two years old. She has now been a folk singer and human rights activist for more than fifty years.

When Joan was ten years old, her family lived for a year in Baghdad, Iraq. Baghdad at that time was occupied by the British army. British soldiers treated her badly because they thought she was Arab. Joan has brown skin and dark eyes she inherited from her father, who was born in Mexico. "Being brown-skinned, I was considered an Arab. . . . That's kind of how it started, my feeling about how people would want to be treated," she said.

Joan began playing folk music in the late 1950s in high school. She taught herself how to sing and play the guitar. Joan had an amazing, powerful voice. She was also an excellent guitar player. She loved to sing songs like "Silver Dagger," which was written sometime in the late 1800s. These old ballads were about strong feelings of love and betrayal. Joan sang these songs because she was attracted to the life-and-death struggles they described.

During the 1960s and 1970s, folk music became extremely popular, particularly among young people. Many songs were about the struggles for peace, justice, and equality that were taking place in the United States and around the world. People sang at rallies and marches to feel united and express their purpose. People sang in jail and when they were being attacked to help keep their spirits strong.

In 1959 Joan traveled to the Newport Folk Festival. This festival was a major event for folk singers, fans, and record companies. She wasn't on the program, but Joan convinced another musician to let her perform with him. She sang the spirituals "Virgin Mary Had One Son" and "We Are Crossing Jordan River" on stage. The crowd loved her. The next year, Joan was the star of the festival. Over the next three years, she released three gold records. That means each of her first three records sold more than half a million copies.

Joan quickly became one of the most famous folk musicians of the 1960s. Her album *Joan Baez in Concert* made it to number ten on the Billboard charts. Joan used her fame to speak and act for peace and justice. She was deeply committed to the civil rights movement and the struggle against the US war in Vietnam. "When I heard Dr. King speak, I knew this was it for me," she said.

Dr. King asked her to march with students trying to attend school in Alabama. And she was twice arrested for trying to stop young men who had been drafted from going to fight in Vietnam. In 1967 she was stopped from playing in a Washington, DC, concert hall because of her antiwar activism. Joan instead played a free concert for 30,000 people at the bottom of the Washington Monument.

Joan has never stopped performing music. She hasn't stopped protesting either. In November 2011 she played the protest song "Joe Hill" for an Occupy Wall Street demonstration in New York.

**—Ben Dalbey**

## Timeline:

| | |
|---|---|
| 1941 | Born Joan Chandos Báez on January 9 on Staten Island, New York |
| 1959 | Begins performing at a coffeehouse in Boston and makes her first appearance at the Newport Folk Festival |
| 1960 | Headlines the Newport Folk Festival and releases her first gold album *Joan Baez* |
| 1961–62 | Releases *Joan Baez, Vol. 2*, and *Joan Baez in Concert*; appears on the cover of *Time* magazine |
| 1963 | Performs at the March on Washington |
| 1964 | Travels to Tuscaloosa, Alabama, at the request of Martin Luther King Jr. to aid the struggle against segregation |
| 1967 | Arrested twice for blocking the entrance of the Oakland Draft Induction Center |
| 1972 | Helps to establish Amnesty International on the West Coast |
| 1972 | Travels with a US fact-finding delegation to Hanoi, Vietnam |
| 1979 | Founds Humanitas International Human Rights Committee |
| 1982 | Premier of the film *There But for Fortune: Joan Baez in Latin America* |
| 1987 | Publishes autobiography *And a Voice to Sing With* |
| 2007 | Receives a Lifetime Achievement Award at the Grammys |

## More you can do:

- Listen to *Joan Baez in Concert*
- Watch the American Masters documentary *Joan Baez: How Sweet the Sound*

## What do you think?

- Can you think of a song that has taught you something important that you did not learn from other sources?
- What do you think about musicians who update or write new words to existing songs? Is it better to write something new from scratch?

**Stokely Carmichael is best known as the civil rights activist who first called for "Black Power."**

He was part of a younger generation of civil rights activists that went from protesting the laws in the southern United States made to keep blacks and whites separate (known as "Jim Crow") to questioning the whole system of racial injustice.

Stokely was the son of immigrants from the West Indies. They came to New York City in 1952 when he was eleven years old. Stokely's first year in college in 1960 was a turning point in the struggle for black equality in the United States. College students began a series of sit-ins at segregated restaurants in the South. Stokely saw the footage on TV and was angered by the vicious treatment these young people endured at the hands of racist mobs. "Suddenly, I was burning," he later told a reporter.

By the end of his freshman year, Stokely hopped aboard the Freedom Rides. He went with other young activists to the South to challenge the Jim Crow laws. The Freedom Riders went as an integrated group into bus station waiting rooms labeled "Whites Only." Stokely later asked, "What could be more harmless?" But the Freedom Riders were attacked and beaten by police and racists. Stokely was arrested in Jackson, Mississippi, for ignoring the "Whites Only" sign at the train station and thrown into prison for forty-nine days.

> ❝Our grandfathers and our great-grandfathers had to run, run, run! My generation has run out of breath. We just ain't runnin' no more.❞
>
> *—Stokely Carmichael, as quoted in "Stokely Carmichael: Young Man Behind an Angry Message," Life, May 19, 1967*

In 1964 Stokely graduated from college and joined the youth-led Student Non-Violent Coordinating Committee (SNCC). In SNCC he helped to organize voter registration drives. He was known as a powerful speaker who voiced the rage of his people and exposed the hypocrisy of racism in the "world's greatest democracy."

The strategy of nonviolent civil disobedience was put to its greatest test during the voter registration campaigns. The elites of the South weren't about to give up their supremacy peacefully. Civil rights workers were jailed, beaten, kidnapped, raped, bombed, and murdered. The federal government in Washington, DC, did nothing to stop this violence.

Stokely and others grew impatient with the slow pace of change. Malcolm X's calls for black resistance "by any means necessary" were appealing to many of these younger activists. They were angry about racist inequality across the country, including the North. Stokely and others were growing tired of asking the federal government for help, particularly when they felt their calls were being ignored. At a civil rights march in Mississippi he said, "We been saying 'Freedom' for six years. What we are going to start saying now is 'Black Power'!"

Though the term would come to mean many different things to different people, in 1966 "Black Power" signaled a new direction for many in the civil rights movement. The focus on nonviolent resistance to Jim Crow laws in the South shifted toward a movement to overturn institutional racism and white supremacy across the entire country.

Stokely believed that white people should organize in their own communities. He disagreed with other activists in the Black Panthers who thought white people would help them. In 1969 he left the United States for Guinea and changed his name to Kwame Ture.
—**Kirstin Roberts**

## Timeline:

| | |
|---|---|
| 1941 | Born on June 29 in Port of Spain, Trinidad |
| 1952 | Stokely and family emigrate from Trinidad to the Bronx in New York City |
| 1960 | Sit-ins against segregated lunch counters begin on February 1 |
| 1960 | Begins attending Howard University |
| 1961 | Joins Freedom Rides |
| 1961 | Arrested in June during Freedom Rides |
| 1964 | Graduates from Howard; joins SNCC |
| 1966 | Becomes chairman of SNCC |
| 1968 | Joins Black Panther Party |
| 1968 | Marries South African singer and activist Miriam Makeba |
| 1968 | Helps organize the All African Revolutionary People's Party, a Pan-Africanist organization |
| 1969 | Leaves Black Panther Party; publicly rejects their willingness to work with white antiracist activists |
| 1969 | Settles permanently in the African nation of Guinea, takes the name Kwame Ture |
| 1998 | Dies of cancer at age fifty-seven |

## More you can do:

- Watch the *Eyes on the Prize* series
- Watch *The Black Power Mixtape (1967–1975)*, which features a segment with Stokely interviewing his mother

## What do you think?

- Stokely broke the law during the Freedom Rides and was put in prison. Would you have done the same thing? Why or why not?
- What does the term "Black Power" mean to you?
- Stokely told a reporter that after watching the sit-ins on the news, "Suddenly I was burning." Have you ever felt that way? What did you do about it?
- Why did Stokely disagree that white antiracists could be allies in the black struggle? Do you agree or disagree?

# #80
# Muhammad Ali
## (1942–)

**Muhammad Ali was a great boxer who became a powerful symbol of the fight against racism. He was born Cassius Clay in Louisville, Kentucky, in 1942. His father, who dreamed of being an artist, was a house painter.**

His mother sometimes cleaned houses to help make ends meet. Louisville back then had "Jim Crow" laws, which treated blacks as second-class citizens. Despite this, young Cassius could box and he could talk. The press called him the Louisville Lip, Cash the Brash, Mighty Mouth, and Gaseous Cassius. But he could also back up the talk. His boxing skills won him the gold medal in the 1960 Greek Olympics at age eighteen.

The week after returning home from the Olympics, Cassius went to a Louisville restaurant with his medal around his neck—and was denied service because of the color of his skin. Cassius then said he threw his beloved medal into the Ohio River.

Cassius looked for political answers and began finding them when he heard Malcolm X speak at a meeting of the Nation of Islam (NOI). The young fighter and Malcolm became fast friends. At this time, he also shocked the world by beating champion Sonny Liston. He boasted, "I'm the greatest of all time!"

The day after he beat Sonny, Cassius announced publicly that he was joining the

NOI. The Olympic gold medalist now stood with a group that called white people "devils" and stood unapologetically for self-defense and racial separation. He changed his name to Muhammad Ali. Some people were outraged, but the new generation of activists loved it.

In early 1966, during the Vietnam War, the army drafted Muhammad. He heard this news surrounded by reporters and blurted out one of the most famous phrases of the decade, "Man, I ain't got no quarrel with them Vietcong." He said he would refuse to go to war. For saying no to serving in the military, Muhammad got sentenced to five years in prison and had his passport seized. He immediately appealed. A divided Supreme Court struck down his sentence in 1970. But he was stripped of his title and suspended from boxing.

Muhammad was vilified in the media as unpatriotic and a racist (against white people). He was abandoned by old friends. But a young generation wanted to hear what he had to say. And Muhammad obliged. In 1968, he spoke at two hundred campuses.

He returned to the ring in 1971 a slower fighter but as intelligent as any who ever laced up the gloves. The slower Muhammad discovered something: he had a jaw of iron and could take a punch. Unfortunately, his bravery in taking punches aggravated the disease that would cripple him: Parkinson's.

The new, slowed Muhammad, with slurred speech due to the disease, was now celebrated and much loved. Louisville named a street after him and presidents invited him to the White House. Today, he is considered a walking saint. But his resistance to racism and war is a key chapter in our struggles for social justice to remember.

—Dave Zirin

## Timeline:

1942 January 17, born Cassius Clay in Louisville, Kentucky

1960 Wins the gold medal at the Rome Olympics in light-heavyweight boxing

1964 February 25–26, in a monumental upset, knocks out Charles "Sonny" Liston in seven rounds, becoming the second youngest heavyweight champion in history; publicly joins the Nation of Islam

1964 Takes the new name Muhammad Ali

1967 April 28–29, refuses induction into the US Army, declaring himself a conscientious objector to the war in Vietnam; is stripped of his championship title

June 20, found guilty of draft evasion in Houston, Texas; fined $10,000 and sentenced to five years in prison, but remains free on appeal

1974 "Rumble in the Jungle" championship match against George Foreman

1981 December 11, fights future world champion Trevor Berbick and loses badly; it is his last fight

1984 Announces he has Parkinson's disease

1996 In an emotional ceremony, lights the torch at the Summer Olympic Games in Atlanta

2005 Receives the Presidential Medal of Freedom

## More you can do:

- Watch the movie *When We Were Kings*
- Chart the various ways in which Muhammad has been portrayed in the media from his early days as a boxer, draft resister, and NOI adherent through to winner of the Presidential Medal of Freedom

## What do you think?

- Imagine that you are gold-medal-winning Cassius Clay on the night he was denied service at the restaurant in his hometown. What do you think he was thinking as he threw his gold medal into the river?
- In 1967, Muhammad Ali was found guilty of draft evasion and sentenced to prison time. Do you think refusing to serve in the military is a crime? Why or why not?

# Huey P. Newton

## (1942–1989)

In October 1966, two young black men met in Oakland, California. One of them was named Huey Percy Newton. The other was Bobby Seale.

They decided to form a political party to gain black freedom and equality. Little did they know that their party would soon become one of the most respected and feared organizations in the country. This group was called the Black Panther Party.

Huey was born in Louisiana, the youngest of seven children in a poor family. He grew up in Oakland, California, during the height of the civil rights movement. Public schools were integrated but still unequal, and Huey got a terrible education. He could barely read when he finished high school. He often landed in jail for minor crimes. He saw that racism persisted—in education, housing, jobs, and most of all, in the way the police treated black people.

Huey educated himself and went to college. There, he met Bobby. Together they founded the Black Panther Party for Self-Defense (BPP). They chose the black panther as their logo because it was a symbol of courage, determination, and freedom. They adopted Malcolm X's slogan: "Freedom by any means necessary."

The BPP grew—and grew quickly. By 1969, the party had more than ten thousand members with chapters across the country. Their newspaper sold 250,000 copies each issue. One of the key problems the Black Panthers organized around was police violence. Police regularly beat, jailed, and even killed black people with few consequences. The BPP called for black people to defend themselves from police attacks. They fought for the right to carry guns.

The Black Panthers also made demands on the government. They called for good housing, quality education, and jobs for every black person. They argued for structural change to end both racism and capitalism. They also started free health clinics, free breakfast programs for poor children, and even an ambulance service.

Because the Black Panthers were so popular, they were also feared—most of all, by the police and the federal government. In 1969, FBI head J. Edgar Hoover called the BPP the "greatest threat to the internal security of the country."

Authorities waged a years-long campaign to bring down the group. At times, this campaign included shocking levels of violence. In 1969 Chicago police killed young Panthers Fred Hampton and Mark Clark as they lay sleeping in their beds. No police officer was ever convicted for these crimes.

Huey himself was soon targeted by law enforcement. He was arrested and convicted in September 1968 for killing a police officer. He served two years in prison. He was eventually freed after people all around the world rallied to his defense. Yet the illegal government campaign against the Panthers eventually succeeded. The organization fell apart by the late 1970s. Huey fell prey to depression and drug addiction. In 1989, he was shot dead by an Oakland drug dealer. But the legacy of Huey Newton and the Black Panthers looms large today for all those who strive to end racial oppression and police brutality.

—Zach Zill

## Timeline:

| | |
|---|---|
| 1942 | Born on February 17 in Monroe, Louisiana |
| 1956 | Arrested at fourteen for gun possession |
| 1960 | Graduates from high school illiterate |
| 1966 | Founds the Black Panther Party in Oakland with Bobby Seale |
| 1967 | April, publishes the first issue of the *Black Panther* |
| | May, dozens of Black Panthers march on the California state capital carrying guns to protest a recent change in gun law |
| | October, stopped for a traffic check by police and there is a scuffle; Huey suffers from a bullet wound in his stomach; police officer John Frey dies from a bullet wound |
| 1968 | September, convicted of killing Frey |
| 1969 | January, Panthers' Free Breakfast for School Children Program begins |
| 1970 | May, released from prison |
| 1974 | Flees to Cuba to escape charges; marries Gwen Fontaine |
| 1977 | Returns to the United States to face charges |
| 1980 | Earns a PhD degree in social philosophy from the University of California at Santa Cruz |
| 1987 | Serves time in prison on the 1977 gun charge |
| 1989 | Is murdered by a drug dealer |

## More you can do:

- Read Huey's book of essays, *To Die for the People*
- Watch the movie *The Huey P. Newton Story*
- Write three questions that you would want to ask Huey if he were alive today

## What do you think?

- Was the perception that racism was deep-seated in the United States even after the gains of the civil rights movement correct?
- Read the BPP's Ten-Point Program. Do you agree with it? Why or why not?
- Do you agree with the BPP's criticisms of the civil rights movement? Why or why not?

**In the late 1960s, a growing women's movement demanded equality. This fight was expressed in the world of sports in many challenges to the idea that sports were for men only.**

But two moments stand above all others. The passage of Title IX—the 1972 law that stated, "No person in the United States shall, on the basis of sex, be excluded from participation in, be denied the benefits of, or be subjected to discrimination under any education program or activity receiving Federal financial assistance"—was one. The emergence of tennis great Billie Jean King was the other.

The roar of the new movement was heard when Billie Jean faced off against Bobby Riggs

in their 1973 "Battle of the Sexes" tennis match. Riggs, a 1939 Wimbledon champion, was public in his contempt for all women athletes, saying, "The male is king. The male is supreme. I've said it over and over again. I still feel that way. Girls play a nice game of tennis for girls." Billie Jean later said, "I thought it would set us back fifty years if I didn't win that match. . . . It would ruin the women's tour and affect all women's self-esteem."

The "Battle of the Sexes" captured everyone's imagination in the country, not just that of tennis fans. On September 20, 1973, Billie Jean was carried out on the Houston Astrodome court like Cleopatra, in a gold throne held up by four muscular men dressed as ancient slaves. Riggs was wheeled in on a

In the seventies we had to make it acceptable for people to accept girls and women as athletes. We had to make it okay for them to be active. Those were much scarier times for females in sports.

—Billie Jean King, as quoted in "Ahead of Her Time," Chicago Sun-Times, March 16, 1997

rickshaw pulled by female models in tight outfits and named "Bobby's Bosom Buddies."

Billie Jean, then twenty-nine, ran Riggs ragged, winning 6–4, 6–3, 6–3. As Neil Amdur wrote in the *New York Times*, "Most important perhaps for women everywhere, she convinced skeptics that a female athlete can survive pressure-filled situations and that men are as susceptible to nerves as women."

Billie Jean was far more than just a symbol or an athlete. She was an activist and a participant in the women's movement for equal rights. Billie Jean fought for a women's tennis players' union and forged the Women's Tennis Association. She was elected its first president in 1973. Billie Jean called for a strike by women players if the prize money at tournaments wasn't equal to the men's. In 1973, the US Open became the first major tournament to offer an equal winners' purse for men and women. Then Billie Jean became the first prominent athlete ever to be open as a lesbian.

*Life* magazine named her one of the "100 Most Important Americans of the Twentieth Century." She was the only female athlete on the list, and one of only four athletes. (Of the other three, two—Jackie Robinson and Muhammad Ali—are also strongly associated with social movements; Babe Ruth was the other.)

As for Title IX, today one in three young girls play sports. Twenty-five years ago, that number was one in thirty-five. This law has improved the quality of life for tens of millions of girls and women across the country. One person to thank for this is the great Billie Jean King.

—**Dave Zirin**

## Timeline:

| | |
|---|---|
| 1943 | November 22, born in Long Beach, California |
| 1959–65 | Has her Grand Slam debut at the US Championships at the age of fifteen; she loses, but over the next six years goes on to win local, regional, and international championships |
| 1966–75 | Dominates women's tennis, winning championships in the United States, the United Kingdom, France, and Australia |
| 1973 | Competes with Riggs, former male tennis star, in the "Battle of the Sexes" live on television; forms the Women's Tennis Association |
| 1981 | Is forced to publicly acknowledge her sexuality as the result of a lawsuit, becoming the first female athlete to come out as a lesbian; within twenty-four hours of the lawsuit's filing, loses all her advertising endorsements contracts, worth an estimated $2 million |
| 1983–1990 | Continues to play competitive singles tennis until 1983 and competitive doubles until 1990, when she retires from the sport |
| 1990–present | Continues her advocacy and work in numerous areas |
| 2009 | Awarded the Presidential Medal of Freedom |

## More you can do:

- In the context of a rising woman's right's movement, the "Battle of the Sexes" tennis match took on a much larger meaning. Write a dialogue between a husband, wife, son, and daughter as they watch the game together

## What do you think?

- What has been the impact of Title IX, especially in schools?
- Within twenty-four hours of being outed as a lesbian in 1981, Billie Jean King lost all of her advertising endorsements and was vilified in the press. In 2009, she was awarded the Presidential Medal of Freedom, the nation's highest civilian honor. Compare and contrast the reactions to Billie Jean King in 1981 and 2009.

# #83
# Angela Davis
## (1944–)

**Author. Scholar. Black freedom fighter. Prison abolitionist. Feminist. Communist. Revolutionary. Icon. Angela Davis is one of the most recognizable living changemakers in the United States.**

Angela's life is inseparable from the biggest social movements of the twentieth century. She is widely known as a leader of the Black Power movement of the late 1960s and early 1970s. Images of Angela from that era, wearing her afro proudly, became engraved in popular culture.

Angela hails from a family of teachers in Birmingham, Alabama. Her mother was also an organizer of the Southern Negro Congress. During the Jim Crow era, Birmingham was scarred by racist violence. The city became a battleground for important civil rights struggles. These events influenced Angela's thinking as she grew up.

Angela was a student during the height of the civil rights movement. She joined the movement as it turned toward more radical solutions to racism and inequality. Angela worked closely with the Black Panther Party and its radical leaders, such as Stokely Carmichael and Huey Newton. Angela also spoke out against the war in Vietnam and supported the struggles for women's and LGBT rights.

During this era, the black movement was full of debate about how to win freedom and equality. Some black leaders wanted to

> "The idea of freedom is inspiring. But what does it mean? If you are free in a political sense but have no food, what's that? The freedom to starve?"

—Angela Davis, "The Meaning of Freedom," talk in Denver, February 15, 2008

separate themselves from white society altogether. But Angela insisted on a joint struggle that united blacks and whites in fighting racism. Angela also saw racism as a product of capitalism. She led a wing of the movement that wanted to do away with capitalism and replace it with socialism. In 1968 she joined the Communist Party.

Because of her radical ideas and involvement in militant actions, Angela became a target of the government and other authorities. In 1970, Angela was fired from her teaching job at the University of California, Los Angeles. Soon afterward, she found herself on the FBI's Ten Most Wanted List.

In August, guns owned by Angela were used in a deadly clash between black activists and the police. A judge was kidnapped and killed along with three other people. Angela was charged with kidnapping and murder, even though she was not present during the showdown.

Thousands upon thousands of people rallied to Angela's defense. Activists in the United States and around the world created hundreds of local Angela Davis Defense Committees. Famous musicians such as John Lennon, Yoko Ono, and the Rolling Stones wrote songs about Angela. In the end, this people power helped win her freedom. The jury at her trial found Angela not guilty.

Angela went on to become a leading fighter for social justice in the United States. She has continued to promote women's rights and racial justice. In the 1980s, she ran for vice president twice on the Communist Party ticket. Her recent work has focused on opposing the death penalty and the prison system. She helped popularize the notion of the "prison industrial complex."

For decades, Angela's scholarship and activism have championed the struggles of all oppressed people.
—Zach Zill

## Timeline:

| | |
|---|---|
| 1944 | Born in Birmingham, Alabama |
| 1962 | Is one of three black freshmen at Brandeis University |
| 1965 | Graduates from Brandeis with high honors, goes to Frankfurt, Germany, for graduate school, and participates in antiwar protests |
| 1967 | Returns to the United States to take part in the civil rights movement |
| 1968 | Joins the Communist Party after Martin Luther King's assassination |
| 1969 | Fired by UCLA for being a Communist |
| 1970 | Weapons registered in her name are used in an attempted prison escape in San Rafael, California |
| 1970 | Found and jailed |
| 1972 | Acquitted |
| 1980 | Publishes *Women, Race, and Class*; runs for vice president on the Communist Party ticket |
| 1984 | Runs again for vice president on the Communist Party ticket |
| Early 1990s | Breaks from Communist Party |
| 1991 | Becomes professor at UC Santa Cruz |
| 1997 | Helps found Critical Resistance; comes out as a lesbian |
| 2011 | Speaks at the Philadelphia and New York Occupy encampments |

## More you can do:

- **Read** *Angela Davis: An Autobiography*
- **Watch** *The Black Power Mixtape 1967–1975* **and read the companion book**

## What do you think?

- **The jury at Angela's 1972 trial consisted only of white people. Why would this raise concerns among Angela's supporters at her trial?**
- **Angela once said, "Racism, in the first place, is a weapon used by the wealthy to increase the profits they bring in by paying black workers less for their work." Explain**

# 84

# Leonard Peltier

(1944–)

Leonard Peltier is a Native American activist, writer, and political prisoner. Leonard was born in Grand Forks, North Dakota. His father was Ojibway and his mother was Dakota Sioux.

He grew up with his grandparents on the Turtle Mountain Reservation in North Dakota. More than a hundred years before, Native American peoples had lived freely on the Great Plains. The US government sent troops to go to war with Indians, which often resulted in treaties. But by the 1880s, the US government broke these promises. It forced many nations onto tiny reservations.

Like many on the reservation in the 1940s, Leonard lived in poverty, without running water and electricity. He often went hungry. At age nine, Leonard was taken to the Wahpeton Indian School. Wahpeton was a boarding school that the US government forced Indian children to attend against their will. Indian students had to change their dress and speak English. Boys had to cut off their long hair. Leonard was one of many children who were punished for trying to hold on to their traditional ways.

Leonard began to question the way that the US government treated Native Americans. In the 1950s, the US government began to relocate Native Americans from reservations to big cities. Leonard explained, "We pleaded with the government to let us stay on our land . . . but it was all in vain."

> " The destruction of our people must stop! We are not statistics.
> We are the people from whom you took this land by force and blood and lies. . . .
> America, when will you live up to your own principles? "
>
> —*Leonard Peltier*, Prison Writings: My Life Is My Sun Dance, *2000*

In 1959 Leonard moved to Seattle. While relocation was difficult, he met other Indian people from different nations. Many of them shared his concerns about poor housing, illiteracy, and poverty among Seattle's Indian residents.

Across the United States, the civil rights movement inspired others to fight for their rights. The American Indian Movement (AIM) began organizing Native Americans around the country. Leonard joined this movement and committed himself to fighting for his people.

AIM took militant actions to force the United States to acknowledge that it had betrayed Native Americans. In 1973, AIM occupied Wounded Knee, South Dakota, to express their anger. They stayed there for more than two months until the FBI used force to get them to leave.

In 1975, AIM members, including Leonard, went to the Pine Ridge Reservation to support the rights of traditional Indians who were being terrorized by Tribal Police and Bureau of Indian Affairs agents. These officers had unjustly attacked and killed dozens of Lakota Sioux on the reservation.

As AIM helped defend the Lakota on Pine Ridge, a shootout took place between AIM and the FBI in which two FBI officers were killed. Leonard was blamed for their deaths. In 1977, Leonard was convicted, even though he did not receive a fair trial.

Millions of people have learned about Leonard's case and have come to support him. Despite the difficulties he has faced in prison, Leonard has continued to work for justice for his people.

—**Michele Bollinger**

## Timeline:

| | |
|---|---|
| 1944 | Born in Grand Forks, North Dakota |
| 1953 | Sent to Wahpeton Indian School |
| 1957 | Returns to Turtle Mountain Reservation |
| 1959 | Moves to Seattle, Washington |
| 1970 | Fort Lawton occupation |
| 1972 | Joins the American Indian Movement (AIM) |
| | Travels to Washington, DC, as part of the "Trail of Broken Treaties" caravan |
| 1973 | AIM occupies Wounded Knee, South Dakota; Leonard supports it but does not participate |
| 1975 | With AIM, goes to Pine Ridge Reservation in South Dakota; FBI shootout |
| 1977 | Leonard is convicted in an unfair trial |
| | Fort Lawton (in Seattle) becomes an Indian Cultural Center |
| 1985 | Denied a new trial |
| 1987 | Conviction upheld even though the court acknowledges FBI misconduct |
| 1992 | The film *Incident at Oglala* is released; international support grows for Leonard's release |
| 2009 | George W. Bush denies clemency to Leonard |

## More you can do:

- Write a letter to Leonard in prison and ask him questions about his life, his case, or issues facing Native Americans today
- View the documentary *Incident at Oglala*

## What do you think?

- Why did Leonard's experiences as a child lead him to activism?
- In what ways was relocation a negative experience for Native Americans? In what ways was it beneficial?
- Why did some conflicts between Native Americans and the US government turn violent?
- Why are Americans guaranteed the right to a fair trial? What should happen if someone is denied that right?

168

# 85

# Alice Walker

## (1944—)

**Alice Walker, an African American writer and activist, is living proof that a person doesn't need to become less radical to achieve success.**

Alice's life itself has often been about defeating despair and emerging stronger, more determined, but still compassionate. She and her seven older siblings were born in the Jim Crow South. Most black children then were expected to help their sharecropper parents farm. But Alice's mother sent her to school, to learn to read and write. At only four years old, she began first grade.

When Alice was eight years old, her brother accidentally shot her in the right eye with his BB gun. Her family didn't own a car and couldn't bring Alice to the doctor for a week. So Alice lost vision in that eye. After it scarred over, children began to make fun of how she looked. This caused Alice to become very shy, and she began writing poetry. But the scar tissue was eventually removed, and Alice was voted most popular in her high school. She also graduated as the highest-ranking student in her class.

Alice went to Spelman College in Atlanta on a full scholarship. She took classes with Howard Zinn, the renowned historian and activist. He encouraged his students to protest unjust laws through civil disobedience. Among many actions, Alice and other students sat in at lunch counters where black people were not allowed to eat.

Alice married Melvyn Leventhal and the couple moved to Jackson, Mississippi. They were the first legally married interracial couple in the entire state. They were threatened by the Ku Klux Klan.

In 1982 Alice wrote her most famous book, *The Color Purple*. The book takes place in Georgia, and the main female characters deal with racism from whites and sexism within the black community. The book has been censored because of its frank portrayal of these themes. Steven Spielberg later made the book into a film. In 2005 it was adapted as a Broadway musical.

Alice has marched on Washington as part of the civil rights and antiwar movements. She has brought aid to Gaza, Palestine. While these actions are considered quite radical by mainstream US culture, her work has been read by many. There are ten million copies in print of more than thirty of her published works. She was the first black woman to win the Pulitzer Prize for fiction.

One theme running throughout Alice's work is hope amid hopelessness. Many of her characters struggle to retain their humanity despite racism or sexism. As one critic wrote of *The Color Purple*, Alice's portrayals of "political and economic issues finally give way to what can only be described as a joyful celebration of human spirit."

Alice continues to stand up for what she believes in. As the US invasion of Iraq was beginning, she was one of many arrested in front of the White House. Alice later said of the protest, "I was with other women who believe that the women and children of Iraq are just as dear as the women and children in our families."

**—Jason Farbman**

## Timeline:

| | |
|---|---|
| 1944 | February 9, born in Eatonton, Georgia |
| 1952 | Right eye is wounded when her brother accidentally shoots her with a BB gun |
| 1961 | Attends Spelman College on a full scholarship |
| 1963 | Participates in the March on Washington |
| 1965 | Alice graduates from college after transferring to Sarah Lawrence |
| 1967 | Marries civil rights lawyer Melvyn Leventhal, a white, Jewish civil rights lawyer |
| 1983 | Wins the Pulitzer Prize for Fiction for *The Color Purple* |
| 2003 | Arrested, along with many other activists, after marching to the White House to protest the US invasion of Iraq |
| 2009 | January, Alice and more than fifty others send an open letter protesting the Toronto Film Festival's spotlight on Israeli filmmakers; the letter calls Israel an "apartheid regime" |
| | March, Alice and dozens of female activists from Code Pink travel to Gaza; they deliver aid and attempt to convince Israel and Egypt to open the borders they share with Gaza |

## More you can do:

- **Read *The Color Purple* or watch the film adaptation**
- **Watch video of Alice Walker reading Sojourner Truth's "Ain't I a Woman?" speech and Rachel Corrie's "Letter from Palestine"**

## What do you think?

- **Do you agree with Alice's "As long as we are all here . . ." quote above? What makes it difficult to "share the planet, rather than divide it"? What makes it possible?**
- **The same year Alice married Melvyn Leventhal, the Supreme Court declared interracial marriage between black and white people legal across the country. Do you see similar struggles today?**

# 86

# Fred Fay
## (1944–2011)

Fred Fay was an important leader in the movement to win equal rights for people living with disabilities. He pushed for the development of new technology to give people living with disabilities more control over their lives.

He also worked to get many federal laws passed to protect people living with disabilities. His work touched and improved the lives of millions.

Fred was born in 1944. After a spinal cord injury, he began using a wheelchair at the age of sixteen. The next year, he became an activist when he and his mother founded a counseling and information center called

Opening Doors. Soon after that, he entered the University of Illinois. It was one of the few wheelchair-accessible universities in the United States at the time. Yet there were many campus businesses and lounges that were still not accessible. He joined with other activists to open these places up. As he said in a documentary filmed at this time, "I'm really a back-door citizen, or a second-class citizen, when it comes to getting into the buildings my taxes pay for."

Many oppressed people began fighting for dignity, respect, and equal rights in the 1960s. People living with disabilities were no different. In the '60s, Fred began working as an adviser to both presidents and Congress. He faced legislative and physical barriers to

> "I think one of the sea changes in attitude in the '60s was the realization on the part of people with disabilities that it was the environment and attitudes of people that limited us and not our own disabilities."
>
> —Fred Fay, from a video clip in the "Fred Fay" section, UC Berkeley Disability Rights and Independent Living Movement collection

getting around the city because the capital was not wheelchair accessible at that time. For example, in 1964 he was invited to the White House for the signing of the Urban Mass Transportation Act. This law was supposed to make it easier for people living with disabilities to get around on buses and subways. But passing laws was not enough. When Fred arrived at the White House, there were no ramps or elevators. He had to be bumped up the stairs in his wheelchair. This convinced him to keep fighting for accessibility.

Fred helped create and lead several important organizations in the 1970s. These organizations helped pass several important federal laws, including the Americans with Disabilities Act in 1990 (ADA). The ADA was a landmark civil rights law. It prohibits discrimination against people living with disabilities and ensures that they have equal access to all areas of public life, including education. For many decades, people with disabilities were completely excluded from society. They lived and went to school in places where they had no contact with the rest of the world. They were not considered valuable members of society. The ADA also helped challenge these ideas and made sure that people with disabilities had all the same opportunities to contribute to society as everyone else. In 1995, Fred cofounded Justice For All (JFA), which spread disability rights information to people all over the world. JFA has helped make sure laws like the ADA are maintained and strengthened.

Fred was a key figure in the disability rights movement. He believed that people living with disabilities could lead their own struggles for rights and dignity. He was an activist for most of his life. His work, his leadership, and his example live on and continue to inspire the work of many activists.

—Christine Darosa

## Timeline:

| | |
|---|---|
| 1944 | Born in Washington, DC |
| 1961 | Breaks neck, is paralyzed; cofounds support network Opening Doors |
| 1964 | Urban Mass Transportation Act passed |
| 1968 | Architectural Barriers Act passed |
| 1974 | Cofounds Boston Center for Independent Living |
| 1975 | Cofounds American Coalition of Citizens with Disabilities |
| 1975 | Individuals with Disabilities Education Act passed |
| 1980 | Cofounds Massachusetts Coalition of Citizens with Disabilities |
| 1990 | Americans with Disabilities Act passed |
| 1995 | Cofounds Justice For All |
| 1997 | Receives Henry B. Betts Award from the American Association of People with Disabilities, for improving life for people with disabilities |
| 2004 | Individuals with Disabilities Education Act passed |
| 2011 | Dies in Concord, Massachusetts |

## More you can do:

- Watch *A Life Worth Living*, a documentary film about Fred
- Check out the Youth Organizing! Disabled and Proud site: www.yodisabledproud.org
- Explore the University of California, Berkeley Disability Rights and Independent Living Movement Collection online
- Look around your school. What is or is not accessible to people with disabilities?

## What do you think?

- What kinds of challenges do people with disabilities face when using a public facility (a library, a school, sidewalks)? How is a wheelchair user's experience different from a blind person's? How about a deaf person's?
- Why is it important that people with disabilities are involved in the fight for equal access and protections?

# 87

# Wilma Pearl Mankiller

(1945–2010)

**Wilma Mankiller was the principal chief of the Cherokee Nation from 1985 to 1995. She was the first woman to be elected chief.**

Wilma's accomplishments as an activist and leader were important for the Cherokee people and many others, including Native American children. As Wilma once noted, "prior to my election, young Cherokee girls would never have thought that they might grow up and become chief."

Wilma was born in Tahlequah, Oklahoma, the capital of the Cherokee Nation. Tahlequah was established in 1838 when President Andrew Jackson forced thousands of Cherokee to relocate against their will. The Cherokee were made to leave their original home in the southeastern United States. This horrible tragedy is known as the "Trail of Tears." It was just one of many times when the US government took American Indian land and gave it to white settlers, plantation owners, and businessmen.

Growing up in the 1940s and 1950s, Wilma and her family faced many hardships, including poverty. Although her family drew strength from their community and their land, their home had no running water or electricity.

In the 1950s, Wilma's family was forced to relocate to San Francisco due to US government policy. The authorities intended to break up Native American nations and separate them

> **"The torch of protest and change was grasped by Native Americans. In 1969, the rage that helped to give a voice and spirit to other minority groups spread through Native people like a springtime prairie fire. . . . We too were given a renewal of energy and purpose."**
>
> —*Wilma Mankiller, in* Mankiller: A Chief and Her People *by Wilma Mankiller and Michael Harris, 1993*

from their land. Wilma later described her move to San Francisco as "total culture shock" and her "own little Trail of Tears."

Most Native Americans who relocated found it painful to leave their land and people behind. However, many were able to meet and work with people from different Indian nations for the first time. In San Francisco, Wilma's father worked as a longshoreman and became a union organizer. Wilma became active at the Indian Center in the Mission District. Campaigns for Indian rights began to grow along with other movements for civil rights and social justice.

In 1969, Native Americans involved in a group called Indians of All Tribes (IAT) took over Alcatraz Island, a small island off the San Francisco coast with a famous prison on it. IAT occupied Alcatraz in order to draw attention to injustices done to Native Americans. It also demanded that the United States honor promises made in past treaties with Native tribes.

During the nineteen-month occupation, Wilma went to the island repeatedly. She later said, "For the first time, people were saying things I felt but didn't know how to articulate. It was very liberating." Around the country, people joined the American Indian Movement to demand justice from the US government.

Wilma returned to Oklahoma in 1977 and went to work for the Cherokee Nation. Over the years, she worked on issues of education and community development while becoming a leading voice for justice for Native Americans. While her work in later years was a step back from the grassroots activism that changed America in the 1960s and 1970s, she made many contributions to improve the lives of her people. In 1991, she was reelected chief, winning 83 percent of the vote.

**—Michele Bollinger**

## Timeline:

| | |
|---|---|
| 1945 | Born in Tahlequah, Oklahoma |
| 1956 | Is forced to move to San Francisco |
| 1960s | Attends San Francisco State University |
| 1963 | Marries Hector Hugo; they have two children |
| 1969 | Occupation of Alcatraz Island begins |
| 1977 | Moves back to Cherokee land in Oklahoma |
| 1983 | Elected deputy chief of the Cherokee Nation |
| 1987 | Elected principal chief of the Cherokee Nation |
| 1991 | Reelected chief |
| 1995 | Steps down as chief |
| 2010 | Dies in Tahlequah |

## More you can do:

- Locate the Cherokee Constitution of 1827 and articles from the original *Cherokee Phoenix* newspaper. Identify issues and concerns of the Cherokee during this era

- Research the Trail of Tears and imagine you are with the Cherokee during this experience. Write a letter to another Native American of the Southeast—such as a member of the Seminole Nation—in which you describe your experience and give them advice about how to deal with the US government

## What do you think?

- What impact did the history of the Cherokee Nation have on Wilma's life?
- Why are Indian reservations important to Native American people? What makes reservation life difficult?
- Why might relocation have been a difficult experience for children like Wilma?
- Why was Wilma Mankiller's election important?
- How does Wilma's election compare to the election of women into positions of power in the US government today?

# 88

# August Wilson
## (1945–2005)

**Many black playwrights have given the world a glimpse of what it meant to be an African American. But few have created a body of work more celebrated than that of August Wilson.**

August wrote ten plays, known as the Pittsburgh Cycle (or the Century Cycle), that depicted the experience of African Americans from the 1900s to the 1990s.

He was born Frederick August Kittel on April 27, 1945, in Pittsburgh. August was named after his father, a white German immigrant who was mostly not there in August's life. August later took the last name of his black mother, Daisy Wilson. He grew up as a black child in a mostly white suburb at a

time when the civil rights movement had yet to emerge. He was the only black child in his class at a Catholic high school. He was bullied in school and got into many fights. In an interview August recalled, "There was a note on my desk every single day. It said, 'Go home, n----r.'" Eventually he left that high school. He left his next school, too, when his shop teacher punched him and August fought back. In this racially hostile setting, August sought to educate himself.

August left school for good when one of his teachers failed him on a paper that the teacher believed August did not write. He didn't tell his mother for months. Instead he spent time in the library. He immersed himself in the mostly black section of Pittsburgh called the Hill District, also known then as Little Harlem. Inspired by the everyday comedy and tragedy of the neighborhood men and women, August put what he heard around him on paper, into poetry.

Around the same time that August bought his first typewriter, black Americans across the nation began to adopt a new sense of racial pride. August and his friends founded their own journal, theater, and art gallery to promote black art. "As a twenty-three-year-old poet concerned about the world and struggling to find a place in it, I felt it a duty and an honor to participate," August later said. Without any formal training, the members of the Black Horizon Theater began staging plays about and for the black residents of Pittsburgh.

About ten years later, August earned a prestigious fellowship at the Playwrights Center in Minneapolis. There he wrote *Ma Rainey's Black Bottom*, a play about the effects of racism on a group of black musicians in 1927. *Ma Rainey* became the second play by a black writer to be produced on Broadway. It would also become the first play in August's cycle. The second, *Fences*, earned him a Pulitzer Prize in drama. He won another Pulitzer for his fourth play in the cycle, *The Piano Lesson*.

For the next fifteen years August continued to write and see his Pittsburgh Cycle plays produced. He continued to be vocal about the need for black theater made by black writers, actors, and directors. In 2005 August completed his cycle with *Radio Golf*. This was his last work for the stage.

Although August wrote plays for "blacks [to] see the content of their lives being elevated into art," his cycle of plays continues to influence generations of theatergoers from all walks of life.

—Idris Goodwin

## Timeline:

| | |
|---|---|
| 1945 | April 27, born Frederick August Kittel in Pittsburgh |
| 1960 | Drops out of high school |
| 1965 | Death of biological father, Frederick Kittel; changes name to August Wilson |
| 1968 | Cofounds the Black Horizon Theater with Rob Penny, Sala Udin, and others |
| 1980 | Fellowship at Minneapolis Playwrights Center |
| 1982 | National Playwrights Conference at O'Neill Theater Center in Connecticut accepts *Ma Rainey's Black Bottom*; meets O'Neill chief Lloyd Richards, who then directs Wilson's first six plays on Broadway |
| 1984 | *Ma Rainey* premieres at Yale Repertory Theatre, moves right to Broadway and wins August's first New York Drama Critics Circle Best Play award |
| 1987 | *Fences* opens on Broadway, starring James Earl Jones, wins NYDCC Award and August's first Pulitzer Prize, grosses a record $11 million in its first year |
| 1990 | *The Piano Lesson* opens on Broadway, wins NYDCC Award and second Pulitzer Prize |
| 2005 | *Radio Golf* premieres at Yale Repertory Theatre in March; August dies October 2, at age sixty, in Seattle; funeral takes place in Pittsburgh with a procession through the Hill District |

## More you can do:

- Listen to the *New York Times* interactive feature on August
- Watch an interview with August with Bill Moyers on YouTube
- Pick a scene from one of August's plays and act it out
- Watch the film of *The Piano Lesson* on YouTube

## What do you think?

- Given the difficulties August faced in school with both peers and teachers, do you think it was a good or bad decision to drop out?
- What do you think August meant in the quote above about blacks speaking "their own language"?

# 89

# Barbara Young

## (1947–)

**Barbara Young is one of the key organizers of the National Domestic Workers Alliance (NDWA). She is a former care provider who mobilizes domestic workers to improve their conditions.**

There are about 2.5 million domestic workers in the United States. Even though their work is enormously valuable, they often face long hours for low pay. Many have no health insurance through their employers and are often denied paid time off when they are sick. Immigrant women, some undocumented, make up most of the workforce. They sometimes experience racism as well as physical and other forms of abuse. Some are even modern-day slaves, illegally sold and forced to work in terrible conditions. These are

some of the issues Barbara tries to address. She speaks to activists, trade unionists, government officials, and many others to get her message across: domestic workers deserve to be treated with fairness, respect, and dignity.

Barbara grew up in a small town on the tropical island of Barbados in the Caribbean. Her mother was a homemaker and her father worked on a sugarcane plantation. He was very active in a union that defended the rights of his fellow workers. When Barbara finished school she moved to St. James, a bigger town on the island. There she worked as a bus conductor and was an activist in her union. "I'm very friendly and outgoing," she said. "And I just want to see people treated in a fair way." She worked for twenty years as a conductor

> "It was quite a shock to me when I came to the United States in 1993 to discover that domestics were excluded from the country's labor laws and regulations and they didn't have the rights of other workers. It was an eye-opener for me."
>
> —*Barbara Young, as quoted in "Been up North," profile,* Nation News *(Barbados), April 15, 2012*

until the government cut hundreds of jobs. The conductors were replaced by fare boxes and Barbara could not find well-paying work.

She decided to join her daughter in New York City in 1993. When Barbara first arrived she worked as a caregiver for an elderly person in Queens. Later she took a job as a live-in childcare provider, or nanny, and looked after the young children of working couples. She worked as a nanny for seventeen years. Barbara's work in this country has always been caring work. And it is "work that makes all other work possible." But she has had to endure a lot over the years. She recalls how one employer paid her the bare minimum for her daily nannying work and then expected her to sleep in the room with and feed an infant overnight, all for no extra pay. She explains: "Because you work in the home, people don't see you as an employee. It's seen as women's work, not proper work."

By 2001 she was talking to other care providers about banding together to better conditions for domestics. Domestic workers, like farmworkers, are specifically excluded from the National Labor Relations Act of the 1930s, the law that allows workers to form unions. Workers in private homes regularly operate in the shadows. Their pay and conditions are set by their employers without proper regulation. Barbara and others joined forces with Domestic Workers United to win basic labor rights for nannies, housekeepers, and caregivers.

In 2010 workers won a domestic worker bill of rights in New York that says they should have basic rights and protections including a forty-hour week, paid days off, overtime pay, and the right to organize as a group.

Barbara knows more rights like these for domestics would make a huge difference. "It recognizes domestic work as real work."

**—Dao X. Tran**

## Timeline:

**1947** Born Barbara Scantlebury in St. Peter, Barbados

**1965–85** Works as Barbados Transport Board conductor; represents Transport Board workers on the Barbados Workers' Union's executive council

**1993** Emigrates to New York; works as a caregiver in Queens

**1993–2010** Works as a nanny in Long Island and New York City

**2001** Begins agitating for better conditions for domestics and joins forces with Domestic Workers United (DWU)

**2003** Successful campaign for New York City mayor Michael Bloomberg to sign a bill protecting domestic workers working through an agency

**2004** Joins DWU's steering committee; helps expand DWU's membership and deepen its impact; works to build a global domestic workers' movement

**2010** Domestic Workers' Bill of Rights in New York passes; Barbara takes job organizing full time for NDWA

**2011** NDWA launches Caring Across Generations, a national campaign to address the working conditions of people providing direct care to our nation's elderly and people with disabilities

## More you can do:

- **Watch some of the stories of domestic workers and those they care for at domesticworkers.org and www.caringacrossgenerations.org**
- **Read the New York State Domestic Worker Bill of Rights and design a flyer promoting its key points**

## What do you think?

- **Why have domestic workers historically been excluded from labor laws and protections?**
- **Do you think work done in the home—housekeeping and taking care of the elderly, the disabled, and children—is "real" work? Why or why not?**
- **Does your city, county, or state offer similar protections to the New York State Domestic Worker Bill of Rights? If not, what could you do to help pass them?**

# 90

# Sylvia Rae Rivera
## (1951–2002)

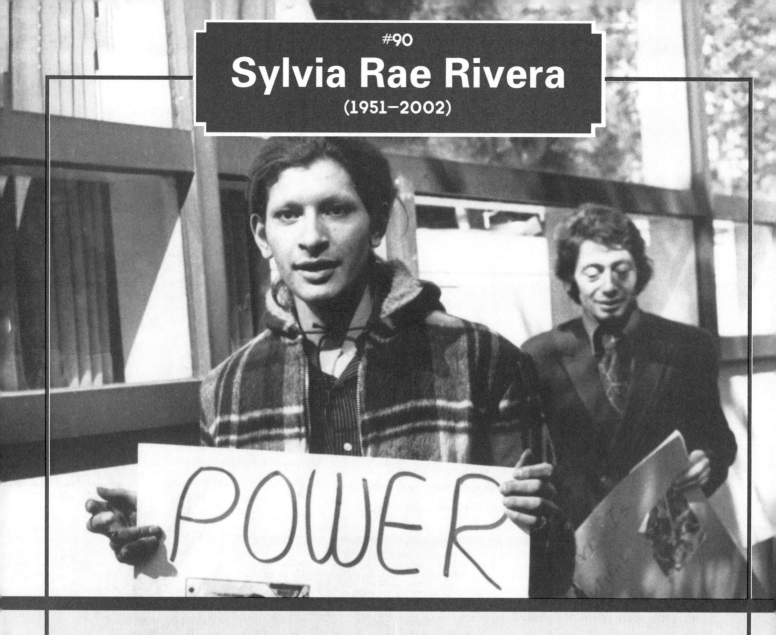

**Sylvia Rae Rivera was a pioneer in the fight against gay, lesbian, bisexual, and transgender (LGBT) oppression. She was a transgender woman, meaning she was born male but felt more female.**

Even though Sylvia played a leading role in the fight for gay civil rights in the 1960s, she was often not recognized in that history. Today she is known to some as the founder of the transgender rights movement and is given credit for adding the "T" in LGBT.

Sylvia was born in New York City in 1951 as a boy named Rey Rivera Mendoza. She was Venezuelan and Puerto Rican. Her father left when she was a baby and her mother died a few years later. Sylvia became an orphan when she was

three years old. She was raised by her grandmother, who treated her terribly for being dark-skinned, wearing makeup, and behaving "like a girl." Sylvia's life was painful and hard. She said that she grew up without love. At the very young age of eleven, Sylvia left home and lived on the streets. Sometimes she did illegal things in order to survive. This was when she changed her name to Sylvia Rae Rivera.

During the 1960s and '70s, Sylvia was known as a Puerto Rican street "drag queen" because the word *transgender* didn't exist yet. Life on the street was hard. Drag queens faced constant beatings by police and bigots. Sylvia and others like her even ended up in jail. Despite this, she was active in many movements against racism, the war in Vietnam, the sexism, and

> "I've had a very hard struggle. I tell these stories of my life because I know that my children, in later years, my transgender community, will understand we have to stand up and speak for ourselves. We have to fight for ourselves!"
>
> —*Sylvia Rivera, from the documentary* Sylvia Rivera: A Trans Life Story

economic inequality. But she is most well known for her efforts in the gay rights movement.

At seventeen, Sylvia helped lead the Stonewall Rebellion in 1969. These were several days of protests after police raided a bar called the Stonewall Inn. Sylvia was there the night of the raid and became a founding member of the Gay Activists Alliance and the Gay Liberation Front after the riots. She was a fearless leader of the new gay rights movement, but she was constantly sidelined and harassed because she was transgender and Puerto Rican. Trans people like young Sylvia played an important role during the Stonewall Rebellion. However, they were not included in the gay rights movement. Some of its leaders thought trans people made the movement look bad. They didn't like the way transgender people dressed and considered them not "normal." Some in the movement thought transgender women like Sylvia were not "real" women.

This made Sylvia very angry. She felt it was wrong for those in the gay rights movement to leave out the rights of transgender people, poor people, and minority people of all ethnicities. They were often homeless, poor, and oppressed but were not included or defended in the mostly white, male gay rights movement. Silvia went to meetings to speak passionately in support of the people left out of the movement. She kept up this fight by being a "mother" to many homeless LGBT kids and demanding policies to promote equality for transgender people.

Sylvia was a fighter against all forms of oppression who saw all struggles for social change as connected. Her legacy lives on through efforts like the Sylvia Rivera Law Project, which provides transgender people with services and aids in the fight for their rights.

—Akua Gyamerah

## Timeline:

| | |
|---|---|
| 1951 | Born in New York City to Puerto Rican and Venezuelan parents |
| 1954 | Moves in with her grandmother after her father leaves and mother dies |
| 1962–63 | Leaves home to live on the streets |
| 1969 | June, fights alongside others at the Stonewall Inn when the police attack it and participates in the riots that follow; helps found the Gay Liberation Front (GLF) and the Gay Activists Alliance (GAA) |
| 1970 | Founds the Street Transvestite Action Revolutionaries along with close friend Marsha P. Johnson because GLF and GAA are not welcoming enough to poor and transgender people of color; continues to participate in GLF and GAA |
| 1970s–92 | Leaves gay rights activism because the gay rights movement excludes transgender people in a gay rights bill she fought for; focuses on transgender rights issues |
| 1994 | During the Stonewall 25th anniversary march, leads a separate march in protest of the exclusion of transgender people from the history of Stonewall |
| 1995 | Attempts to drown herself in the Hudson River |
| 2002 | Dies from liver cancer |

## More you can do:

- Watch "Sylvia Rivera Trans Movement Founder" on YouTube and the "OutRage '69" episode of the PBS documentary series *The Question of Equality*

## What do you think?

- Do you think that everyone's gender identity does, or should, match their apparent biological sex?
- How are transgender rights different from and similar to gay and lesbian rights?
- Do you think Sylvia's hope for LGBT civil rights has been realized? Why or why not?

# 91

# Mary Beth Tinker

(1952–)

**Mary Beth Tinker is a nurse, union organizer, and activist. Mary Beth, her brother John, and their friend Chris were at the heart of the landmark Supreme Court ruling *Tinker v. Des Moines* (1969).**

Mary Beth grew up in Iowa with her family. Her father was a minister. Her parents were dedicated to social justice. As she grew older, Mary Beth became more aware of issues and conflicts in her community.

In 1964 Mary Beth's parents took her to Mississippi to support the work of civil rights activists. By 1965 many people also became concerned about the US war in Vietnam.

The people of Vietnam wanted to decide their government for themselves, but the US government interfered in the conflict. The war became unpopular because tens of thousands of US soldiers and millions of Vietnamese and other Southeast Asian people were killed or wounded.

In 1965 Mary Beth was thirteen and in the eighth grade. She and her brother began to publicly oppose the war in Vietnam. She had seen images of the war on the news and was alarmed by the "gruesome things that were being done to the Vietnamese people. . . . I could not sit by and watch this happening to kids thousands of miles away on the other side of the world."

Mary Beth, her brother, and their friends decided to wear black armbands to school to express their views. The administration found out about their plan. The school board banned the armbands, calling them "disruptive," and promised to suspend students who wore them.

The students wore the armbands and were suspended. After they returned to school, they wore black clothes in protest of how they were treated. The Tinkers believed that the school system violated their right to free speech, which is guaranteed in the First Amendment to the Constitution. With the help of the American Civil Liberties Union, they filed a lawsuit against the school system.

Not everyone supported the Tinkers in their fight. There was a backlash against their actions. Some people even threatened Mary Beth and her family with violence. But in 1969 the Supreme Court sided with the Tinkers. The highest court in the United States agreed that the school board had no right to prevent students from wearing the armbands and expressing their views. Justice Abe Fortas famously wrote that students and teachers do not "shed their constitutional rights to freedom of speech or expression at the schoolhouse gate."

The precedent set by the Tinker case has been applied to more recent cases involving student activists. For example, in 2003 sixteen-year-old Michigan student Bretton Barber went to court for his right to wear a T-shirt that criticized President George Bush. In 2008 Florida student Heather Gillman successfully challenged school officials' attempts to ban rainbows and other symbols of LGBT expression.

Today, Mary Beth educates students and community groups about their constitutional rights and encourages them to fight for their rights.

—Michele Bollinger

## Timeline:

| | |
|---|---|
| 1952 | Born in Des Moines, Iowa |
| 1963 | March on Washington takes place |
| 1964 | President Lyndon Johnson sends more troops to Vietnam |
| | Tinker family travels to Mississippi with a group of minorities to support the civil rights movement |
| 1965 | Wears armband to school; is suspended |
| 1968 | US District Court rules against Mary Beth and her friends |
| 1969 | US Supreme Court rules in favor of their right to free speech |
| 1970 | Graduates from St. Louis University |
| 1970s-present | Works as a pediatric nurse; speaks and educates students about free speech and standing up for their rights |

## More you can do:

- Explore resources at www.band-of-rights.org and www.aclu.org on the case
- Mary Beth and her friends wore armbands to protest the war—think of something you want to speak out about and design an item of clothing or other symbol you could use to make a statement

## What do you think?

- Where did the "right to free speech" come from? Why is it important?
- Why did Mary Beth and others choose to wear armbands? What did they hope to accomplish?
- What reasons do school officials give for limiting or banning students' views? Do you agree that these limits are unacceptable? Why or why not?

Julia "Judy" Bonds was an activist who fought against what is called "mountaintop removal." This type of mining was ruining her community and destroying the environment.

She died on January 3, 2011, of cancer but she left behind a movement for the environment that was stronger than before.

Judy was an ordinary person. She worked most of her life as a waitress in the tiny community of Marfork Hollow in West Virginia. But as she got older she was inspired to fight the coal companies who were ruining the area her family had lived in for over a hundred years.

Her inspiration came from her young grandson. One day her grandson went fishing in the local creek where people in the area had fished for years. That day, he found dead fish on the ground and floating in the water. It turned out that the dust from coal companies blowing up the mountaintops got in the creeks and killed the fish.

Another day Judy and her grandson were sitting on the porch at their house. They were talking about the Massey Energy company building a new dam in the area. It would be used to hold back dirty water from mining the coal. If the dam failed it would flood their valley with poisonous water. Other dams had failed in other valleys not far from them. Judy's seven-year-old grandson told her he wanted to plan an escape route in case their dam broke.

> **In southern West Virginia we live in a war zone. Three and one half million pounds of explosives are being used every day to blow up the mountains. Blasting our communities, blasting our homes, poisoning us . . . I don't mind being poor. I mind being blasted and poisoned.**
>
> —Judy Bonds, in an October 10, 2008, speech to the Maine People's Alliance

Hearing her grandson's stories and concerns worried Judy. Also, a lot of families like hers were moving away because of the mountaintop removal. She once showed a reporter a flower near her house and said, "That's the ironweed. They say they're the symbol of Appalachian women. They're pretty. And their roots run deep. It's hard to move them!" These were words she lived by. Others left, but Judy decided to stand and fight.

She began to volunteer at Coal River Mountain Watch (CRMW). This was a local group that protested the companies and the government to get them to stop mountaintop removal. Judy was so good at organizing protests and talking to people about the issue that she became the director of the group.

In 2003 she received the Goldman Environmental Prize for her work in trying to protect the environment. She paid some personal bills with the award money. But she donated a large part to CRMW so it could continue its work.

In 2010 CRMW sued Massey Energy for violating the Clean Water Act. Judy was key in organizing thousands of people in support of this lawsuit to march in Washington, DC, as part of "Appalachia Rising." This is a movement to convince the US Congress to stop giving permits that allow mountaintop removal. More than one hundred people were arrested for refusing to leave the offices of the Environmental Protection Agency. This protest made the cause of stopping mountaintop removal a well-known issue all over the United States.

More people are aware of the problems that mountaintop removal causes than ever before. Judy inspired a whole new generation of young people who want to work for clean energy and against the destruction of the environment and communities.

**—Joe Cleffie**

## Timeline:

| | |
|---|---|
| 1957 | Born in Marfork Hollow, West Virginia |
| 1998 | Joins Coal River Mountain Watch |
| 1999 | Leaves Marfork Hollow because it is no longer safe |
| 2001 | Becomes outreach director for Coal River Mountain Watch |
| 2003 | Receives the Goldman Environmental Prize for her work |
| 2010 | CRMW sues Massey Energy |
| 2010 | September "Appalachia Rising" march in Washington, DC; around a hundred arrested |
| 2011 | Dies in January at the age of fifty-eight |

## More you can do:

- **Read** *Coal River* **by Michael Shnayerson**
- **Watch these documentaries:** *Coal River; Coal Country;* **and** *Black Diamonds: Mountaintop Removal* **and** *the Fight for Coalfield Justice*
- **Watch the music video "The Hand of Man" by Magnolia Mountain. The lyrics include the line: "We have no wealth, we have no voice / we have no power and no choice." What does this mean to you?**

## What do you think?

- **What is mountaintop removal? In what ways is it harmful to the environment?**
- **People sometimes argue that industry is good for poor communities and that environmental worries like Judy's are exaggerated. Do you agree or disagree?**
- **Did Judy make the right choice in fighting the coal companies? Would you have done the same in her position?**

**Cleve Jones has been a leader in the struggle for lesbian, gay, bisexual, and transgender (LGBT) rights since the 1970s.**

Cleve was bullied as a teenager for being gay. He often felt alone and angry. But he found an outlet in activism. At Arizona State University, Cleve joined Gay Liberation Arizona Desert (GLAD), one of the first gay rights groups at a major university. When Cleve was seventeen, he told his father he was gay. His family responded badly. Feeling rejected, Cleve moved to San Francisco, where there was a large gay community. This was at a time when LGBT people were largely invisible in most places and had almost no rights.

In the mid-1970s, Cleve met Harvey Milk, a leader in the gay rights movement. In 1976, orange juice spokesperson Anita Bryant launched a campaign to overturn a law banning discrimination against gays and lesbians in Florida. Cleve worked with Milk to stand up to this attack. He led marches of thousands in opposition. Bryant was successful, but the forces that opposed her were part of what grew to become the gay rights movement.

The next year, Cleve worked with Harvey to help launch a major campaign against the Briggs Initiative, an attempt by State Senator John Briggs to ban openly gay teachers from California schools. Briggs led an attack on gay teachers based on lies. He smeared gays as predators and said that they posed a "threat" to children. Cleve organized a conference of students from across the state. Harvey led a campaign involving everyone from Democrats to labor unionists and socialists. The campaign that Cleve helped lead ultimately defeated the Briggs Initiative. It was a major victory for the gay rights movement.

In the early 1980s, the HIV/AIDS epidemic hit the gay community. Thousands of gay men died of AIDS during the 1980s. President Ronald Reagan refused to even mention the disease until 1987. Government funding for treatment or a cure was almost nonexistent. Cleve organized the first public forum on AIDS in 1982 and helped found the San Francisco AIDS Foundation. Cleve was diagnosed with HIV in 1985.

After his diagnosis, Cleve devoted his life to a new project. He founded the NAMES Project AIDS Memorial Quilt. The AIDS quilt is a giant quilt made up of thousands of quilts stitched together. Each quilt was made by the family or friends of someone who had died of AIDS. The project grew to include thousands of quilts and was displayed yearly on the National Mall in Washington, DC, from 1987 to 1996. The quilt became famous around the world. It helped raise awareness about AIDS, educated people, and raised money for AIDS service organizations.

In recent years, Cleve has worked for the union UNITE HERE, connecting the labor and LGBT rights movements with his "Sleep with the Right People" campaign. In 2009, Cleve was a key organizer of the grassroots National Equality March. About two hundred thousand people marched on the Capitol Building in Washington, DC, to demand full equality for LGBT people.

—**Gary Lapon**

## Timeline:

| | |
|---|---|
| 1954 | Born in West Lafayette, Indiana |
| 1972 | Moves to San Francisco |
| 1976–78 | Meets Harvey Milk; helps lead a campaign against the attack on gay rights in Florida and around the country; helps defeat the Briggs Initiative |
| 1978–79 | Milk and Mayor George Moscone are killed by San Francisco Supervisor Dan White; Cleve organizes a memorial march. When White is sentenced to five years in prison, riots erupt. Cleve is brought before a grand jury for his role but refuses to apologize for the spontaneous outpouring of anger |
| 1980 | Hired in Sacramento by a consulting firm attached to the state Democratic Party; hears about a new disease killing gay men, which turns out to be AIDS |
| 1982 | Helps found the San Francisco AIDS Foundation and organizes the first public forum on the AIDS epidemic |
| 1985 | Is diagnosed with HIV; organizes a march in San Francisco marking Milk's assassination in which activists paste placards with the names of those who had died of AIDS on a government building; forms the idea for the AIDS quilt |
| 1987–1996 | The NAMES Project AIDS Memorial Quilt is displayed on the National Mall |
| 2009 | Is a leading organizer of the National Equality March |

## More you can do:

- **Read Cleve Jones and Jeff Dawson's** *Stitching a Revolution: The Making of an Activist*
- **Check out Cleve's website: www.clevejones.com**

## What do you think?

- **What is Cleve's approach to changing the world?**
- **Why do you think it took so many years of struggle to get the government to devote resources to addressing the AIDS epidemic?**
- **LGBT people still don't have equality today. What do you think it will take to change that?**

# Lam Duong
## (1954–1981)

**Lam Duong was a student, activist, community worker, and journalist. Born in Hanoi, Vietnam, Lam was ten years old when the war in Vietnam broke out. He was the middle child in his family and was bright and ambitious.**

Lam came to Athens, Georgia, in 1971 as a high school senior through an exchange program. Even though this was after the civil rights movement, racism was still alive. He saw how African Americans were treated and faced discrimination himself while living there.

He soon moved to Oberlin, Ohio, which was more accepting of people from diverse backgrounds. At Oberlin College, Lam became

more and more critical of the war in Vietnam and US military actions. During this time, he sponsored his sisters and brothers to come to Oberlin.

Soon after graduating, Lam moved to San Francisco with his college girlfriend. He began working for a Vietnamese refugee aid organization. Dissatisfied with the way it was run, he started his own center, called the Vietnamese Youth Development Center. It was the first center dedicated to helping Vietnamese refugee youth and developing their leadership skills.

Soon after the war in Vietnam ended in 1975, more than two hundred thousand Southeast Asian refugees came to the United States. Several thousand resettled in San Francisco. Lam wanted to educate them on their rights as new Americans. He also helped them apply for social services such as housing, food stamps, and health care. Lam's dream was to organize this new community so that they could advocate for their rights.

Lam also started a Vietnamese radio show at the University of San Francisco and a Vietnamese-language newspaper. As well as running original stories, the newspaper, *Cái Đình Làng* (the *Village Temple*), also reprinted articles from Vietnam's state-run press.

Lam was educated in America and had liberal and radical ideas about politics and freedom of speech. Many Vietnamese refugees disliked Lam's views and thought he was a Communist agent. Most of the refugees who came after the war were conservative anticommunists who fled Vietnam when the Communists came to power. They had a lot of anger and hatred toward Communists. Many were soldiers during the war who still had dreams of going back to Vietnam and reclaiming the country. Within this war mentality, some started a militant group called the Front.

On July 27, 1981, Lam Duong was shot and killed outside his apartment in broad daylight in San Francisco's Tenderloin neighborhood. His murder remains unsolved, but many in the community believe members of the Front did it. Lam's was the first in a string of murders of Vietnamese American journalists. Between 1981 and 1990, four other Vietnamese journalists who were thought to be "Communists" were killed in the United States. None of the cases was ever solved. Many believe Lam was targeted for exercising his freedom of speech by publishing his newspaper. The youth center he founded still exists and continues to serve low-income Southeast Asian and multiracial youth in San Francisco.

—**Momo Chang and Tony Nguyen**

## Timeline:

| | |
|---|---|
| 1954 | June 19, born in Hanoi, Vietnam |
| 1964 | US Congress signs Gulf of Tonkin Resolution, giving President Johnson full authority to escalate the war in Vietnam |
| 1971 | Moves to Athens, Georgia, to attend school in the United States |
| 1972–76 | Studies math and philosophy at Oberlin College |
| 1975 | The war in Vietnam ends and more than 200,000 new refugees arrive in the United States |
| 1976 | Moves to San Francisco |
| 1976 | Works at the Center for Southeast Asian Refugee Resettlement |
| 1977 | Starts the Vietnamese Youth Development Center, the first organization for Vietnamese refugee youth in the United States |
| 1978 | Produces and hosts a Vietnamese radio program on refugee rights and services |
| 1980 | Begins publishing *Cái Đình Làng*, for which he writes and reprints articles from Vietnam |
| 1978–80 | Is labeled a Communist agent and protested against by conservative Vietnamese Americans |
| 1981 | Shot and killed outside his apartment in San Francisco; his murder remains unsolved |

## More you can do:

- **Watch *Enforcing the Silence*, a documentary on Lam by Tony Nguyen**
- **Read "Silenced: The Unsolved Murders of Immigrant Journalists in the United States," a report from the Committee to Protect Journalists**

## What do you think?

- **How was Lam different from many other Vietnamese in the United States?**
- **What do you think Lam meant when he said, "The only thing a young Vietnamese man wants is to see peace?"**
- **Is freedom of speech the same in all communities?**

# 95

# Fernando Suarez del Solar
## (1955–)

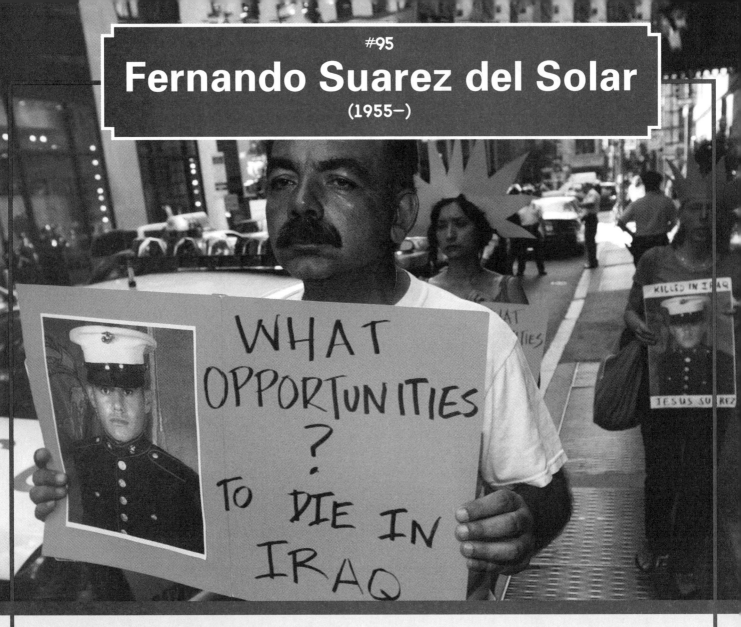

**Fernando Suarez del Solar is an antiwar activist working to see no more "green card marines." Since 2003 he has discouraged low-income immigrant youth from joining the military.**

Fernando was against an invasion of Iraq from the beginning. But he became much more active after his son Jesus, a marine, died in Iraq.

In the first week of its invasion of Iraq, the US military dropped many cluster bombs, which each released hundreds of small bomblets over a wide area. Unexploded bomblets look like cans of beer or soda, are easy to step on, and often explode randomly. On March 27, 2003, Jesus's marine unit was ordered to en-

ter part of the Iraqi desert on foot. None of the soldiers (or the Iraqis living nearby) were told that cluster bombs had been dropped in the area the day before.

When Jesus stepped on an undetonated cluster bomb, the blast ripped into his body. The other marines were told to leave the area. The commanding officer refused to let anyone help Jesus because it was too dangerous. He lay there, alone, suffering for two hours. Twenty-year-old Jesus left behind his wife and one-year-old son, his mother, three sisters, and his father, Fernando.

Before moving to the United States, the Suarez family lived in Tijuana, Mexico. Fernando was a noted activist there, fighting for

"Immigrants are generally the first on the front lines. They should know where they'll end up."

—Fernando Suarez del Solar

poorer neighborhoods to have running water and working sewage systems. Many of Jesus's friends died from violence related to the drug war. Jesus wanted to move to the United States so he could work for the Drug Enforcement Agency (DEA) to prevent any more deaths.

A military recruiter working in Mexico told Jesus he could be working at the DEA within a year if he came to the United States and joined the Marine Corps. Jesus was promised he would be safe in the marines. The Suarez family crossed the border so Jesus could pursue this goal.

To help support his family in the United States, Fernando worked as a newspaper deliveryman and a cashier at a 7-Eleven. After Jesus died, Fernando began speaking out.

Fernando had deep experience as an organizer in Tijuana. He connected the issues of war, racism, and immigration to social justice. Hearing Fernando tell the vivid and tearful story of Jesus's death has convinced many young Latinos not to join the military.

Fernando's message has been heard far beyond the Latino/a community. He has visited Iraq more than once, bringing thousands of letters of greeting and peace from US children—for both soldiers and Iraqi children. He continues to campaign today and has spoken at more than 150 different schools across the United States and Mexico helpng students to understand what war means and to find alternatives to joining the military.

—Jason Farbman

## Timeline:

| | |
|---|---|
| 1955 | Born in Mexico City, Mexico |
| 1990s | Moves with wife Rosa and their four children, Karla, Olivia, Jesus, and Claudia, to Tijuana |
| 1995 | Receives a "Civic Service" award for outstanding citizen of the year for organizing neighborhood committees so that poor communities will have running water and sewer systems |
| 1996 | Jesus Suarez first meets Marine Corps recruiters on a shopping trip at age thirteen |
| 1997 | Family emigrates from Tijuana |
| 2003 | Jesus Suarez dies on March 27 |
| 2003 | Founds Aztec Warrior Peace Project |
| 2004 | Appears in documentary *Hijacking Catastrophe: 9/11, Fear and the Selling of American Empire* |
| 2004–2005 | Travels with Rosa as part of an antiwar delegation to Fallujah, Iraq; they bring $600,000 in cash and humanitarian aid for civilians on "the other side" |
| 2004–2006 | Testifies in antiwar tribunals in Massachusetts, New York, Italy, Japan, and Venezuela |
| 2007 | Appears in documentary *Camilo: The Long Road to Disobedience* |

## More you can do:

- Invite counter-recruiters from a local antiwar or peace group to your school to do a workshop and discussion
- Watch *Camilo: The Long Road to Disobedience*

## What do you think?

- What is a "green card marine"?
- Why do you think poorer communities—including many immigrants—are targets for military recruiters?
- Billions of dollars have been spent on wars in Iraq and Afghanistan. At the same time, schools and hospitals are being closed across the United States. What would you do with the money spent on war if you could make that decision?
- Why are US military recruiters talking to students in Mexico?

# 96

# Tony Kushner

(1956—)

**Tony Kushner is one of the most important left-wing playwrights in the United States today. His most famous play is *Angels in America: A Gay Fantasia on National Themes*.**

It is a two-part play about the AIDS disease in New York during the Reagan era. Tony won the Pulitzer Prize and the Tony Award for *Angels*. It was later made into a miniseries. Tony wrote the screenplay and it earned him an Emmy in 2004.

Tony was born in New York City in 1956. His parents were both musicians who grew up in the Depression era. They were also activists. His family later moved to Louisiana, where Tony was raised. His experiences growing up in a Jewish community in the South during the sixties inspired one of his later plays, *Caroline, or Change*. The musical is set in Louisiana during the civil rights era. It is about the struggles of an African American maid working for a Jewish family.

Tony went to Columbia University in New York City from 1974 to 1978. He became more involved in theater during this time, and also became more politically active. He participated in a movement to stop the city from shutting down a local public library. And he was involved in the struggle against apartheid, a racial system of segregation and discrimination in South Africa.

After graduating from college, Tony continued

> " Marx was right: The smallest divisible human unit is two people; not one; one is a fiction. From such nets of souls societies, the social world, human life springs. And also plays. "
>
> —*Tony Kushner, from the afterword to* Angels in America: Perestroika

to work in theater. He graduated from New York University's Graduate Acting program in 1984. In 1991, Tony reached national fame with *Angels in America*. Over the next two years, both parts of the play, *Millennium Approaches* and *Perestroika*, were performed in San Francisco, Los Angeles, New York, and London.

Tony also wrote many other plays. *A Bright Room Called Day* is about a group of friends in Germany during Hitler's rise to power. *Homebody/Kabul* is a play about the war in Afghanistan. He also wrote *The Intelligent Homosexual's Guide to Capitalism and Socialism with a Key to the Scriptures*. This play tells the story of Gus Marcantonio, a retired longshoreman, union activist, and former member of the Communist Party in Brooklyn. It played to a sold-out audience at the Public Theater in New York City in 2011.

Tony's plays have a wide appeal because they give voice to people in society who are often ignored. All of his plays explore the relationship between the personal and the political. They all deal with themes of social justice.

Tony is also a political activist. He has been a fighter for gay rights and in the movement for marriage equality. Tony has spoken out against the wars in Iraq and Afghanistan. As a member of Jewish Voice for Peace, he has also opposed Israel's violence against Palestinians. In 2011, a trustee of the City University of New York tried to prevent Tony from getting an honorary degree because of his comments about Israel. This led to public protest. As a result, Tony was given the honorary degree in May. Later that year, he was awarded the annual Puffin/Nation Prize for Creative Citizenship. This award is given to artists and others for "socially responsible work" and "challenges to authority."

**—Megan Behrent**

## Timeline:

**1956** Born in New York City

**1958** Moves to Louisiana

**1978** Graduates from Columbia University

**1985** *A Bright Room Called Day* is first performed in New York City

**1991** *Angels in America: Millennium Approaches* is first performed in New York City

**1993** Awarded the Pulitzer Prize for Drama and the Tony Award for Best Play for *Angels in America: Millennium Approaches*

**1994** Awarded the Tony for Best Play for *Angels in America: Perestroika*

**2003** Speaks at massive protest against the war in Iraq; commitment ceremony with Mark Harris is the first same-sex ceremony to be reported in the "Vows" section of the *New York Times*

**2004** Awarded an Emmy for *Angels in America*

**2007** Receives the Laurence Olivier Award for Best New Musical for *Caroline, or Change*

**2008** Marries Mark Harris in Massachusetts

**2011** Awarded an honorary degree by the City University of New York (despite political opposition) and the Puffin/Nation Prize for Creative Citizenship; *Intelligent Homosexual* is performed in New York City

## More you can do:

- See the film adaptation of *Angels in America*
- Read the interview "Finding the Truth Where Certainties Collide" in *ISR* magazine

## What do you think?

- How do you think Tony's experiences growing up as a gay Jewish man in the South might have influenced his ideas and/or his plays?
- Why do you think *Angels in America* touched so many people? What made it so powerful? Can you think of plays or movies today that might have a similar impact?
- Was it right to take away an honorary degree from Tony (or any writer) for his political views?

# 97

# Chuck D
## (1960—)

Legendary rap artist and political activist Chuck D was born Carlton Douglas Ridenhour on August 1, 1960, in Queens, New York. He went to college at Adelphi University on Long Island, studying graphic design.

On campus, Carlton delivered furniture and worked at the college radio station. During this time, he helped to start the groundbreaking hip-hop group Public Enemy (PE). Other members were Flavor Flav, Professor Griff, the S1Ws, DJ Lord (who replaced Terminator X in 1999) and a group of musical composers and producers known as the Bomb Squad. Journalist Harry Allen is the group's "Media Assassin."

In PE, Carlton was reborn as Chuck D, a politically conscious poet-rapper with a distinctive, booming, deep voice. His music and lyrics are in the tradition of what is known as the Black Arts movement. Chuck D considers himself part of this movement, the cultural grandson to writers such as Amiri Baraka, Sonia Sanchez, Nikki Giovanni, Gil Scott-Heron, and the Last Poets. In the conservative 1980s, Chuck D's lyrics and the music of Public Enemy helped to educate a generation of listeners about the importance of history, love for one's community, and having the power and courage to stand up and speak out for what you believe in. PE's second and third albums, *It Takes a Nation of Millions to Hold Us Back* and *Fear of a Black Planet*, are considered classics. Songs like "Don't Believe the Hype,"

> "My beloved let's get down to business
> Mental self-defensive fitness"
>
> —Chuck D, "Fight the Power"

"Bring the Noise," "911 Is a Joke," and "By the Time I Get to Arizona" became anthems of their era.

The 1989 Spike Lee film *Do the Right Thing* highlighted what remains PE's most iconic song, "Fight the Power." "Fight the Power" plays a large role in telling the story through a central character, Radio Raheem. In this song, which has become a classic song of hip-hop resistance, Chuck D advocates for the inclusion of *all* peoples into US history. He rhymes:

"I'm Black and I'm proud / I'm ready and hyped plus I'm amped / Most of my heroes don't appear on no stamps / Sample a look back you look and find / Nothing but rednecks for four hundred years if you check"

This insistence that people of color be included fully in the media and in the story of America remained a consistent theme in PE's music and in Chuck D's raps. He criticized Hollywood, radio stations, and the state and federal governments for excluding diverse images, ideas, and celebrations of black culture and expression.

To ensure these stories are told, Chuck D started his own website, Rapstation.com, and record company, SlamJamz. Rapstation was one of the first sites on which you could download music. Chuck D was an early advocate and champion of distributing music over the internet via MP3s, a format virtually unknown at the time. He wanted to give artists more freedom and financial rewards. In doing so, he helped to change the music industry in another way.

Chuck D remains a voice for resistance as a musician, performer, and radio host. Whenever there is injustice, Chuck D is there.

**—Kevin Coval**

## Timeline:

1960   Born on August 1 in Queens, New York

1982   Meets Flavor Flav and forms Public Enemy

1987   Releases *Yo! Bum Rush the Show*

1988   *It Takes a Nation of Millions to Hold Us Back*

1990   *Fear of a Black Planet*

1991   *Apocalypse 91... The Enemy Strikes Black*

1996   *Autobiography of Mistachuck*

1998   *He Got Game* (soundtrack); publishes the book *Fight the Power: Rap, Race, and Reality* with Yusuf Jah

1999   Launches Rapstation.com

2000   Appeared on May 12 episode of the *Charlie Rose Show*, in a debate with Lars Ulrich (famous for leading the charge against Napster), addressing the need for a more democratic media and music industry

2004   Hosts radio show, *Unfiltered*

## More you can do:

- Thinking about the importance Chuck D places on knowing your history, document in what ways you do or don't see yourself represented in the media
- Watch the Spike Lee film *Do the Right Thing* and look for how the song "Fight the Power" is used
- Listen to "911 is a Joke," "Black Steel in the Hour of Chaos," and "Fight the Power." Compare the messages in each song

## What do you think?

- What is "the power" Chuck D talks about fighting?
- Who are your favorite rappers?
- How do you listen to new music?
- Why does Chuck D think it is important to distribute music over the internet? Do you agree?
- Research the economic, social, and political problems in Los Angeles between 1988 and 1993. How did these problems lead to the LA Rebellion in 1992?

# 98

# Bhairavi Desai
## (1972–)

**Bhairavi Desai is an Indian American activist who has been involved in many causes including women's, immigrants', and workers' rights. She is best known as one of the founders of the New York Taxi Workers Alliance (NYTWA).**

She was born in Gujarat, India, in 1972 and moved to New Jersey with her parents and older brother when she was six years old. As she grew up she saw the tough life that is common to immigrant families. Her father worked constantly in the family grocery store and her mother and brother worked hard in factories. The family experienced racism, too. As a child Bhairavi was chased down the street by men who tried to hurt her because she was a person of color and an immigrant.

She feels strongly that people who work hard for a living deserve respect and a decent life, no matter what country they are from or how much money they make.

Through her family's hard work, Bhairavi was able to go to college. She went to Rutgers University and graduated with a degree in women's studies. Even though she might have made more money by becoming a college professor, she was set on helping others. After graduating she joined the South Asian women's group Manavi, working with women who are survivors of domestic violence.

At age twenty-three she joined the Committee Against Anti-Asian Violence (CAAAV), which organizes people of Asian origin and

We've got to have a plan of action. The best way to get inside City Hall is to make noise on the street.

—Bhairavi Desai, as quoted in "Thin Yellow Line," New Yorker, April 18, 2011

descent. This group helped to form the Lease Drivers Coalition. Its members talked to taxi drivers about their work and lives and tried to find ways to help to make their conditions better. They saw that most taxi drivers were being treated unfairly. Drivers work around sixty to seventy hours a week. But because of very high fees to rent the cab and to pay for permission to drive it, they may only take home around $300 to $400 per week. It is very hard to live on that little money in New York City. Most cab drivers have to work other jobs to feed their families and pay rent. It is also a very dangerous job. Taxi drivers are often the victims of robbery and violence.

In August 1997, CAAAV organized a demonstration of more than two thousand drivers and cabs. The people who set the high fees, the Taxi and Limousine Commission (TLC), saw this and realized they would have to talk about lowering fees.

In February 1998, Bhairavi and others formed the NYTWA to bring cab drivers together to fight for a better life. New York mayor Rudy Giuliani proposed increased costs and new rules that drivers thought were unfair. In May 1998, the cab drivers went on strike. More than 90 percent of New York City's twelve thousand cab drivers did not work during the strike. The strike did not stop all the unfair fees and treatment. And New York City and the TLC still make it hard for taxi drivers to make a living. But they showed that striking—a collective action—could have an effect.

Thanks to Bhairavi and people like her, cab drivers are now organized to fight for their rights. Today the NYTWA has more than fifteen thousand members and it keeps growing. Bhairavi continues to fight for taxi drivers and others in the immigrant communities of New York.

—Joe Cleffie

## Timeline:

| | |
|---|---|
| 1972 | Born in Gujarat, India |
| 1979 | Family moves to Harrison, New Jersey |
| 1991 | Accepted to Rutgers University |
| 1994 | Graduates with a degree in women's studies |
| 1994 | Joins the South Asian women's group Manavi |
| 1996 | Joins CAAAV at age twenty-three |
| 1997 | Helps organize a protest of two thousand taxi drivers in New York City |
| 1998 | Creates the NYTWA with other activists |
| 1998 | Strike of 90 percent of New York City's taxi drivers |
| 2011 | Taxi drivers win the right to say no to some ads on their taxis. They are currently fighting to have some of the money that companies pay for the ads |

## More you can do:

- **Read *Unruly Immigrants: Rights, Activism, and Transnational South Asian Politics in the United States* by Monisha Das Gupta and *Taxi! A Social History of the New York City Cab Driver* by Graham Russell Hodges**
- **Create a flyer for the strike that includes demands you would make if you were a cabdriver**

## What do you think?

- **What gave Bhairavi the motivation to want to help people, especially immigrants?**
- **Do you think that she made the right choice to live a life of helping others?**
- **What are some reasons that the taxi drivers had a strike? Do you think these are good reasons?**
- **What makes taxi drivers' jobs hard and dangerous? Can you think of changes that could make their jobs better?**

# 99

# Elvira Arellano

## (1975–)

On August 15, 2006, Elvira Arellano refused to be deported to Mexico, her home country, by taking refuge in the Aldaberto United Methodist Church in Chicago.

Elvira was an undocumented immigrant. Her seven-year-old son, Saul Arellano, was a US citizen. If Elvira's deportation was successful, she would not be allowed to stay with her son. Elvira and her supporters made her case public. In doing so, they showed how unjust laws can break families apart.

In 1997, Elvira left her home in Michoacán, Mexico, for the United States to find work and support her family. Farming in the community where Elvira grew up had been destroyed by US food exports. It was almost impossible for Mexican farmers to make a living from their work. Elvira found a job working as a cleaner at O'Hare International Airport in Chicago. She was working there when she was arrested by Immigration Customs Enforcement (ICE).

ICE targets undocumented immigrants and raids many workplaces. ICE agents arrested Elvira and others like her for the crime of not having the correct papers. There are an estimated twelve million undocumented immigrants living in the United States. Elvira explains the unfairness of this: "For more than two decades the government accepted our [immigrants'] cheap labor, our taxes, our social security payments, but oh no, they didn't want to legalize us." Immigrants like Elvira did not have the chance to get the necessary documents for staying and working in the country legally.

Elvira was an activist in the group Familia Latina Unida. She stood up against her own deportation. Elvira's actions helped inspire the immigrant rights movement of 2006. Churches and towns across the country made themselves sanctuaries, or safe places, for undocumented immigrants. Activists organized vigils and rallies in support of Elvira and Saul. They called for an end to deportations and workplace raids until immigration law was changed.

In late August 2007, Elvira went on a speaking tour to continue building the movement. During the tour, she was detained and deported to Mexico. She had to leave Saul in the United States. Saul stayed with the pastor of the church until he could join his mother in Mexico. "They were in a hurry to deport me because they saw that I was threatening to mobilize and organize the people to fight for legalization," Elvira said afterward.

Elvira has continued to organize for immigrants' rights in the United States and in Mexico. In 2008, she helped found Casa Refugio Elvira. The shelter in Tijuana was named after Elvira. It takes in women and families who have been separated by deportation from the United States. In 2009, Elvira led a demonstration to the US embassy in Mexico for humane immigration reform.

Many immigrant rights activists have called Elvira Arellano the Rosa Parks of the immigrant rights movement.

—Akunna Eneh

## Timeline:

| | |
|---|---|
| 1975 | Born in Michoacán, México |
| 1997 | Arrives in the United States |
| 2002 | Arrested during an ICE workplace raid |
| 2005 | Sensenbrenner bill, criminalizing undocumented immigrants, passes the House |
| 2006 | May, a million people around the United States protest to support immigrant rights and to stop the Sensenbrenner bill from passing the Senate; Senate eventually rejects Sensenbrenner bill |
| | August, refuses deportation orders; takes sanctuary in the Aldaberto United Methodist Church |
| | November, Saul Arellano speaks before the Mexican Congress to ask that his mother not be deported |
| 2007 | Deported to Tijuana |
| 2008 | Helps found Casa Refugio Elvira in Tijuana |
| 2009 | Leads a protest for immigration reform to the US embassy in Mexico; runs for a seat in the Mexican Congress on a pro-immigrant and indigenous rights platform |

## More you can do:

- Read transcripts of Elvira's story on *Democracy Now!*, from April 17, 2009, and November 15, 2006
- Research the New Sanctuary Movement and write a letter to your local city council explaining why you do or don't support it

## What do you think?

- What experiences in Elvira's life do you think influenced her decision to take sanctuary in a church and refuse to be deported?
- Do you think undocumented immigrants, especially those with children and family who are US citizens, should be deported?
- Do you think the comparison activists make between Elvira and Rosa Parks is accurate? Why or why not?

# 100

# Laila Al-Arian

(1981—)

**Laila Al-Arian is a journalist, television producer, and activist. She has brought to light many injustices committed by the US government during its "war on terror."**

The federal government targeted Laila's father, Professor Sami Al-Arian, for exercising his right to free speech. Laila was active in the campaign to defend her father. Sami is the son of Palestinians forced from their land by Israel, in 1948. He spoke out strongly for Palestinian rights. Since 2003, federal prosecutors have spent $50 million trying to convict Sami Al-Arian of wrongdoing. They have failed to persuade a jury to do so. As Laila explains:

Attorney General John Ashcroft personally ordered the indictment against my father, a mandate that puzzled the many career professionals assigned to the case. The political nature of the charges was apparent from the beginning. A jury empaneled by the federal government would reach the same conclusion three years later, concluding that the Bush administration's case was not much of a case at all. But first my father would suffer under extremely restrictive, inhumane conditions clearly meant to psychologically break him before trial, including being placed in solitary confinement for 27 months.

In 2007 Sami Al-Arian went on a sixty-day hunger strike to protest his ongoing imprisonment. He was in a wheelchair and required medical treatment. When he was moved to a federal prison in Virginia, a guard there told him: "If I had my way, you wouldn't be in prison. I'd put a bullet in your head and get it done with." In the same year, a Norwegian filmmaker released the award-winning documentary *USA vs. Al-Arian*. This film recounted the Al-Arian family's legal battle to free Sami.

In 2006 Laila began interviewing US soldiers who served in Iraq. They gave firsthand accounts of horrible crimes committed against Iraqi civilians. The soldiers, Laila wrote, "described how the mechanics of war—home raids, convoys, patrols, detentions, and military checkpoints—led to the daily abuse and killing of innocents. How the killing of civilians became routine, how rules of engagement changed all the time, and how there was a culture of impunity [or getting away with anything] in the military when it came to noncombatant deaths."

Laila now works as a journalist and producer for the news channel Al Jazeera English. In January 2011 she helped to produce the network's report on the release of the Palestine Papers. The Palestine Papers are documents, such as notes and transcripts of meetings between Israeli and Palestinian officials, that were leaked to journalists. The Palestine Papers show that Palestinian negotiators were willing to make major compromises with Israel, but Israeli negotiators demanded still-greater concessions.

Laila has exposed how the United States mistreats Arabs and Muslims—both here and abroad. Her actions are a shining example of how to fight for justice, even when it means standing up to the entire political establishment.

—Eric Ruder

## Timeline:

**1981** Born in Durham, North Carolina, on December 11

**2003** Sami Al-Arian, Laila's father, is arrested on trumped-up terrorism charges

**2006** Receives an MS degree from Columbia University's Graduate School of Journalism

**2007** Documentary *USA v. Al-Arian* is released; the *Nation* publishes an article coauthored by Laila, with interviews with US soldiers who fought in Iraq, in "The Other War"; this article is selected by Project Censored as one of 2008's most underreported news stories

**2007** Sami Al-Arian goes on a sixty-day hunger strike

**2008** Coauthors *Collateral Damage: America's War Against Iraqi Civilians*

**2011** Reports for Al Jazeera English on the Palestine Papers

## More you can do:

- Read *Collateral Damage* and other pieces of Laila's reporting
- Watch a clip of Laila speaking about her father's case on YouTube
- View the full-length version of *USA vs. Al-Arian* at www.usavsalarian.com

## What do you think?

- Laila maintains that the Bush administration targeted her father, "who was an activist who just spoke his mind," while the government's case charged he was involved in supporting a "terrorist" Palestinian group. Who do you agree with and why?
- Why do you think that Laila's interviews with US soldiers about their experiences in Iraq got so little attention in the mainstream media?

## #101
# Constance McMillen
## (1992—)

**Constance McMillen was an ordinary high school senior who became a changemaker because she wanted to bring her girlfriend to the prom.**

Constance is a lesbian, and in 2009 she was a student at Itawamba Agricultural High School in Fulton, Mississippi. In December, Constance asked her assistant principal about wearing a tuxedo and bringing her girlfriend to the prom. AP Mitchell told her she could not attend the prom with her girlfriend, but she and her friend could go with "guys." Constance responded, "I explained to [my vice principal] that you can't pretend like there's not gay people at our school, and if you tell people they can't bring a same-sex date, that's discrimination." School officials gave students a memo that said dates must be of the opposite sex.

Discrimination against lesbian, gay, bisexual, and transgender (LGBT) people is legal in many states. Mississippi doesn't protect LGBT people from job discrimination. The state also bans same-sex marriage. Activists struggling for equal rights for LGBTs have made a lot of progress in changing laws and minds. But inequality and intolerance are still major problems for LGBT people.

When Constance stood up for her right to go to the prom with a girl, the school canceled the event. She was bullied at school. Many students blamed her for the canceling of the prom. Constance filed a lawsuit against the

"I don't think you should have to hide who you are to go to a school event.
. . . I'm not gonna pretend. I was raised to be proud of who you are."
—Constance McMillen, on CBSNews.com video clip, "Teen Sues District for Discrimination," March 12, 2010

school district. She had the help of the American Civil Liberties Union (ACLU, a group of lawyers who support civil rights and free speech causes). The lawsuit demanded that the school district hold the prom and allow Constance to bring her date and wear a tuxedo. The school district invited Constance to a fake prom that only seven students attended. The rest of the students went to a secret event that Constance wasn't told about.

Many people supported Constance and her struggle for justice. A Facebook group backing Constance gained more than three hundred thousand fans in five days. Constance took her case to the public and was heard by millions. She appeared on several national news and talk shows.

In July 2010, the Itawamba County School District gave in. They agreed they had violated Constance's rights and owed her $35,000 in damages. They also promised to create a policy banning discrimination against LGBT students. They became the first public school district in Mississippi to do so.

Constance was the target of unfair treatment and stood up for her rights. She had to fight for her right simply to bring her date and wear what she wanted. She won a victory not only for herself but for every LGBT student in her school district. By standing up for her rights, Constance inspired people around the world and won a victory against intolerance and discrimination. She continues to advocate for equal rights and protection from mistreatment at school for LGBT youth.

—Gary Lapon

## Timeline:

**1992** Born in Mississippi

**2009** December, asks a vice principal at her school if she can bring her girlfriend to the prom

**2010** February–March, school officials circulate a memo stating that prom dates must be of the opposite sex and eventually cancel the prom

March, Constance and the ACLU file a lawsuit against the school district to allow her to bring her girlfriend to the prom and wear a tuxedo; appears on the *Ellen Degeneres Show* and is given a $30,000 scholarship

April, in response to a media uproar, the school hosts a prom Constance can attend with her girlfriend; Constance finds out that most of her classmates were at an alternate private prom

June, serves as grand marshal at New York City's LGBT Pride March

July, wins lawsuit against the Itawamba County School District; the school district agrees to pay Constance $35,000, cover her legal fees, and create a policy banning discrimination against LGBT people

November, named a Woman of the Year by *Glamour* magazine

## More you can do:

- See the ACLU website for a page on Constance's case
- Share Constance's story with the student government in your school to find ways to support LGBT students

## What do you think?

- What do you think about Constance's challenge to what she thought was an unjust rule?
- Are there any rules, laws, or ideas supported by leaders in society today that you disagree with? If so, what do you think it will take to change them?
- Why do you think LGBT people face discrimination?

# Glossary

**abolition:** (n) to get rid of something permanently, such as slavery

**abolitionist:** (n) someone who fights to abolish, or get rid of, something. This term is usually used to describe people who fought to abolish slavery before the Civil War

**abortion:** (n) a medical procedure that ends a pregnancy

**advocate:** (v) to speak up about something; (n) someone who speaks up on behalf of another person or a cause

**agent:** (n) someone or something that can make something happen

**anarchism:** (n) a viewpoint or opinion in which one rejects various forms of authority; a radical political movement

**annex:** (v) to add something on, usually to a piece of land or a building

**annexation:** (n) territory or land that is taken over or absorbed by another entity

**apartheid:** (n) a system of separating people on the basis of race that is enforced by law; a system of minority rule by whites in South Africa until 1994

**backlash:** (n) a negative or hostile reaction to something

**blackball:** (v) to ban or bar someone from something; usually used to mean someone is prevented from gaining a job because of their political views

**bayonet:** (n) a long blade or spike that attaches to the barrel of a rifle, commonly used in war

**bigotry:** (n) to treat someone badly or unfairly because of his or her race, gender, sexual orientation, religion, or another part of his or her identity. See also discrimination

**boycott:** (v) to stop buying or taking part in something as a way of protesting

**brutality:** (n) extreme violence, especially the use of unnecessary violence to make people obey out of fear

**capitalism:** (n) an economic system that is based on some people making a profit from work that is done by other people; people produce goods and services for sale in a market, based on what will earn profits for corporations

**Chicano/Chicana:** (adj) a term used by many Mexican Americans to identify themselves

**civil disobedience:** (n) when someone deliberately disobeys a law that he or she thinks is unjust in public as a way of protesting

**Cold War:** (n) the political and military standoff between the United States and the Soviet Union between the 1940s and the 1980s

**Communism:** (n) a system of government in which the government owns and runs all the workplaces; and in which the state determines how goods and services will be produced. Communism was the form of government in the Soviet Union (Russia) from the 1920s to the 1980s. Communism came into power after the defeat of socialism, but it is different from socialism. See also socialism

**contract:** (n) an agreement made between two individuals or entities; an agreement between a workers' union and the bosses that spells out the workers' pay, benefits, time off, work rules, and other important parts of the workers' jobs

**constitution:** (n) an official document that describes the structure and powers of a government and its citizens

**constitutional:** (adj) determined to be in keeping with (in support of) the principles stated in the Constitution of the United States

**controversial:** (adj) something about which many people disagree

**deportation:** (n) when a government sends someone back to the country where he or she was born, even if he or she doesn't want to go

**diagnosed:** (v) to be told that you have an illness

**direct action:** (n) ways of protesting that involve taking action to change something right away. Many kinds of protest, like marches and rallies, are symbolic, meaning that they show what people want to change; in direct action, people actually try to change something right now.

**discrimination:** (n) to treat someone unfairly because of his or her race, immigration status, gender, sexual orientation, religion, ethnicity, nationality, class, or another part of his or her identity

**draft:** (n) an order by the government to join the military and fight in a war

**epidemic:** (n) when a disease spreads to many people very quickly

**exploit:** (v) to benefit unfairly from the work that someone else does; to take advantage of someone

**fascism:** (n) a system of government where a state run by an individual or small group has complete power and takes people's rights away in order to gain control over them

**feminism:** (n) the belief that women are equal to men and should be treated fairly

**feminist:** (n) someone who believes that women and men are equal and works to achieve equal rights for women

**gay:** (adj) a man who is romantically attracted to other men. Sometimes used to refer to all LGBT people. See also homosexual, LGBT

**gender:** (n) behavior, culture, and traits associated with being male, female, or transgendered

**Ghost Dance movement:** (n) a religious movement that was popular among Native Americans of many tribes during the nineteenth century

**grassroots:** (adj) a movement that springs up from "below," from ordinary people

**Great Depression:** (n) a very severe economic crisis in the late 1920s and early 1930s in which millions of people lost their jobs and homes

**homophobia:** (n) fear and mistreatment of someone because he or she is (or is thought to be) gay, lesbian, bisexual, or transgendered

**homosexual:** (adj) someone who is romantically attracted to people of the same sex; this term is somewhat outdated. See also gay, lesbian, LGBT

**hunger strike:** (n) a way of protesting in which people starve themselves publicly to bring attention to an issue and show that they are willing to die for their cause

**hypocrisy:** (n) dishonesty; to say one thing but do another

**immigrant:** (n) someone who is born in one country and moves to another

**impeachment:** (n) to charge someone who holds a powerful office, such as the president, with a crime

**indigenous:** (adj) originating in a particular place; the first people to live in a place (such as Native Americans in the United States)

**industrialization:** (n) a process in which farms and open land are replaced with factories and towns for workers; economic activity in which labor is used to make or produce goods and services for sale; an era in which these changes happen more quickly

**influence:** (n) the ability or power to have an effect on; (v) to have sway over; to impact

**injustice:** (n) something that is unfair and wrong

**insurrection:** (n) a violent uprising against the existing government or system

**integration:** (n) when people of all backgrounds who used to be separated live together. The civil rights movement fought to integrate black and white people.

**interracial:** (adj) across races; for example, interracial marriage is when someone of one race marries someone of another race

**intolerance:** (n) when people are not willing to treat others as equals. See also bigotry, discrimination

**lawsuit:** (n) a legal act in which one party makes charges against another in court

**legislation:** (n) a bill that becomes law

**lesbian:** (n) a woman who is romantically attracted to other women

**LGBT:** (adj) lesbian, gay, bisexual, and transgendered; this term is often used because it includes more people than "gay" does

**liberal:** (n) someone who wants to make the existing system better without changing the whole system; (adj) open to ideas of social justice; not conservative

**liberation:** (n) complete freedom

**lynching:** (n) a violent kind of racism in which white people murder black people, often by hanging them from trees, in order to make all black people live in fear. Lynching was very common in the southern US in the late nineteenth century and early twentieth century, and white people often had parties to celebrate the murder

**Ku Klux Klan:** (n) a terrorist group that believes in white supremacy that arose in response to black people winning freedom from slavery

**Manifest Destiny:** (n) the belief that God wanted the United States to take over the whole continent of North America; this belief was very popular among white people in the nineteenth century and had a strong influence on government policy

**martyr:** (n) someone who dies heroically for a cause

**maternity leave:** (n) time off from a job for a woman after she gives birth or adopts a baby

**McCarthyism:** (n) a period of anticommunist panic in the 1950s in which Congress, led by Senator Joseph McCarthy, accused many people of being Communists. Many people were driven out of their jobs, jailed, and treated very badly because of their political beliefs.

**migrant:** (n) someone who moves around to find work, usually farm work

**militant:** (n) someone who stands up very strongly for his or her political beliefs, even if it means confronting others

**miscegenation:** (n) an old, racist term for interracial marriage that was used by people who were against it

**missionary:** (n) a person of the Christian faith who attempts to convert others to Christianity

**mobilize:** (v) to get people together and organize, protest, or otherwise work for a cause

**monarch:** (n) royalty; a ruler

**negotiate:** (v) to make a deal; to discuss different views in order to settle a conflict

**New Deal:** (n) a series of laws and programs put in place by President Franklin D. Roosevelt to help make people's lives better during the Great Depression

**nominate:** (v) to decide on a candidate to run for office

**nonviolence:** (n) ways of protesting that do not use violence, not even in response to violence; this way of protesting became popular in India in the 1940s and became an important part of the civil rights movement in the United States

**occupation:** (n) taking over a space and refusing to leave; this can be used as a way of invading other people's land and stealing it (like the United States occupying Native American land), or it can be used as a way of protesting (like when strikers occupy a factory)

**oppression:** (n) the use of power and authority in an unjust, cruel manner; the state of being burdened by that power

**parley:** (v) when people who represent both sides of a war or battle get together to try to make a deal

**perpetuate:** (v) to help something bad continue to exist

**pesticides:** (n) toxic chemicals that are used to kill insects and other pests, but can also harm people, especially workers, and the environment

**poverty:** (n) the state of being very poor

**progressive:** (n) someone who wants things to change for the better; (adj) forward-thinking; enlightened

**Prohibition:** (n) a name for the national ban on alcohol in the United States from 1919 to 1933

**property:** (n) something you own, especially something that you can use to make a profit, like factories

**public assistance:** government programs that help people who are poor by giving them money, food, and places to live; welfare

**Quakers:** (n) a mostly Christian religious movement whose members believe that all people are equal under God, that it is wrong to profit from or exploit others, and that everyone should seek to live in peace together

**racism:** (n) a system of treating some people as being worth less than others because of their race, skin color, or ethnic background

**radical:** (adj) something that is very different from, or part of changing, what is considered normal; (n) someone who wants and works for big, fundamental changes in the world; someone who goes to the root of an issue

**refugee:** (n) someone who has to flee from his or her home because of war, hunger, or other problems

**relocation:** (n) to move from one place to another; often this word is used to describe when people are forced to move against their will

**renaissance:** (n) a period when arts, culture, and new ideas blossom and grow

**repression:** (n) when the government or people in power use force or fear to try to stop others from talking about new ideas or fighting for change; a process where unaccepted thoughts, feelings or behavior are denied; unfair and persecution (harsh punishment) of a person due to their political beliefs and actions

**reproduction:** (n) when people or animals have babies and help them grow

**resistance:** (n) when people fight back against something that is wrong or unfair

**revolution:** (n) when people are so unhappy with their government that they take it over and form a new one

**scab:** (n) someone who takes a worker's job while the worker is on strike

**sedition:** (n) to convince people to rebel against the government. The Sedition Act of 1918 made it a crime to say anything bad about World War I or the way the government was acting.

**segregation:** (n) a system in which white people and people of color (such as black, Asian, Native American, or Latino/a people) are forced to live in separate places, use separate facilities (such as school, buses, and water fountains), and stay away from each other. This system was the law in most of the southern United States until the civil rights movement changed the law. Today segregation is not part of the law, but systems still exist to keep people of different races apart. See also apartheid

**sexism:** (n) the system of treating women and girls as less than men and boys because they are female

**sit-in:** (n) a way of protesting in which people sit down in a place (such as a lunch counter, a factory, or a school administrator's office) and refuse to leave until their demands are met

**social justice:** (n) economic, social, and political equality between and dignity for all people; complete fairness and respect for all members of a community

**socialism:** (n) a system of government in which all ordinary working people make decisions together, democratically, about how society should be run; a system where the needs and desires of all human beings are the basis for organizing society; a way of organizing society where all people would be free from poverty, oppression, and war; a society characterized by complete political, economic, and social democracy

**strike:** (n) a way of protesting in which workers refuse to do any work until their demands are met

**suffrage:** (n) the right to vote

**temperance:** (n) a movement in the late nineteenth and early twentieth century to ban alcohol. Many people who were feminists also believed in temperance because they blamed alcohol for domestic violence.

**transgender:** (adj) someone who was born with the body of one sex but feels that they are another sex or gender; (n) someone who feels, identifies, and lives in a way that is different from social norms based on their biological sex

**undocumented:** (adj) someone who immigrates to another country but does not have all the legal paperwork. In the United States and many other countries, being undocumented is treated as a crime. Many employers take advantage of undocumented workers by paying them less and threatening to report them.

**unemployment insurance:** (n) a government program that pays people who lose their jobs part of what they used to make; introduced as part of the New Deal, during a depression when many people lost their jobs.

**voter registration:** (n) a procedure in which people fill out official forms in preparation for voting during an election. When black people first won the right to vote, many white people tried to stop them from voting by making it hard for them to register. Activists in the civil rights movement helped black people register to vote, and some were threatened and even killed for this.

**whistleblower:** (n) someone who speaks out when his or her employer is doing something wrong or harmful. Many whistleblowers lose their jobs or are treated very badly.

**white supremacy:** (n) the belief that white people are better than people of color; a kind of racism

**yellow fever:** (n) a deadly disease that was very common in the United States in the nineteenth century

# About the Contributors

**Michele Bollinger** is a high school social studies teacher in Washington, DC, where she has been an activist since 1997. She is a member of the Washington Teachers' Union, AFT Local 6. She is also the proud mama of Sasha, 8, and Jacob, 4.

**Dao X. Tran** was born in Vietnam and grew up in Philadelphia, where she was an activist since her youth. She is currently an editor based in the Bronx, New York, focusing on the Domestic Worker Oral History Project. When not reading for work and pleasure, she enjoys time with her daughter Quyen, a changemaker of a different sort.

**Anthony Arnove** wrote, directed, and produced *The People Speak* with Howard Zinn, Chris Moore, Josh Brolin, and Matt Damon, the film companion to Zinn's best-selling book *A People's History of the United States* and its primary source companion, *Voices of a People's History*, which Arnove coedited with Zinn. Arnove is the editor of several books including *The Essential Chomsky*, *Iraq Under Siege: The Deadly Impact of Sanctions*, and *Terrorism and War*. He is also the author of *Iraq: The Logic of Withdrawal*. He sits on the editorial boards of Haymarket Books and *International Socialist Review* magazine.

**Megan Behrent** is a high school English teacher in Brooklyn, where she has been teaching since 1999. She is also currently a graduate student pursuing a PhD in English literature at SUNY Stony Brook. She is a union activist and a UFT delegate from her school. As a longtime activist, she has been involved in campaigns for education reform, for social justice, and for a more democratic and militant union. She is a frequent contributor to *SocialistWorker.org* on labor and education issues, and has also been published in *Labor Notes*, *New Politics*, and the *Harvard Educational Review*.

**Dana Blanchard** is an elementary school teacher and instructional coach in Berkeley Unified School District. She is involved in social justice organizing efforts in her community and is an activist in the Berkeley Federation of Teachers.

**Brian Chidester** is an activist and foreign language teacher in Rhode Island.

**Nick Chin** is a socialist living in Boston. He has been an activist for global justice, against the wars in Afghanistan and Iraq, against the death penalty, and for labor rights. He is a native of Washington, DC.

**Momo Chang** is a freelance journalist based in Oakland, California. She writes about Asian American communities, youth, and social issues. She is an editor for *Hyphen*, a magazine focused on Asian American politics, art, and culture.

**Joe Cleffie** is a socialist and activist living in Philadelphia. He writes for the *International Socialist Review*.

**Amy Cohen** is a teacher and social studies department chairperson at Masterman School in Philadelphia. After many years of teaching seventh-grade world geography, she has been teaching African American history since 2005. She writes frequently for the "Teachers' Turn" and "Teachers' Page" sections of the Historical Society of Pennsylvania's *Legacies Magazine* and has had commentaries published in the *Philadelphia Inquirer*. In summer 2011, Ms. Cohen had the distinct pleasure of meeting her hero, Congressman John Lewis.

**Kevin Coval** is the author of *L-vis Lives!* and *Everyday People and Slingshots (A Hip-Hop Poetica)*. He has performed in seven countries on four continents, appeared on four seasons of HBO's *Def Poetry Jam*, and is cofounder of Louder Than a Bomb: The Chicago Youth Poetry Festival, the largest youth poetry festival in the world. Coval is the artistic director of Young Chicago Authors and teaches at the School of the Art Institute in Chicago.

**Ben Dalbey** is a parent, early childhood educator, and music lover living in Baltimore, Maryland.

**Paul D'Amato** is the managing editor of the *International Socialist Review* and author of *The Meaning of Marxism*.

**Christine Darosa** is a socialist involved in a wide range of grassroots struggles for social justice. Most recently, she has focused much of her activism on campaigns for equality and health care for transgender people. She is based in San Francisco.

**Akunna Eneh** earned a master's degree in library science from Simmons College in 2008. She is currently an activist and youth services librarian in Boston.

**Jason Farbman** is a New York City–based activist. For two years Jason was a Foreign Language and Area Studies Fellow at New York University's Center for Latin American and Caribbean Studies. There, he focused on social movements in Bolivia and Argentina. His writing has appeared in a number of online and print publications, including *SocialistWorker.org*, *International Socialist Review*, *North American Congress on Latin America*, *Latin America News Dispatch*, and *Z Communications*.

**Phil Gasper** teaches philosophy and works at the Center for Excellence in Teaching and Learning at Madison College in Madison, Wisconsin.

**Rose Golder-Novick** graduated from Connecticut College with a major in Religious Studies and went on to complete a Fulbright in Munich, Germany, for one year. She currently is an ESL and Social Studies high school teacher in New York City at a school for immigrant youth.

**Idris Goodwin** is an NEA award-winning playwright, Pushcart-nominated essayist, and critically acclaimed spoken word performer. He teaches performance writing and hip-hop aesthetics at Colorado College.

**Sarah Grey** is a Philadelphia-based freelance writer, editor, and indexer who specializes in social and political texts (www.greyediting. com). Her writing has been published in the *International Socialist Review, SocialistWorker.org, Monthly Review, GRID,* and *Motivos*. She enjoys knitting, mic-checking the powers that be, creative writing, and reading books with her two-year-old daughter Lucia.

**Akua Gyamerah** is a Ghanaian-born activist based in New York City. She is also a doctoral student at the Columbia University Mailman

School of Public Health, where she is studying government AIDS policies on the most at-risk populations in Ghana.

**Jesse Hagopian** is a public high school teacher in Seattle and a founding member of Social Equality Educators (SEE), a rank-and-file organization of union teachers. Hagopian serves on the board of directors of the Haiti solidarity organization Maha-Lilo (Many Hands, Light Load). His writing has appeared in the *Seattle Times*, *TheProgessive.org*, *Black Agenda Report*, *Common Dreams*, *Truthout*, and *Counterpunch*.

**Brian Jones** is an educator, actor, and activist in New York. He co-narrated the film *The Inconvenient Truth Behind Waiting for Superman* and contributed to the book *Education and Capitalism: Struggles for Learning and Liberation*. He has also lent his voice to several audiobooks, including Howard Zinn's one-man play *Marx in Soho*.

**Danny Katch** is a writer, activist, and tutor who lives in Queens, New York. He writes a political humor (hopefully) column for *SocialistWorker.org* and he tries every day to be a changemaker. OK, almost every day.

**Nicholas Klinovsky** is a US history teacher for emerging bilingual students at a Queens high school. Working in classrooms throughout NYC since 2009, he has always tried to create a learning experience and curriculum that comes from his perspective as a teacher interested in justice and equity, as well as sharing his love for the details of history and its little-known heroes.

**Sarah Knopp** is a public high school teacher in Los Angeles. She has been teaching economics and government since 2000. A fre-

quent contributor to the *International Socialist Review*, Knopp has also written for *Rethinking Schools*, *Counterpunch*, and *United Teacher*. She is an activist with United Teachers Los Angeles, a union co-chair at her school, and a dedicated participant in the movements for public education, immigrants' rights, and social equality.

**Peter Lamphere** wears a bowtie and teaches math to emerging bilingual immigrant students in Queens, New York. He is also an activist in the United Federation of Teachers fighting against budget cuts and for a more democratic and social justice–oriented union. He occasionally writes about education and teacher union issues for *GothamSchools.org* and *SocialistWorker.org* and works with the Movement of Rank and File Educators—MORE—(inside the UFT) and the Grassroots Education Movement.

**Gary Lapon** is originally from Springfield, Massachusetts, and currently resides in New York City where he is an activist and frequent contributor to *SocialistWorker.org*. He hopes that this book will inspire readers to write their own chapters in the struggle to build a better world.

**Don Lash** is a lawyer who has developed affordable housing and advocated for children and youth with disabilities and for young people in foster care. He lives in the Bronx, New York.

**Bill Linville** has been a high school and middle school math teacher in New York City since 2006. When not grading or lesson planning, he is involved in struggles for social and educational justice.

**Laura Lising** is a longtime activist in the DC

area. Her work has focused on police brutality and criminal justice issues, housing, women's and LGBT rights, and antiwar organizing, among others.

**Sarah Macaraeg** is the publicity director for Haymarket Books in Chicago, where she is currently at work on the Domestic Worker Oral History Project. She likes writing and activism, and talking about changing the world with her five young nieces.

**Alpana Mehta** was born in Kashmir, India, and spent her formative years in Zambia. She was a women's rights and gay rights activist at Brandeis and is currently an activist with the International Socialist Organization in Boston.

**Jessie Muldoon** is a special education teacher in Oakland, California. She is a member of and activist in the Oakland Education Association and has written for the *International Socialist Review* and *SocialistWorker.org* on topics including labor and education reform.

**Tony Nguyen** is an emerging documentary filmmaker and a second-generation Vietnamese American. His first feature film, *Enforcing the Silence*, has screened in festivals, colleges, and community venues around the country.

**Melissa Pouridas** was born in New York City and relocated to the Washington, DC, area in 1980. After working as a day care provider, housekeeper, administrative assistant, and editor, she has been a public high school English teacher for the past thirteen years.

**Kirstin Roberts** is an early childhood teacher and activist in Chicago.

**Eric Ruder** is a longtime antiwar activist, a journalist for *SocialistWorker.org*, and a frequent contributor to the *International Socialist Review*.

**Adam Sanchez** is a social studies teacher in Portland, Oregon. His writing has been featured in *Rethinking Schools*, *SocialistWorker.org*, and the *International Socialist Review*.

**Helen Scott** is associate professor of English at the University of Vermont, where she is a delegate for the faculty union, United Academics: AFT/AAUP. She is author of *Caribbean Women Writers and Globalization: Fictions of Independence* (Ashgate, 2006), editor of *The Essential Rosa Luxemburg* (Haymarket Books, 2008), and has contributed to anthologies and journals including *Callaloo*, *International Socialist Review*, *Journal of Haitian Studies*, *Socialist Studies*, and *Works and Days*.

**Caitlin Sheehan** is an activist in Chicago.

**Sharon Smith** is the author of *Subterranean Fire: A History of Working-Class Radicalism in the United States* and *Women and Socialism: Essays on Women's Liberation* (an updated edition of which will be published in 2012).

**Mike Stark** is an activist in the Washington, DC, metro area. His focus includes abolishing the death penalty and advocating for the rights of prisoners and their families.

**Alex Tronolone** is a born-and-bred New Yorker who currently resides in Greenpoint, Brooklyn, with his wife and puppy. Alex earned his MSEd in adolescent special education as a NYCTF at Long Island University after graduating from New York University with a BA in history. He has years of experience working in

NYC schools and cultural institutions, leading groups of all ages and abilities, and developing content through archival research.

**Dan Troccoli** is a social studies teacher in a Seattle public school and a founding member of Social Equality Educators. He has been a union representative since 2007 in the Seattle Education Association and is an activist in a number of other areas.

**Wally Showman** is an activist and lawyer living in New York City.

**Jon Van Camp** is a longtime activist for peace and social justice causes in the Washington, DC, area. He teaches world history and geography at Northwestern High School in Hyattsville, Maryland.

**Erik Wallenberg** has a degree in environmental studies from the University of Vermont. He is currently working on a master's in history, researching twentieth-century US social movements and environmental history. He is an activist against racism and war.

**Brian Ward** is an activist based in Washington, DC. He has worked and organized with indigenous people in North, South, and Central America in their struggles for liberation. When he is not in DC, he spends his time on the Pine Ridge Indian Reservation working with the Oglala Lakota Oyate.

**Sherry Wolf** is the author of *Sexuality and Socialism: History, Politics, and Theory of LGBT Liberation* (Haymarket Books, 2009). Wolf is also a public speaker on many social and economic justice issues and is the associate editor of the *International Socialist Review*.

**Leela Yellesetty** is an activist in Seattle, Washington. She is a regular contributor to *SocialistWorker.org* and the *International Socialist Review*.

**Zach Zill** is a carpenter, writer, and activist from Washington, DC. His writing has appeared in *AlJazeera.com*, the *International Socialist Review*, and the *Nation*.

**Annie Zirin** is an art teacher and activist who lives in the Chicago area.

**Dave Zirin** is the coauthor, most recently, of *The John Carlos Story*. He writes about the politics of sports for the *Nation* magazine. In 2009 he was named one of *UTNE Reader*'s "50 Visionaries Who Are Changing Our World." Winner of Sport in Society and Northeastern University School of Journalism's 2011 Excellence in Sports Journalism Award, Zirin is also the host of Sirius XM Radio's popular weekly show, *Edge of Sports Radio*. Robert Lipsyte called him "the best sportswriter in the United States." Zirin is, in addition, a columnist for *SLAM Magazine* and the *Progressive*. ●

# Photo Credits

Crispus Attucks: As he is shot during the Boston Massacre, March 5, 1770, lithograph, Bettmann/Corbis/AP Images (hereafter, "AP")

Tom Paine: A life-size memorial by sculptor George J. Lober shows Paine writing "The Crisis" near Morristown, New Jersey, photographed July 12, 1949, AP

Tecumseh: Undated painting, AP

Angelina Grimké and Sarah Grimké: Wood engraving, Library of Congress, LC-USZ61-1609 and LC-USZ61-1608

David Walker: Walker's Appeal, Library of Congress, LC-USZ62-63775

Nathaniel "Nat" Turner: "Discovery of Nat Turner," undated print of wood engraving by William Henry Shelton, Bettmann/Corbis/AP

John Brown: Undated engraving, Bettmann/Corbis/AP

William Lloyd Garrison: Portrait, Bettmann/Corbis/AP

Elizabeth Cady Stanton: Speaking during the first Women's Rights Convention in Seneca Falls, New York, July 19, 1848. Undated screened illustration, Bettmann/Corbis/AP

Frederick Douglass: Undated photo, AP

Lucy Stone: Undated portrait, Bettmann/Corbis/AP

Harriet Tubman: Photo dating from 1860–85, AP/Library of Congress

Susan B. Anthony: With an original letter she wrote in 1898, part of the "Man's Inhumanity Toward Man" exhibit at the Karpeles Manuscript Library Museum in Buffalo, New York, January 10, 2005, David Duprey, AP

Sitting Bull: Undated photo, Bettmann/Corbis/AP

Mark Twain: Undated photo, AP

Mother Jones: December 18, 1918, Bettmann/Corbis/AP

Queen Liliuokalani: Circa 1881, AP/PBS

Albert and Lucy Parsons: 1886, AP

Mary E. Lease: Undated photographic print, Library of Congress, LC-USZ62-36676

Eugene Debs: Undated photo, AP

Clarence Darrow: Outside the White House in Washington, DC, 1927, AP

Jane Addams: With a child at fortieth anniversary of Hull House, May 12, 1930, Bettmann/Corbis/AP

Ida B. Wells: Circa 1891, Library of Congress, LC-US762-107756

W. E. B. Du Bois: Addressing the World Congress of Partisans of Peace at the Salle Pleyel, Paris, France, April 22, 1949, AP

William "Big Bill" Haywood: On November 4, 1922, AP

Albert Einstein: On March 14, 1954, AP

Joe Hill: Bettmann/Corbis/AP

Frances Perkins: Discussing the Chrysler auto strike, March 20, 1937, AP

Helen Keller: Smelling roses, circa 1955, Bettmann/Corbis/AP

Henry Wallace: Speaking at a meeting sponsored by labor and civic groups in Michigan, July 25, 1943, AP

A. Philip Randolph: Speaking at a press conference in Washington, DC, in preparation for the March on Washington, August 8, 1963, AP

Elizabeth Gurley Flynn: In New York City, March 22, 1949, AP

Paul Robeson: Testifying before the Senate Judiciary Committee that he is willing to go to jail before answering questions about his political beliefs, Washington, DC, May 31, 1948, AP

Langston Hughes: Testifying before the House Un-American Activities Committee, Washington, DC, March 26, 1953, AP

Ella Baker: Speaking at a news conference, January 3, 1968, Jack Harris, AP

Clifford Odets: Returning from Cuba to New York on July 5, 1935, Arthur Brooks, AP

Rachel Carson: Testifying before members of the United States Senate, in Washington, DC, June 4, 1963, AP

Anita Andrade Castro: In 1972, courtesy of Sherna Berger Gluck

Richard Wright: In New York, March 21, 1945, Robert Kradin, AP

Harry Hay: Speaking at a press conference outside the Stonewall Inn in New York, June 24, 1994, Marty Lederhandler, AP

Bayard Rustin: In New York City, outside of the National Headquarters for the March on Washington, August 1, 1963, AP

Studs Terkel: On a Chicago radio show, 1977, Bettmann/Corbis/AP

Rosa Parks: Booking photo, February 22, 1956, AP/Montgomery County Sheriff's office

Genora Dollinger: Organizer of Women's Emergency Brigade Auxiliary of the UAW, circa 1937, Walter P. Reuther Library, Wayne State University

Carlos Bulosan: University of Washington Libraries, Special Collections, UW513

Grace Lee Boggs: At the closing panel of the US Social Forum in Detroit, 2010, photo by Skip Schiel ©2012, teeksaphoto.org, skipschiel.wordpress.com

Billie Holliday: At a recording session, undated, AP

Jacob Lawrence: With his work at a Boston exhibit, 1945, Library of Congress, Prints & Photographs Division, NYWT&S Collection, LC-USZ62-129809

Fannie Lou Hamer: Speaking to Mississippi Freedom Democratic Party sympathizers outside the Capitol in Washington, September 17, 1965, William J. Smith, AP

Fred Korematsu: Photo by Shirley Nakao, courtesy of the Korematsu Institute

Betty Friedan: Speaking during the Women's Strike for Equality event in New York, August 26, 1970, AP

Del Martin and Phyllis Lyon: At their home, December 17, 2004, Eric Risberg, AP

Philip and Daniel Berrigan: Watching two baskets of draft board records burn, May 17, 1968, Bettmann/Corbis/AP

Howard Zinn: ©The People Speak by Greg Federman

Mary and Carrie Dann: At their ranch, October 3, 2002, Laura Rauch, AP

James Baldwin: In Istanbul, Turkey, December 1969, AP

Shirley Chisholm: Speaking in San Francisco, May 16, 1972, Richard Drew, AP

Malcolm X: Speaking at a rally, June 29, 1963, Bettmann/Corbis/AP Images

Elizabeth Martinez: Taken in the 1980s, ©Margaret Randall

Cesar Chavez: Speaking to the press in San Francisco, California, on April 8, 1966, AP

Noam Chomsky: In Turkey, February 13, 2002, Murad Sezer, AP

Martin Luther King, Jr.: Speaking at a news conference in Greenwood, Mississippi, on July 21, 1964, Jim Bourdier, AP

Dolores Huerta: At the dedication of the Cesar Chavez Monument at San Jose State University, September 4, 2008, Paul Sakuma, AP

Harvey Milk: Outside his camera shop in San Francisco, November 9, 1977, AP

Lorraine Hansberry: On May 5, 1959, AP

Daniel Ellsberg: With photos of himself as a US Marine in Vietnam, in Washington, DC, April 21, 2000, Ron Thomas, AP

Richard and Mildred Loving: On June 12, 1967, Bettmann/Corbis/AP

Audre Lorde: In 1989, ©Dagmar Schultz

Ralph Nader: Speaking to reporters about his call for a national march in response to the Three Mile Island nuclear disaster, in Washington, DC, April, 18, 1979, Schwarz, AP

Gloria Steinem: On January 30, 1971, AP

Edward Said: Speaking to reporters, March 26, 1988, Bettmann/Corbis/AP Images

Sylvia Mendez: February 15, 2011, ©Alex Wong, Getty Image

Claudette Colvin: At age 15 in 1953, AP Photo/Farrar, Straus and Giroux

John Lewis: In New York, June 1967, G. Marshall Wilson/Ebony Collection via AP

Bob Dylan: Performing in March 1963, AP

Jesse Jackson: Speaking in Little Rock, Arkansas, November 30, 2006, Mike Wintroath, AP

Joan Baez: With children at a refugee camp in Thailand, February, 1980, AP

Stokely Carmichael: In Atlanta, Georgia, as chairman of the Student Nonviolent Coordinating Committee, May 23, 1966, Bettman/Corbis/AP

Muhammad Ali: In 1970, G. Marshall Wilson/Ebony Collection via AP

Huey Newton: In a jail cell in the Alameda County Courthouse in Oakland, California, July 18, 1968, AP

Billie Jean King: At Wimbledon in London, England, July 8, 1967, AP

Angela Davis: In New York, April 3, 1973, AP

Leonard Peltier: In prison, February 1986, Cliff Schiappa, AP

Alice Walker: At a poetry reading in New York, in the mid-1980s, Bettman/Corbis/AP

Fred Fay: In 1972, courtesy of Trish Irons

Wilma Mankiller: In front of the tribal emblem of the Cherokee Nation, in Oklahoma, July 19, 1985, AP

August Wilson: In Seattle, May 30, 2003, Ted S. Warren, AP

Barbara Young: At the podium, courtesy of the National Domestic Workers Alliance

Sylvia Rivera: At a demonstration in New York, 1970, Diana Davies photographs, Manuscripts and Archives Division, The New York Public Library, Astor, Lenox and Tilden Foundations

Mary Beth Tinker: Displaying armbands with her brother, John, in Des Moines, Iowa, March 4, 1968, Bettman/Corbis/AP

Judy Bonds: Speaking at a rally in Washington, DC, in 2009, Bob Bird, AP

Cleve Jones: Speaking at a rally in Salt Lake City, Utah, June 7, 2009, Steve C. Wilson, AP

Lam Duong: Courtesy of *Enforcing the Silence*

Fernando Suarez del Solar: Protesting outside a New York hotel where former president George W. Bush was speaking, August 31, 2004, Ted S. Warren, AP

Tony Kushner: At the Guthrie Theater in Minneapolis, MN, April 30, 2009, Craig Lassig, AP

Chuck D: Performing in London, July 19, 2012, Jon Furniss/Invision/AP.

Bhairavi Desai: Picketing in New York, September 6, 2007, Peter Morgan, AP

Elvira Arellano: At a news conference with her son, Saul, in Chicago, Illinois, December 27, 2006, Nam Y. Huh, AP

Laila Al-Arian: Courtesy of Sarah Nasr

Constance McMillen: Outside the federal courthouse in Aberdeen, Mississippi, March 22, 2010, Rogelio V. Solis, AP

**Haymarket Books** is a nonprofit, progressive book distributor and publisher, a project of the Center for Economic Research and Social Change. We believe that activists need to take ideas, history, and politics into the many struggles for social justice today. Learning the lessons of past victories, as well as defeats, can arm a new generation of fighters for a better world. As Karl Marx said, "The philosophers have merely interpreted the world; the point, however, is to change it."

We take inspiration and courage from our namesakes, the Haymarket martyrs, who gave their lives fighting for a better world. Their 1886 struggle for the eight-hour day reminds workers around the world that ordinary people can organize and struggle for their own liberation.

For more information and to shop our complete catalog of titles, visit us online at www.haymarketbooks.org.

**Also available from Haymarket Books**

**Education and Capitalism**
*Struggles for Learning and Liberation*
Edited by Jeff Bale and Sarah Knopp

**Howard Zinn Speaks**
*Collected Speeches 1963 to 2009*
Howard Zinn
Edited by Anthony Arnove

**The John Carlos Story**
*The Sports Moment That Changed the World*
John Carlos with Dave Zirin
Foreword by Cornel West

**Schooling in Capitalist America**
*Educational Reform and the Contradictions of Economic Life*
Samuel Bowles and Herbert Gintis

**For young adults**
**IraqiGirl**
*Diary of a Teenage Girl in Iraq*
IraqiGirl

**A Little Piece of Ground**
Elizabeth Laird with Sonia Nimr

**Oranges in No Man's Land**
Elizabeth Laird

**Red Sky in the Morning**
Elizabeth Laird